D0537205

advanced

Gold

coursebook

Richard Acklam

with Sally Burgess

Longman

Contents

Exam information

Overview

The Cambridge Certificate in Advanced English consists of five papers. Each paper tests a different area of your ability in English and is worth 20% of your total result. A candidate's overall CAE grade is based on the total score gained by the candidate in all five papers. It is not necessary to achieve a satisfactory level in all five papers in order to pass the exam. After you take the exam you will receive a grade: A, B and C are pass grades. D and E are fail grades.

Paper 1 Reading

This paper contains four parts. Each part has at least one text with a task. There is a total of approximately 50 questions. A text may consist of several short pieces. A variety of types of texts may be used, including extracts from newspapers, magazines, non-literary books, brochures etc. You will have 1 hour and 15 minutes to answer all the questions.

There are three main types of task:

1 **Multiple matching: (Parts 1 and 4)** this will generally involve matching prompts from a list to different parts of a text. *(See example on pp.70–71 Unit 6 Exam focus, Paper 1, Part 1 and pp.132–133 Unit 11 Exam focus, Paper 1, Part 4.)*

2 **Multiple choice: (Part 3)** in this case you will have to choose answers or finish sentences. *(See example on pp.156–157 Unit 13 Reading, Exercise 3.)*

3 **Gapped text: (Part 2)** in this case you are given a number of paragraphs which have been removed from a text. You must decide where they should go in the text. *(See example on pp.116–117 Unit 10 Exam focus, Paper 1, Part 2.)*

Paper 2 Writing

In this paper you have two tasks. You will have 2 hours to complete the two tasks and you will be required to write approximately 250 words for each task.

Part 1 is compulsory and requires you to read about 400 words of input material and then do a related task e.g. write a formal letter and a note. *(See example on pp.124–125 Unit 10 Exam Focus, Paper 2, Part 1.)*

In **Part 2** you have a choice from four tasks. These could include the following:
- an article *(See example on p.150 Unit 12 Writing and p.210 Writing reference.)*
- a report *(See example on pp.112–113 Unit 9 Writing and p.208 Writing reference.)*
- a review *(See example on pp.56–57 Unit 5 Writing and p.206 Writing reference.)*
- a competition entry *(See example on pp.186–187 Unit 15 Writing.)*
- a leaflet *(See example on pp.88–89 Unit 7 Writing.)*
- an information sheet *(See example on pp.26–27 Unit 2 Writing and p.203 Writing reference.)*
- a contribution to a brochure *(See example on pp.136–137 Unit 11 Writing.)*
- a letter *(See example on pp.38–39 Unit 3 Writing and p.204 Writing reference.)*

One question always relates to a work situation.

Paper 3 English In Use

This paper contains six parts with a total of 80 questions. You will have 1 hour and 30 minutes to answer all the questions. The six different parts are as follows:

Part 1: This consists of a multiple-choice cloze text. *(See example on p.102 Unit 8 Exam focus.)* This is a text with 15 gaps, followed by 15 four-option multiple-choice questions. The focus is on vocabulary.

Part 2: This consists of an open cloze text. *(See example on p.160 Unit 13 Exam focus.)* This is a text with 15 gaps which you must fill with an appropriate word. The focus is on grammar.

Part 3: This consists of an error correction text. *(See example on p.28 Unit 2 Exam focus and p.64 Unit 5 Exam focus.)* The errors are either a) additional words or b) wrong spelling or punctuation. You decide for each line of the text if it is correct or if there is a mistake.

Part 4: This consists of a word formation exercise. *(See example on p.167 Unit 14 Exam focus.)* You will read two short texts in which there are a total of 15 gaps. You are given the stem of the word which you must use to complete each gap.

Part 5: This consists of two texts. You must transfer information given in one text to the other. *(See example on p.140 Unit 11 Exam focus.)* The two texts are different in terms of register. Words contained in the first text cannot be used in the second.

Part 6: This consists of a gapped text. This is a text from which several phrases / short sentences have been removed and placed below the text with additional phrases. *(See example on p.37 Unit 3 Exam focus.)* You must select the correct options to complete the text.

Paper 4 Listening

This paper contains four parts with a total of 30–40 questions. In Parts 1, 3 and 4 you will hear the text(s) twice; the text in Part 2 is heard **once only**. The texts will be a variety of types, possibly including announcements, radio broadcasts, telephone messages, talks, lectures, interviews, meetings. There will be a mixture of native and non-native speaker accents. This paper will last approximately 45 minutes.

Part 1: You will hear a monologue lasting about 2 minutes. You will have to take notes or complete sentences. *(See example on p.119 Unit 10 Listening.)*

Part 2: You will hear a monologue lasting about 2 minutes. (There may be prompts from a second speaker.) You will only hear this **once**. You will have to take notes or complete sentences. *(See example on p.172 Unit 14 Listening.)*

Part 3: You will hear a conversation between two or three speakers lasting about 4 minutes. You will have to complete sentences or answer multiple-choice questions. *(See example on p.30 Unit 3 Listening.)*

Part 4: You will hear five short, related extracts of about 30 seconds each. You will then have to either
a) complete a multiple-matching task. In this case there are two parts. In each part you must select the correct option from a list of eight. *(See example on p.114 Unit 9 Exam focus.)*
b) answer ten multiple-choice questions. There are two questions for each speaker. *(See example on p.184 Unit 15 Exam focus.)*

Paper 5 Speaking

This paper contains four parts. The standard format involves an interview between two candidates and two examiners. One of the examiners is an interlocutor who speaks to the candidates; the other examiner only assesses the candidates and does not speak. The different parts are as follows:

Part 1: The interlocutor asks the candidates to respond to one another's questions about themselves or to respond to the interlocutor's questions. The questions generally involve giving personal information of some kind. *(See example on pp.10–11 Unit 1 Exam focus.)* This will last approximately 3 minutes.

Part 2: Candidates comment on visual prompts e.g. photographs. Each candidate will speak for about one minute. The second candidate will make a short response after the other candidate has finished. *(See example on p.22 Unit 2 Speaking.)* This will last approximately 3–4 minutes.

Part 3: Candidates are given visual prompts (e.g. photographs, line drawings, diagrams) and are asked to carry out a problem-solving task together which may involve sequencing, ranking, comparing and contrasting, selecting etc. *(See example on pp.54–55 Unit 5 Speaking.)* This will last approximately 3–4 minutes.

Part 4: The interlocutor develops the topic covered in Part 3 and asks the candidates to discuss and give opinions on more general questions related to the same theme. *(See example on pp.54–55 Unit 5 Speaking.)* This will last approximately 3–4 minutes.

In total this paper will last approximately 15 minutes. *(For an example of a complete Paper 5 interview see pp.146–147 Unit 12 Exam focus.)*

UNIT

1

What a spectacle!

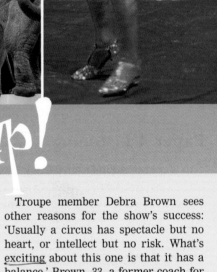

Reading

▶ P1, Pt3 (multiple choice)

1 Discuss with other students:

- any memories you have of going to a circus
- what a 'traditional' circus is like
- what an 'alternative' circus might be like

2 Read the first two paragraphs of the text below and find a description of one of the photos above.

Roll up! Roll up!

Hurry! Hurry! Hurry! Step right up to Cirque du Soleil, the greatest ... well, one of the greatest shows on earth. You'll thrill to the sight of a single
5 circus ring that has never been marked with the hoofprint of a wild beast. You won't see packs of elephants stand on their heads, but you will be awestruck[1] by the multiple talents of performers
10 who play clowns and then transform themselves into acrobats, trapeze artists and jugglers. You won't see an alligator tamer wrestle with the jaws of death, but you will be treated to the
15 spectacle of two tango dancers concluding their romance with an amazing hand-balancing act. And you'll gasp[2] as a tightrope walker strides across the wire while playing a
20 haunting[3] theme on the oboe.
    Easily as compelling, if not more so, is the body-bending act by contortionist Elena Lev of Russia (Cirque du Soleil has a penchant[4] for what could be
25 seen as physical extremism), who twirls[5] a batch of golden metal hoops around herself. Other acts of jaw-dropping expertise include a bare-chested aerialist who twirls a giant

cube in midair, and Andrei Lev's Flying
30 High Bar Act, seven Russians who do their whizzing flips dangerously close to the top of the circus' blue-and-gold tent.
35 At the heart of the Cirque du Soleil is the desire to combine acrobatics with refined acting. Perfectly designed, everything – wailing music, dramatic lighting, elaborate costumes, strange
40 images and mystical themes – meshes[a] into a spellbinding[b] whole, Cirque du Soleil's productions are entertainments without comparison which have a charm all their own.
45 This relatively new troupe has captured the imagination of audiences around the world by replacing circus pomp with up-close, unusual thrills and surprises. In a comparatively tiny 1,754-
50 seat tent, one lone Cirque trapeze artist can stop heartbeats by swooping[c] just a few feet above the heads of spectators without a net. 'Because you're so close,' said one satisfied customer,
55 Sandy Willis, 21, 'you can see their facial expressions, beads of sweat and muscles tensing up. You feel like you're part of the performance.'

    Troupe member Debra Brown sees
60 other reasons for the show's success: 'Usually a circus has spectacle but no heart, or intellect but no risk. What's exciting about this one is that it has a balance.' Brown, 33, a former coach for
65 the Canadian Olympic gymnastics team, carefully plans every move in the ring. 'When you think of dance, you think of people on two feet,' she says, 'but my choreography explores four
70 feet because of the way acrobats use their hands.'
    Founder and director, Guy Laliberté, a college dropout, whose mother is a pianist and whose father is a vice
75 president of an aluminium company, was once just another itinerant musician–fire breather–stilt walker. He honed[d] his skills in Baie Saint Paul, an artists' colony 55 miles northeast of
80 Quebec City where performers congregate each summer. 'I came up with our name,' he says, 'when I was looking in a dictionary of symbols and saw "soleil, sun". It means youth,
85 power, freshness. Everything was there. I just knew at that moment that we would be a success.'

6

3 In Paper 1, Part 3 of the exam you will be required to read a text and then answer 5–7 multiple-choice questions. Read the procedure suggested for tackling this task type in the box below.

Suggested procedure

1 Read the whole text through once quickly to get an idea of the main areas referred to.

Give yourself three minutes to do this. Then work with another student to identify and note down the main point in each paragraph.

2 Read each question and locate the part(s) of the text which relate(s) to it.

Do this and check with another student that you have identified the same parts of the text.

3 Read the relevant part(s) of the text carefully and underline key words/phrases.

Do this and check with another student that you have identified the same key words/phrases.

4 Consider the possible options for each question carefully. The incorrect options will be wrong for different reasons:

- They are not referred to in the text (but may be true).
- They contradict what is in the text.
- They are partially (but not completely) true.
- They are irrelevant to the question.

5 Select the best option.

Compare your answers with another student. Discuss why the incorrect options are wrong in each case.

Remember: A question may ask you to infer the attitude of the writer to the subject of the text. To do this you will need to look for evidence throughout the text. The choice of vocabulary will often give you clues.

4 Use the procedure in Exercise 3 to complete the questions below.

1 The Cirque du Soleil is a different kind of circus because

  A of the number of different acts.

  B the animals who perform are treated humanely.

  C of how dangerous the acts are.

  D there are only human performers who often have more than one skill.

2 The Cirque du Soleil includes an act where someone

  A spins a large ball.

  B throws knives whilst blindfolded.

  C plays music whilst on the trapeze.

  D manipulates her body in unbelievable ways.

3 The Cirque du Soleil has made a big impact partly because

  A the audience gets to know some members of the circus personally.

  B of the colours of their costumes.

  C they involve members of the audience in the acts.

  D of the proximity of the audience to the acts.

4 Debra Brown believes

  A the Cirque is more exciting than other circuses.

  B the essence of the Cirque is planning.

  C she has more scope for creativity than a normal choreographer.

  D her background as an Olympic coach is essential in her present work.

5 Guy Laliberté

  A always knew he would end up in a circus.

  B got a poor college degree.

  C initially was a fairly typical circus performer.

  D seems to owe his success to his parents.

6 He chose the name for the circus because

  A he associated the sun with success.

  B it had all the characteristics symbolised by the sun.

  C he only wanted young people as performers.

  D of a previous experience at an artists' colony.

7 The reviewer's attitude to the Cirque du Soleil is

  A quite sarcastic.

  B essentially positive with one or two minor criticisms.

  C unreservedly enthusiastic.

  D largely neutral and objective.

5 Discuss with other students.

Does this review make you want to see this circus? Why/why not?

Vocabulary: deducing from context and choosing a dictionary

1 The following words are numbered and underlined in the text on p.6.

1 awestruck (1.8)   4 penchant (1.24)
2 gasp (1.18)   5 twirls (1.26)
3 haunting (1.20)

1 Decide what part of speech they are.
2 Look at the context around them. Write down possible meanings for each one.
3 Compare your ideas with other students. (Justify your ideas with reference to the context.)

D **2** Now check your ideas by looking at the dictionary extracts on p.215 which come from the *Longman Dictionary of Contemporary English.*

3 Discuss with other students.

1 What do you expect from a good dictionary?
2 What did you think of the dictionary extracts you have just looked at? Were the meanings and examples clear? Did you get all the information you wanted about the words?
3 How do these dictionary extracts compare with other dictionaries you have used?
4 When do you find it helpful to use a dictionary?

Grammar plus: verb patterns (1)

- *You won't* see *an alligator tamer wrestle with the jaws of death …*
- *… my choreography explores four feet because of the way acrobats* use *their hands.*
- *… a tightrope walker* strides *across the wire …*

1 Read the information in the box in the right hand column. Then decide if the underlined verbs in the sentences above are transitive or intransitive or if they can be both. (If you are not sure, check in a dictionary.)

- Certain verbs are usually followed by a direct object e.g. *He stole some money*. These are called **transitive** verbs. (They can have a passive form e.g. *Some money was stolen.*)
- Certain verbs which are transitive can be followed by two objects (indirect and direct) e.g. *Can you give me the dictionary?* Usually the first object is a person and the second object is a thing. With many of these verbs, we can reverse the order of the objects by using *to* or *for* e.g. *He gave me his phone number* OR *He gave his phone number to me.* Some verbs can only have a second object if this is a prepositional object with *to* e.g. *He described the missing necklace to the police.* NOT *He described the police the missing necklace.*
- Certain verbs are not usually followed by a direct object e.g. *They laughed for hours.* These are called **intransitive** verbs. (They cannot have a passive form.)
- Certain verbs can be both transitive and intransitive e.g. *The old man turned slowly.* – (intransitive) / *He turned the handle as far as it would go.* – (transitive). These verbs often describe change e.g. *open, increase, break* etc.

D **2** Decide which category(ies) each of the following verbs goes into. Use a dictionary if necessary

burn describe wait invite pull lose sit start want send happen surprise eat sleep shut explain wake warn fall make spoil

transitive	transitive with two objects
take	*give*
intransitive	**transitive and intransitive**
laugh	*turn*

3 Sometimes transitive verbs can have their objects left out because the meaning is obvious from the context. Which of the underlined objects in these sentences can be omitted?

1 I can't find anywhere to park the car.
2 He really enjoys cooking food.
3 They found the cat under the stairs.
4 She's been smoking cigarettes for years.
5 He slowly and carefully opened the briefcase.

 4 Look at the following pairs of sentences. Decide if neither, one or both of the sentences is/are correct English. What can you say about any 'rules' for how the main verb in each pair of sentences is used?

1 a) He sent me a picture of his new family.
   b) He sent to me a picture of his new family.
2 a) Could you explain this grammatical point to us?
   b) Could you explain us this grammatical point?
3 a) Do you need to borrow me some money?
   b) Do you need to borrow?
4 a) She built a beautiful wooden doll's house for her children.
   b) She built for her children a beautiful wooden doll's house.
5 a) I can't believe that we won!
   b) I can't believe that we won the match!
6 a) I haven't seen Simon for two months and I miss terribly.
   b) I haven't seen Simon for two months and I miss him terribly.
7 a) They announced their engagement to the whole family.
   b) They announced the whole family their engagement.
8 a) Would you bring some more serviettes for us please?
   b) Would you bring us some more serviettes please?

D **5** Now choose two verbs from Exercise 2. Check in your dictionary if they can be used transitively or intransitively (or both). Write two sentences for each verb as above. Show them to another student and see if they can decide if neither, one or both of the sentences is/are correct.

▶ Grammar reference p.197

▶ *Exam Maximiser* **M**

Listening: Elena Lev

▶ P4, Pt3 (sentence completion)

1 The photo shows Elena Lev with her mother. What do you imagine it is like to live and grow up in a circus environment as a young person? How would your life be different from that of other young people?

 2 Listen to this interview and summarise in a few words

1 how Elena (junior) feels about being part of the Cirque du Soleil.
2 Elena (senior)'s attitude to her daughter.

3 Before you listen to the interview again, read questions 1–12 and predict how the sentences should be completed. (There are no more than three additional words.) Make sure that your ideas work grammatically with the rest of the sentence.

EXAMPLE: *Elena Lev comes from* **Moscow**.

1 Her original training was as a ....
2 She is quite insistent that any success she has is due to her ....
3 She is with her mother constantly except for her time at ....
4 She aims to please her mother as a result of her total ....
5 Her freedom is limited by ....
6 Since she left Moscow she cannot call any particular city her ....
7 From an early age Elena wanted to be .... her mother.
8 Her mother wanted to coach her full-time because she recognised Elena's ....
9 Her mother's method of teaching is to encourage Elena to ....
10 When Elena is not working, she and her mother like to do everyday things together such as ....
11 One reason why people might not think that they are mother and daughter is that Elena is very ....
12 Her mother doesn't think she will ever .... from Elena.

4 Listen to the interview again and check your answers.

5 Discuss with other students. What do you think of:

1 Elena's lifestyle?
2 Elena's relationship with her mother?

Vocabulary: word formation (suffixes)

Her act combines the grace and <u>agility</u> of a gymnast with the <u>flexibility</u> of a contortionist and the <u>dexterity</u> of a juggler.

1 Look at the above extract from the listening text. What part of speech are the underlined words? How do you know?

2

1 Decide if the suffixes in bold below generally indicate that the word is a noun, adjective or verb.

alterna**tive** opt**ion** success**ful** responsibi**lity** organ**ism** weak**ness** count**able** brown**ish** modern**ise** enjoy**ment** delic**ious** leg**al**

2 What is the correct word stress for each of these words?

3 Which suffixes from Exercise 2 make

- nouns from adjectives?
- nouns from verbs?
- an adjective meaning 'can be done'?
- an adjective less precise?
- verbs from adjectives?

Watch Out! *responsible*

What's the difference in the meaning of *responsible* in these two sentences?

1 He's a very *responsible* person.
2 He's the person *responsible* for making all financial decisions.

---

4 Now make a note of two more words you know with each of the endings in Exercise 2.

5 Complete the words in these sentences with the appropriate suffix.

1 What you said is forgiv... . What you did is not.
2 I'd like to make a small donat... to the work you do with the victims of landmines.
3 That's absolutely outrage... . They can't cut our salaries!
4 Your refus... to cooperate leaves us with no alternative I'm afraid.
5 I'm afraid her forgetful... is becoming more and more apparent.

6 We clearly need to standard... our procedures. At the moment everyone has their own particular approach.
7 This discussion has been very product... . We now have a number of possible solutions to the problem.
8 I don't know his exact age. He's probably mid-thirty... .
9 I'm hope... that I will have passed my English exam this time.

6 Work with another student. Practise using suffixes by having a conversation. Include as many words as possible with the suffixes from Exercise 2. Each time you include a word with a suffix correctly and sensibly, you score one point.

EXAMPLE: A: *So, did you have much excite**ment** last night?*
B: *Yes. I had a great time. We went out to this great Italian restaurant where the food is delic**ious**!*

Exam focus

Paper 5 Speaking: Part 1 (introduction)

About the exam: Paper 5 is the part of the exam where your speaking is tested. It lasts 15 minutes and you are paired with another candidate. There are two examiners, one who conducts the test and one who just listens to your English.

In the first part of the interview you will be asked if you know the other candidate. If you do, then you will be asked to tell the examiners about your partner. If you don't, you will be told to ask your partner about certain things. Typical subjects for this part of the speaking paper are:

- where you are from
- your home and family
- your hobbies and interests
- what you do
- why you're learning English
- your plans for your next holiday
- your plans for the future in general

1 Look at these questions. Four of them contain mistakes. Find the mistakes and correct them.

1 So where were you brought up from originally?
2 Tell me little about your family. Do you have many brothers and sisters? What are they like?
3 What kinds of things do you like doing in your free time?
4 Do you have a particular reason of learning English or is it just out of general interest?
5 Have you got anything exciting lined up for your next holiday?
6 Do you have much an idea of what you'll be doing over the next few years?

2 Listen to part of an interview. What is your opinion of the two candidates?

3 Work with another student. Listen to the examiner's instructions on the recording. Practise asking one another about the different subjects. Remember to say as much as possible and sound interested in what you and your partner are saying. Use the questions from Exercise I above where appropriate.

English in Use

▶ P3, Pt3 (error correction, extra word)

1 In Paper 3, Part 3 you will have a short text of about 16 lines. In one task you will have to look at each line and decide if it contains an extra and unnecessary word. These extra words will be 'grammar words' and will often come from the following groups:

- articles (*the, a, an*)
- auxiliaries (*do, have, are* etc.)
- comparatives (*as, than, more* etc.)
- conjunctions (*because, although*)
- prepositions (*to, up, by* etc.)
- personal pronouns (*she, it, them* etc.)
- modifiers (*too, quite, so* etc.)
- relative pronouns (*who, which, that* etc.)

2 Read the text below quickly and see how many unusual things you can discover about Robert Cook. Then compare your answer with another student.

WHITE FOR ALL OCCASIONS

0 ✓	The 17th century Irish farmer Robert Cook was the
00	most startling figure in the region. He never <u>did</u> wore
1	anything but the white linen. Not only were his
2	nightclothes and shirts in purest white but even so were
3	his suits, coats and hats. He became so famous for his
4	clothes and his passion for white although that he was
5	known all over Ireland as 'Linen Cook'. He refused him
6	to have any black cattle in the fields of his farm and even
7	if his horses had to be pure white. On one occasion a
8	fox which had been attacked his poultry was caught.
9	However, he refused to allow it to be killed. Instead
10	of he gave it a lecture on the evils of murder and then
11	gave it up a sporting chance to escape. Cook was
12	a passionate vegetarian and wouldn't have eat the flesh
13	of any animal or wear anything which produced by
14	an animal. He had a long and healthy life and finally
15	died in 1726 when he was over than 80 years old.
16	Unsurprisingly, he was buried in a white shroud.

---

3 Now read the text again. Think about the grammar of each sentence and check that each 'grammar word' needs to be there. If a line does not have an extra word, tick it. If there is an extra word, underline it.

4 Compare your ideas with another student. Note that not more than five lines in the text will usually be correct.

EVERYTHING IS PURGED FROM THIS PAINTING
BUT ART, NO IDEAS HAVE ENTERED THIS WORK.

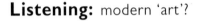

Listening: modern 'art'?

1 Look at the pictures above. Describe what you can see.

2 Listen to the following conversation. Decide which of the pictures above are referred to.

3 Listen to the conversation again. Make notes of the answers to the following questions.

1 When did Pete go to the exhibition?
2 What did Pete and Clare do before going to see the exhibition?
3 What did the exhibition consist of?
4 Why was there originally a fuss about the 'pile of bricks'?
5 What most irritated Pete about the bicycle wheel on the stool?
6 What does Pete think the artist's attitude to their audience might be?
7 What does one of the group believe the purpose of art should be?
8 How would you describe the general attitude of the people in the conversation towards 'modern art'? Were they
   a) intrigued? b) amused?
   c) sceptical? d) confused?

4 In the conversation three different expressions were used to express disbelief. Listen again and write down exactly what they were.

1 In fact .... people can consider that kind of thing to be 'art'.
2 Honestly, ... people can write such rubbish.
3 .... people can come up with such vile notions ...

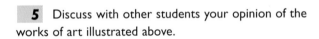

5 Discuss with other students your opinion of the works of art illustrated above.

- Which do you like?
- Which do you not like?
- Do you think they can all be considered to be 'art'?
- Do you think 'art' should have a particular purpose? If so, what?

6 Compare similarities and contrast differences between these two paintings. Which do you prefer and why?

Man with a Pipe 1914
by Picasso

Grammar check: overview

1 Each of the following sentences contains a different basic grammatical mistake in an important area. Find the mistakes and correct them. (This exercise will help to show you any significant gaps in your grammatical knowledge.)

EXAMPLE: *I thought that film was absolutely terrified.*
*terrified > **terrifying***

1 I am knowing that she wants to be on her own tonight.
2 We go never out to restaurants any more.
3 Where are car keys? I had them a minute ago.
4 This computer game is a lot more cheaper than the last one you bought.
5 If I'd have seen him, I'd have invited him to the party.
6 Unless you work a bit harder, you won't fail your exams.
7 They were really helpful and gave us lots of informations.
8 We considered to go to the new French restaurant but it was too expensive.
9 My dad won't let me to stay overnight at John's house.
10 I really wish I would have more time.
11 He went rock-climbing despite of his fear of heights.
12 They might decided to go to the circus after all.

13 Sarah's new boyfriend is absolutely nice. She's very lucky.
14 Last night I dreamt I was being chasing by this huge black dog.
15 Could you tell me whether is there another train to London tonight?
16 She's the girl who brother I went to school with.
17 He apologised for been late.
18 We're having the front of the house painting next week.
19 They've been living here since at least 30 years.
20 I can't get used to start work so early.
21 He's a such terrible liar that no-one ever believes him.

2 Check your answers.

1 Choose two sentences you had problems with.
2 Identify the grammar areas concerned.
3 Research the areas in two different grammar reference books (such as the *Longman Grammar and Vocabulary for CAE*). Make notes of what you learn and be prepared to explain what you read, clearly and simply to another student.
4 Tell another student what you learnt.

3 Discuss with other students which grammar reference book you preferred and why.

4 Look back at some recent pieces of writing you have done in English. Make a note of any grammar areas that you made mistakes with on more than one occasion, like this:

GRAMMAR CHECKLIST	EXAMPLE
Present Perfect v Past Simple	Last summer I ~~have~~ spent 3 marvellous weeks with my sister in the USA.
-ing v. infinitive	She promised coming home by 8pm. (to come)

Add to your Grammar Checklist when you become aware of more typical mistakes. Refer to it each time you do a new piece of writing to help remind you which mistakes to try and avoid.

Boy with a Pipe by Picasso

Writing: drafting

► P2, Pt1 (compulsory)

1 Look at the task and answer on pp.200–202 of the Writing reference. Are the following statements about the answer true or false?

1 The meaning is communicated clearly.
2 It is written in a very formal style.
3 It is slightly longer than the necessary number of words.
4 There is a good variety of grammatical structures.
5 There is a good range of vocabulary.
6 The writing is logically divided into separate paragraphs.
7 A number of linking words/phrases are used.

2 Read the instructions for the task below.

1 Decide what are the key words/phrases. Compare your ideas with another student.
2 Look at the useful language box on p.202 of the Writing reference. Write down any words or expressions that you think might be useful when you come to do the task below.

TASK

You were recently given tickets to see a world famous circus. You went to a performance but were rather disappointed for various reasons.

Write a thank you note to the friends who gave you the tickets without going into what you weren't happy about. Also, write a letter of complaint to the management of the circus, highlighting the various points that you were not happy about.

Read the original letter from your friends and an advert for the circus to which you have added your comments. Then, using the information carefully, write the thank you note [50 words] and letter of complaint [200 words]. You should use your own words as far as possible.

Dear XXX,
Here are the tickets we were telling you about. We're really sorry we can't go but at least you'll be able to enjoy the show! Do let us know what it's like. With any luck, we'll get the chance to go another time.
Love,
Sarah and Pete

CHIPPERHALL CIRCUS
EXTRAVAGANZA

Roll up! Roll up! Come and see an amazing array of high-wire acts, trapeze artists and crazy clowns. Be terrified by the big cats, be awestruck by the Indian elephants.

one lion got outside the ring ... quite frightening

We have travelled the globe and thrilled audiences in every continent.

performance started late and finished early   *seated behind large pillar ... v. restricted view*

Performances in the Grand Marquee every day from 4–6pm and 7–9pm. Fun for all the family.

impossible to get a drink in interval, not enough people serving

Ticket prices start at only £10!

around Grand Marquee extremely muddy field, shoes ruined

3 Look at the underlined linking words in the paragraph below. Can you think of another linking word/phrase with a similar meaning for each one? Record these linking words/phrases in a vocabulary notebook so that you can use them in Exercise 5.

Dear Sir,

I am writing to complain about the service I received at your hotel last weekend.

First of all, on arrival, there was no record of my booking although I had faxed the details several weeks earlier. Secondly, when I got up to my room, I found that it had not been cleaned properly and there were used towels in the bathroom. Furthermore, when I came down to breakfast the next day, I was told that I was too late, even though it was only 10am. Finally, when I was given the bill I was charged for items from the minibar which I hadn't used.

I'm afraid that I have never before been treated so appallingly ...

4 Here is one possible plan of how the thank you note and letter of complaint will be organised. Discuss with another student if this is the plan that you want to use, or whether you would like to change it in some way.

Thank you note
- say 'thanks'
- tell them it was 'an experience'!
- hoping to see them soon

Letter of complaint
- introduce general reason for letter
- list main complaints and effect on children
- request refund for cost of tickets and ruined shoes
- expect reply soon

5 Here are the beginnings of the note and letter. Continue them and write complete draft versions. Check you can say Yes to all the questions below.

Dear Sarah and Pete,
This is just a brief note to say a big 'Thank you!' for sending us the circus tickets. ...

Dear Sir/Madam,

I am writing to you to express my disappointment at a recent visit to the 'Chipperhall Circus Extravaganza' on Saturday 17th March.

To begin with, although the evening performance was supposed to start at 7pm, in fact nothing really happened until 7.30pm which was particularly hard on my children, who had been looking forward to the event all day. The next thing was that we found ourselves sitting behind a large pillar which meant that ...

- Have you responded to all the instructions in the task?
- Have you organised your answers in logical paragraphs?
- Have you avoided copying long phrases from the input texts?
- Have you written approximately the right number of words?
- Have you used appropriate linking words/phrases?
- Have you referred to your Grammar Checklist to remind yourself of possible grammar mistakes?
- Have you used language of an appropriate style in your answers?
- Do the letter and note have the intended effect on the target reader?

6 Show your letter and note to another student. Can she/he see any obvious problems or mistakes with your work? Read your partner's note and letter. Point out any problems you can see.

Speaking: storytelling

1 The pictures below make up a well-known fable, 'The Emperor's New Clothes'. Work with another student and discuss the correct order of the pictures.

2 With your partner, tell the story, by taking it in turns to refer to each picture. (You may wish to use these words: *a weaver, cloth, a loom, a procession*.)

3 Now listen to a version of this story. How similar is it to yours?

4 Discuss with other students.

- What is the point of the story?
- What warning does it give?
- Does it have any relevance to the modern world?

5 Write the story incorporating any new vocabulary you have learnt.

1 The following words are lettered a)–d) and underlined in the text on p.6. From the context decide what you think they might mean.

a) meshes (l.40)
b) spellbinding (l.41)
c) swooping (l.51)
d) honed (l.78)

D Check your ideas in a good dictionary. Find out:

- the meaning appropriate to the context in the review
- the part of speech
- any extra grammatical information e.g. is it generally followed by a particular preposition?
- the pronunciation
- a helpful example sentence

2 Four of the following sentences have mistakes in them. Find the mistakes and correct them.

1 A sudden draught of air blew the door shut.
2 Shaun proposed a wedding to me last night. I didn't know what to say.
3 I'm afraid this will definitely add to the overall cost of the project.
4 Don't shoot! I'm coming out.
5 You surprised when you said you were leaving at the end of the week.
6 I wonder if you could suggest me a good grammar book?
7 Why don't I make you a nice hot cup of tea?
8 He still owes for his share of the holiday we had together last year.

3 Complete the table with the appropriate part of speech.

VERB	NOUN	ADJECTIVE
to alternate		
to opt		
to succeed		
to enjoy		
to weaken		
to count		
x x x x		responsible
		modern

4 Complete the following article with one word in each space.

Itch art – but not as we know it

MARIA FERNANDA CARDOSO (**1**) … never seen a flea circus when she decided (**2**) … resuscitate the lost art of insect performance. And for the (**3**) … three years, Cardoso, a 34-year-old conceptual artist, has painstakingly trained hundreds of fleas.

Fleas dislike light but (**4**) … attracted to all things furry as well (**5**) … heat and carbon dioxide (animals emit both). Cardoso uses these elements (**6**) … motivators. She also manipulates (**7**) … with ultrathin wire leashes, looped around flea heads and bodies. A tug on the leash and a flea is dancing or at (**8**) … looks like it. (**9**) … these impressive results, there are still frustrations. 'Some fleas are just no good,' she says, 'and there's nothing you (**10**) … do.'

Wearing magnifying goggles and a silver cape and brandishing (**11**) … tiny whip, Cardoso conducts the extravaganza. Under a dollhouse-size circus big top, Hercules, 'The Strongest Flea in the World', pulls a toy locomotive many (**12**) … his size. Estrellita, helped by a harness, wobbles (**13**) … a tightrope on hind legs. Fearless Alfredo gears up for his highdive stunt with a drumroll and spotlight. But, alas, after making a ten-inch plunge, he misses his water-filled thimble, hits (**14**) … circus floor and dies.

Is Cardoso upset by the loss? Not really. 'I treat them well and I think they know they are special,' she says. 'And (**15**) … they die, well, that's life.'

UNIT
2 It takes all sorts

Listening: an alien?

1 What might be the connection between the three men and the bulldozer in the photo?

2 Listen to the recording and check your ideas.

3 Read the statements below. Listen to the recording again and then decide if the statements are true or false. Be prepared to justify your answers with references to the text.

  O 1 Arthur knew that his friend, Ford, was not from south London.

  ✓ 2 Ford had done a good job of integrating himself into Earth society.

  ✓ 3 Ford had got work in the theatre.

    4 Ford had made a mistake in his choice of name.

  ✓ 5 Ford was not particularly tall or good-looking.

    6 Ford's eyes tended to water more often than normal. *get crushed*

  0 7 Ford was <u>invited</u> to lots of parties.

  F 8 Ford was pretending to look for flying saucers.

  ✓ 9 Arthur was trying to stop his home from being destroyed. = *demolished*

  ✓ 10 Ford did not understand the real meaning of what Arthur was saying.

4 Read the quotation from the listening text in Exercise 3 and answer the questions below.

'They don't have sarcasm on Betelgeuse.'

> **sar·cas·m** /ˈsɑːkæzəm‖ˈsɑːr-/ *n* [U] a way of speaking or writing that involves saying the opposite of what you really mean in order to make an unkind joke or to show that you are annoyed: **heavy sarcasm** (= very clear sarcasm) *She was an hour late. "Good of you to arrive on time," George said with heavy sarcasm.*

(Longman Dictionary of Contemporary English)

Have you noticed any particular differences between your culture and other cultures? Can this lead to problems? If so, how can these kinds of problems be overcome?

Vocabulary: adverbs of manner

1 These sentences come from the listening text above. Suggest one possible word that could complete each gap and then listen to the complete sentences to hear the actual words that were used.

1 He smiled slightly too ....
2 Then he would start .... for a moment, relax and grin.
3 'Green ones,' he would reply with a wicked grin and laugh .... for a moment.
4 He stared .... into the sky ...

18

2 Can you think of any other adverbs that could complete the sentences in Exercise 1.

3 Decide which two of the adverbs on the right go best with each of the verbs on the left.

EXAMPLE: *laugh – helplessly, uneasily*

laugh	7 intuitively ⁵ irresponsibly
2 dress	4 sincerely 2 neatly 3 attentively
3 listen	6 drastically ¹ helplessly
4 regret	4 bitterly 6 imperceptibly
5 behave	¹⁰ uneasily 5 abominably
6 change	7 intimately 3 patiently
7 know	2 elegantly

4 Make sentences to illustrate the meaning of one combination with each verb.

EXAMPLE: *He **laughed uneasily** when his sister joked that she and her whole family might come and live with them.*

Speaking

1 Look at the picture of commuters reading above. Is this a scene that you could imagine seeing in your country? Why/why not?

2 Discuss with other students.

1 Do people generally read much in your country? What do they read? When do they read?
2 What do you read? When do you read? Do you read much in English? If so, what?
3 Do you think you read quickly or slowly? Have you any ideas about how you might improve your reading speed?

Reading

▶ P1, Pt4 (multiple matching)

1 Read the following questionnaire. Decide if the answer to each question is *Yes* or *No*.

1 Speeds over 1,000 words per minute are possible. Yes/No
2 We all read, by definition, at a natural reading speed. Yes/No
3 Word-for-word reading helps comprehension. Yes/No
4 Your level of motivation does not affect your reading speed. Yes/No
5 You should try and understand 100% of what you read. Yes/No
6 You should try and remember 100% of what you read. Yes/No
7 Your eye should sweep in a continuous flowing movement along the line as it reads. Yes/No
8 You will only truly be able to understand what your eyes focus clearly on. Yes/No
9 Skipping words is a lazy habit and should be eliminated. Yes/No
10 When you miss something while reading, you should skip back to make sure you understand it before you move on. Yes/No
11 When you come to a word that you do not understand, you should have a dictionary close at hand so that you can look it up immediately. Yes/No
12 A good or important book should be read page by page, never reading page 20 until you have read page 19, and certainly not reading the end before you have completed the beginning. Yes/No
13 When you come to important items in a text you should note them in order to improve your memory. Yes/No
14 Your notes should always be in a neat, ordered and structured form – mainly sentences and organised lists of the information you have read. Yes/No
15 For novels and poetry, slower reading speeds are important in order to appreciate the meaning of the information and the rhythm of the language. Yes/No

2 Now check your answers on p.215.

3 Look back at the questionnaire above. With another student decide on two or three methods that you will try in order to improve your reading speed.

4 What do you know about the festivals A–F below?

5 Now speed read the following texts in about five minutes. Tell another student what you remember from each one.

A Halloween

Now a children's holiday, Halloween was originally a Celtic* festival for the dead, celebrated on the last day of the Celtic year, October 31.

5 One story says that, on that day, the disembodied spirits of all those who had died throughout the preceding year would come back in search of living bodies to possess for the next year. It was believed to 10 be their only hope for the afterlife. Naturally, the still-living did not want to be possessed. So, on the night of October 31, villagers would extinguish the fires in their homes, to make them cold and 15 undesirable. They would then dress up in all manner of ghoulish costumes and noisily parade around the neighbourhood, in order to frighten away spirits looking for bodies to possess.

20 The custom of 'trick-or-treating' (when children go from house to house on Halloween to get small presents) is thought to have originated with a ninth-century European custom called 'souling' where 25 early Christians would walk from village to village begging for 'soul cakes', made out of square pieces of bread with currants. The more soul cakes the beggars would receive, the more prayers they would promise to 30 say on behalf of the dead relatives of the donors. At the time, it was believed that prayer, even by strangers, could speed a soul's passage to heaven.

Celts = ancient European people

B Independence Day

Independence Day is the 35 national holiday of the United States of America commemorating the signing of the Declaration of Independence on July 4, 1776.

At the time of the signing, the US 40 consisted of 13 colonies under the rule of England's King George III. There was growing unrest in the colonies concerning the taxes that had to be paid to England. Consequently, King George sent extra 45 troops to help control any rebellion. In April 1775 as the King's troops advanced on Concord, Massachusetts, Paul Revere sounded the alarm that 'The British are coming, the British are coming' as he 50 rode his horse through the late night streets. The battle of Concord would mark the beginning of the war for Independence.

By June 1776 a committee was formed 55 to compose a formal declaration of independence. Thomas Jefferson was chosen to write the first draft which was presented to the Congress on June 28. And although the signing of the Declaration 60 was not completed until August, the 4th of July has been accepted as the official anniversary of United States independence.

By the early 1800s the traditions of 65 parades, picnics, and fireworks were established as the way to celebrate America's birthday. And although fireworks have been banned in most places because of their danger, most towns and 70 cities usually have big firework displays for all to see and enjoy.

C Diwali

Diwali or Deepawali is a Hindu festival of lights symbolising the victory of righteousness and the lifting 75 of spiritual darkness. The word 'Deepawali' literally means rows of diyas (clay lamps). It is a family festival, celebrated 20 days after Dussehra, on the 13th day of the dark fortnight of the month 80 of Asvin (October–November).

This festival commemorates Lord Rama's return to his kingdom after completing a 14-year exile. Twinkling oil lamps or diyas light up every home and 85 there are numerous firework displays. (Another view of the festival is that Deepawali is meant to celebrate the destruction of the arrogant tyrant Bali at the hands of Vishnu.)

90 As part of this festive occasion, Lord Ganesha, the elephant-headed god, the symbol of auspiciousness and wisdom, is worshipped in most Hindu homes. So, also, is the goddess Lakshmi, who is the symbol 95 of wealth and prosperity.

The occasion of Deepawali sees the spring-cleaning and white-washing of houses; decorative designs or 'rangolis' are painted on floors and walls. New clothes are 100 bought and family members and relatives gather together to offer prayers, distribute sweets and to light up their homes.

D Carnival

The origins of Carnival are unclear, but most agree that it 105 started as a pagan celebration in ancient Rome or Greece. Carnival balls were exported from Italy in the late nineteenth century and had their golden age in the 1930s.

110 In Brazil, Carnival rules the country for four days a year, It happens at the peak of summer, attracting thousands of visitors from all corners of the world. 'Carnaval' (as spelled in Portuguese) changes dates every 115 year but it usually happens some time in February or early March.

Carnival is supposed to be a time to 'forget or recall an old love affair, to celebrate new passion or search for new 120 romantic experiences'. It's also a time to 'protest against corrupt politicians, to complain about poverty and give creative suggestions for ways to turn the country into a fair place to live'.

125 According to history, the first Brazilian Carnival is said to have taken place in 1641. Each festival varies depending on the location, but most main attractions are religious ceremonies, performances by the 130 samba schools or huge parades.

E Guy Fawkes' Night

In 1605, Guy Fawkes and a group of co-conspirators attempted to blow up the Houses of Parliament* to kill the King, James I and 135 the entire Parliament. The conspirators were angered because King James had been exiling Jesuits** from England. The plotters wanted to take power away from the king and return the country to the Catholic faith.

140 However, in an attempt to protect a friend, one of the group members sent an anonymous letter warning him to stay away from the Parliament. The warning letter reached the King, and the 145 conspirators were caught, tortured and executed. Guy Fawkes and his

friends had rolled 36 barrels of gunpowder under the Houses of Parliament.

150 These days, Guy Fawkes' Day is also known as Bonfire Night. The event is commemorated every year with fireworks and burning an effigy of Guy Fawkes on a bonfire.
155 The effigies are simply known as 'guys'. Preparations for Guy Fawkes' Day and Bonfire Night celebrations include making the 'guys'. In some parts of England,
160 children keep up an old tradition by walking in the streets, carrying the 'guy' and begging passers-by for 'a penny for the guy'.

> * Houses of Parliament = where Britain's laws get made and national affairs are discussed
> ** Jesuit = member of a Roman Catholic religious order

F Valentine's Day

Every February, across
165 the country, candy, flowers, and gifts are exchanged between loved ones, all in the name of St. Valentine. But who is this mysterious saint and why do we
170 celebrate this holiday?

One legend contends that Valentine was a priest who served during the third century in Rome. When Emperor Claudius II
175 decided that single men made better soldiers than those with wives and families, he outlawed marriage for young, single men. However, Valentine, opposing the
180 decree, continued to perform marriages for young lovers in secret. When Valentine was discovered, Claudius ordered that he be put to death.

185 According to another legend, Valentine actually sent the first 'valentine' greeting himself. While in prison, it is believed that Valentine fell in love with a young
190 girl – who may have been his jailor's daughter – who visited him during his confinement. Before his death, it is alleged that he wrote her a letter, which he signed 'From
195 your Valentine', an expression that is still in use today. Although the truth behind the Valentine legends is murky, the stories certainly emphasise his appeal as
200 a sympathetic, heroic, and, most importantly, romantic figure.

6 For the questions below, choose your answers from the names of the festivals/celebrations on the right. (When more than one answer is required, these may be given in any order. Some choices may be required more than once.)

Before you start highlight the key words in the questions in the left-hand column below. Then, skim the texts looking for 'parallel expressions' (phrases which give the same information as the questions but in different words). The 'parallel expressions' for numbers 1 and 2 have been highlighted in the text.

Which festival/celebration(s)		
involve giving presents?	1 ...	
celebrates the triumph of good over evil?	2 ...	
involves changes in the home	3 ...	
take place in the first three months of the year?	4 ... 5 ...	
come from disagreements with authority?	6 ... 7 ... 8 ...	A Halloween
is celebrated differently in different places?	9 ...	B Independence Day
involve fireworks?	10 ... 11 ... 12 ...	C Diwali
involve begging?	13 ... 14 ...	
came about partly because of anger over money?	15 ...	D Carnival
involves a symbolic food?	16 ...	E Guy Fawkes' Night
arose because of military needs?	17 ...	
came about partly because of an intercepted message?	18 ...	F Valentine's Day
have connections with love and romance?	19 ... 20 ...	
followed a formal political agreement?	21 ...	
involved strange clothes?	22 ...	

7 Discuss with other students.

1 What are the main festivals in your country? What are their origins?
2 How do you celebrate them? Do you have a special routine? What food and drink do you have? What kinds of presents do you give?

Vocabulary: words with similar meaning

D

1 Decide which word in each of these groups is significantly different from the others. What does it mean? (Use your dictionary where necessary.)

EXAMPLE: *a custom, a habit, an anomaly, a tradition*
an anomaly = a strange or unusual feature of a situation

1 to celebrate, to commiserate, to commemorate, to honour
2 a spirit, a phantom, a ghost, a premonition
3 to inflame, to douse, to extinguish, to smother
4 to originate, to terminate, to initiate, to conceive
5 to soothe, to startle, to alarm, to frighten
6 a rebellion, an insurrection, a mutiny, an assembly
7 to ban, to sanction, to outlaw, to prohibit
8 a symbol, a sign, a password, a logo

2 In each of the groups of words in 1–8 above three of the words have a similar meaning. Make distinctions about when you use each of the three words which are similar.

EXAMPLE: *a custom, a habit, an anomaly, a tradition*

*A **custom** is usually something which has been done for a long time by a group. 'It's our **custom** to have a party at the end of every school year.'*

*A **habit** is something someone does again and again, perhaps without realising it. 'He has an annoying **habit** of biting his nails.'*

*A **tradition** is similar to a custom, but may be older and passed down from parents to their children. 'We have a **tradition** in our family to go for a long walk after Christmas lunch.'*

3 Use the most appropriate word from Exercise 1 (in the correct form) in each of the following sentences.

1 Smoking is strictly .... inside the factory.
2 Scientists first .... the idea of the atomic bomb in the 1930s.
3 That cake looks fantastic. It's .... in chocolate. Just how I like it!
4 After several days of reduced rations, there was serious talk of .... amongst the crew.
5 The dove is universally known as a .... of peace.
6 As children we used to terrify one another by telling .... stories at night.
7 I was .... to see Andrea sitting in the corner of the room. I had thought the flat was empty.
8 I felt .... to be chosen to play for the national team.

Speaking

▶ P5, Pt2

1 In Part 2 of Paper 5 (Speaking) each candidate is given the opportunity to speak for about a minute without interruption. Each candidate is asked to react to a different set of pictures. Candidates should pay attention while their partner is speaking, as they are asked to comment briefly (for about 20 seconds) after their partner has spoken.

2 Work with another student. Look at the two photos (on p.218) and read the task. Discuss what you think might be important vocabulary and any possible useful expressions you might need to do the task.

TASK

Student A will have about a minute to compare and contrast the two photographs on p.218, saying how she/he imagines the people are feeling in them.

After this, Student B will briefly say which way of celebrating she/he would prefer and why.

Possible key vocabulary	Possible useful expressions
atmosphere	*The impression I get is that ... On the one hand ...*

3 Do the task twice. Take it in turns to be Student A and Student B. After each turn discuss the contribution of Student A. Note any particular strengths and any ways in which it might have been improved. When you are Student A make sure you:

• follow the instructions and do exactly what you are asked to do
• try and use a good range of vocabulary and grammar as you speak
• sound interested and involved in what you are saying
• speak for one minute and then stop

Grammar plus: noun phrases

1 A noun phrase gives information about a noun. We can combine nouns in the three ways shown in the table below.

Look at the different pairs of words in the table and match each one to the appropriate use:

EXAMPLE: *1b)*

1 when we name a particular thing and it is a well-known combination
2 when we say what things are made of
3 when the second noun is produced by the first noun (often an animal)
4 when we describe a container and its contents
5 when we describe measurement
6 when we describe a certain quantity of something
7 when we talk about parts of inanimate objects
8 when we indicate possession
9 when the first noun is a user of the second noun
10 when the nouns do not refer to a well-known/typical combination

---

noun + noun

a) a 14-year exile, a five-mile run
b) a firework display, mineral water
c) a gold ring, a silk scarf
d) a table leg, a car door

noun + 's + noun

e) America's birthday, Simon's brother
f) a women's sauna, a children's pool
g) goat's cheese, duck's eggs

noun + preposition + noun

h) a piece of bread, a pack of cards
i) a symbol of wealth, a book about indoor plants
j) a box of chocolates, a glass of wine

---

2 Listen to these pairs of sentences. What difference does the position of the stress make to the meaning of the sentences?

1 That's <u>Simon's</u> brother.
  That's Simon's <u>brother</u>.
2 Do you have a <u>book</u> about indoor plants?
  Do you have a book about <u>indoor plants</u>?
3 I'd like to buy my girlfriend a <u>gold</u> ring.
  I'd like to buy my girlfriend a gold <u>ring</u>.
4 I love <u>goat's</u> cheese.
  I love goat's <u>cheese</u>.

3 Four of the following sentences are incorrect. Find the mistakes and correct them.

1 The hair of Susan needs cutting.
2 Could I have a spoonful of sugar in my coffee?
3 There is an excellent shoes shop in the high street.
4 There was a very good documentary about Indian tigers on TV last night.
5 We need an 18-years old girl to play this part.
6 Tom was involved in a minor car's accident at the weekend.
7 Police divers searched along the river bed but they couldn't find the missing knife.

4 Expand these sentences with the information in brackets.

EXAMPLE: They live in a house. (£250,000; the house is in Scotland; an amazing view of the countryside)
They live in a £250,000 house in Scotland with an amazing view of the countryside.

1 There was a delay at the airport. (three hours; Rome; technical reasons)
2 He has a painting in his study. (100 years old; oil; Williamson is the painter)
3 She has been a teacher. (Maths; local secondary school; 25 years)
4 We did a walk for charity. (20 miles; the charity is for children; the weekend)
5 They had a meal. (three-course; a bottle of wine; under £35)
6 A girl was awarded a medal. (13 years old; gold; she was brave; the mayor gave the award)

▶ Grammar reference p.194

Watch Out!   *containers*

What's the difference between the phrases in italics?

1 We need another *wine glass* for the table.
2 Can I get you another *glass of wine*?

English in Use

▶ P3, Pt6 (gapped text)

1 In Paper 3, Part 6 you will have a text from which six phrases/short sentences have been removed and placed below the text with three additional phrases. You will select the appropriate phrase/short sentence for each gap in the text. Gap 0 is always an example filled by sentence J. Read the procedure suggested for tackling this task in the box below.

Suggested procedure

I Read the text through to get the general idea.

What are the two general types of wedding custom that are referred to in the text?

2 Look through the text again and predict possible ways to complete the gaps without looking at the alternatives below.

Discuss your ideas with other students.

3 Go back to each gap in turn. Read what comes before and after carefully. Select a possible phrase to complete it.

- Check the meaning makes sense.
- Check the grammar of linking words (e.g. *but, so*) makes sense.
- Check the referring words (e.g. *she, who*) link backwards or forwards appropriately.

4 Read the complete text again with the added phrases/sentences. Make sure that it all makes sense.

Compare your ideas with other students. If you have any differences, justify your answers by referring closely to the text.

2 Now follow this procedure in relation to the text below.

WAYS TO WEDDED BLISS

For many people their wedding day is the most important planned date in their lives and there are a whole range of symbols and customs associated with it. (**0**) *J.* is the custom of throwing confetti – a colourful mix of small pieces of paper, sometimes in the form of horseshoes, slippers and hearts. (**1**) ... and the practice comes from the Roman tradition of throwing almonds and nuts as fertility symbols. In many countries the wedding guests throw grain – often rice – although increasingly they use a paper substitute. (**2**) ... from which future generations will grow, and the scattering of seeds encourages a fruitful marriage. However, in some parts of the world there are other reasons for throwing sweet things. (**3**) ... raisins, figs and dates are scattered to 'sweeten' the general proceedings. And then again, the Inuit people of North America don't throw sweet things at all, but old shoes as an aid to fertility. (**4**) ... associated with weddings were originally designed to protect the bridal couple from evil influences. Probably the most universal talisman still in use is the veil. (**5**) ... to hide the bride from evil spirits. The Chinese are particularly wary of evil presences during what they see as the 'limbo' period, the time from when the bride leaves her house until her arrival at the ceremony, so she travels inside a closed sedan chair. (**6**) ... in some Russian ceremonies in which all the doors, windows and chimneys are sealed to prevent witches entering the wedding.

A It was used as a disguise,
B In Morocco, for example,
C The idea of the wedding ring
D The word 'confetti' is derived from the Italian for sweetmeats,
E Evil spirits are also literally shut out
F It is hardly surprising that
G Many of the rites and customs
H The journey to the wedding
I The wedding pair represent a new field

J One of the most common

Listening: away from home

▶ P4, Pt4 (multiple choice)

1 In Part 4 of Paper 4 you will listen to a series of five short extracts of about 30 seconds each. You will hear the five extracts twice. The speakers will all be talking about a similar topic. In the multiple-choice task you will answer two questions on each extract you hear.

Suggested procedure

1 Read the stem and the options for each question before you listen.
2 Listen out for key words which relate to the options.
3 Make sure you don't leave any question unanswered.

 2 Read the two questions below. Then listen and read the first extract in which someone is talking about their experience of living in a foreign country. (The tapescript is below the questions.) The correct answers have been circled. Underline those parts of the tapescript that justify the choice of answers.

1 The reason the speaker came to England was

   (A) for her partner's work.
   B because it had always been her dream.
   C in order to have a change.

2 Why didn't the speaker enjoy her time in England?

   A Because of the kind of work she was doing.
   B Because she missed her friends and family in the States.
   (C) Because she felt insecure about her relationships with English people.

Tapescript

I'd been working in Spain when I met Des, my husband to be ... Anyway, he had the chance of a good job back in the UK, in London. So we agreed that we'd go there and try it and see how it worked out. I'd never lived in Britain before but was really quite excited about it. In the end though it was quite different to what I expected. I suppose part of the problem was that I never found a decent job and it was much harder to make friends than I'd imagined it would be. There was also something about the English which I found quite hard ... I often felt I didn't know if people really meant what they were saying to me. I kind of think people are more direct, more straightforward somehow in the States.

---

3 Discuss with other students why the two wrong options in each question are incorrect. Is it because

- they are not referred to?
- they are untrue?
- they are partially but not completely true?
- they are true but irrelevant?
- there is a similar word in the extract but in a different context?

 4 Now listen to the other four extracts in which different people are talking about experiences of living in foreign countries. For questions **3–10**, choose the correct option **A**, **B** or **C**.

3 The speaker didn't know what different local shops sold because he

   A had problems seeing inside them.
   B was unused to these kinds of shops.
   C couldn't read the shop signs.

4 What does the speaker say about the friendliness of the people?

   A It was very unexpected.
   B It was an attractive characteristic.
   C It became rather overwhelming.

5 The speaker's time in Paris was

   A very similar to how she had imagined it.
   B pleasant but a little frustrating.
   C a generally positive experience.

6 What surprised the speaker?

   A How close she became to the French family.
   B How much time was spent at family occasions.
   C How few friends the French family had.

7 The speaker and his girlfriend went to China because they

   A were teachers.
   B needed to earn more money.
   C wanted a change.

8 The speaker felt embarrassed when someone

   A misinterpreted something he said.
   B wouldn't accept a drink from him.
   C made a comment about his watch.

9 The speaker makes the point that English people

   A usually only kiss once on the cheek.
   B only kiss very good friends.
   C feel embarrassed about showing physical affection.

10 The speaker felt embarrassed at first because she didn't

   A want to appear unfriendly.
   B properly understand how to greet people.
   C like kissing people she didn't know very well.

Grammar check: modals

1 Explain the difference in meaning between the sentences in each pair below.

1 You'll be surprised at how friendly they are.
  You may be surprised at how friendly they are.
2 You must kiss people you meet on both cheeks.
  You should kiss people you meet on both cheeks.
3 I can speak French reasonably well.
  I could speak French reasonably well.
4 You may open the window.
  You ought to open the window.
5 That must be the postman.
  That could be the postman.
6 You don't have to come early.
  You mustn't come early.
7 I can't lift those boxes in my condition.
  I mustn't lift those boxes in my condition.
8 I've got to leave work by 3p.m. today.
  I may leave work by 3p.m. today.

2 Give a reason for each of the following statements.

EXAMPLE: *He ought to give up his job because* **now he's won the Lottery he doesn't need to go to work**.

1 The present Prime Minister won't win the next election because ...
2 Jamie doesn't have to go to school tomorrow because ...
3 You mustn't be home late tonight because ...
4 I can't read the instructions on the side of this box because ...
5 This painting could be of some kind of animal because ...
6 You've got to start your revision this weekend because ...

3 Write direct speech for each of the situations below using an appropriate modal verb.

EXAMPLE: 1 *You should join the local gym.*

1 Someone you know wants to get fit. Give them some advice.
2 Someone has asked about your musical abilities when you were a child. Tell them about about your past abilities.
3 A friend has asked to smoke in your bedroom. What question do they ask?
4 Someone has asked you where your friend, Mark, is. You don't know for sure but you have one or two ideas. Tell them your ideas.

5 Someone has offered to give you a lift home. Tell them it is not necessary as you have your bike.
6 You hear the telephone ring. You are sure it is your friend, Sam, because he said he would ring at this time. Tell your flatmate this as you go to answer it.
7 The headteacher has given a pupil permission to leave school early. What does she say?
8 It's necessary for everyone to bring their calculator to the Maths exam. Tell your friend this.

4 Work with another student. Roleplay the above situations and continue the dialogue. Create the most interesting scenario you can think of for the dialogue.

EXAMPLE: Student 1: *You know, I really want to get fit ...*

Student 2: *You should join the local gym. It's great. But, anyway, why this sudden desire to get fit?*

Student 1: *Well, don't laugh, but I want to take part in next year's marathon.*

Student 2: *Really ... Are you sure?*

► *Exam Maximiser*

Writing: information sheet

1 Your local tourist office has asked you to write an information sheet (about 250 words) for visitors to your country. The purpose is to inform foreigners about any culturally sensitive issues so that they avoid offending local people by mistake.

Discuss with other students possible topics for inclusion in your information sheet. Make a list, for example: *gestures, greetings, going to someone's house for dinner* etc.

If you have trouble coming up with ideas, think about
a) times you have accidentally offended people when travelling abroad;
or
b) things that visitors to your country sometimes do that cause offence.

2 Choose three or four areas that are culturally sensitive to include in your information sheet. Make notes of points for inclusion under each heading.

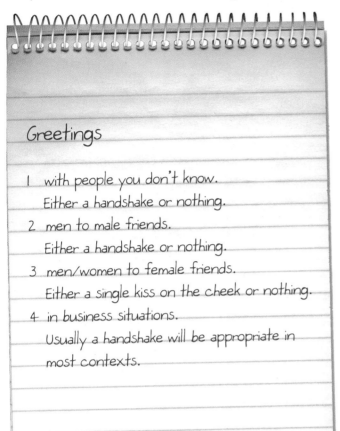

Greetings

1 with people you don't know.
  Either a handshake or nothing.
2 men to male friends.
  Either a handshake or nothing.
3 men/women to female friends.
  Either a single kiss on the cheek or nothing.
4 in business situations.
  Usually a handshake will be appropriate in most contexts.

3 Look at the information sheet on p.203. Make sure you read and understand all the Dos and Don'ts. Plan the information sheet you are going to write.

Planning your information sheet

1 What title will you give your information sheet so as to make it interesting and attractive to your audience?
2 How many sections will you have in your information sheet and what headings will you use for each one?
3 Will you need to use a more formal or informal style with the audience you are writing for?
4 What is the purpose of your information sheet (e.g. to inform, warn and advise)? How will this affect the language you use? (Remember, you don't want to put visitors off coming to your country!)
5 How will you introduce the topics you cover in each section? (Remember, you don't want to make your customs and values seem illogical to visitors.)

4 Write the first draft of your information sheet.

5 Show your first draft to another student for them to check by answering these questions.

Checking a first draft

1 Does the general heading make you want to read the sheet?
2 Is there a helpful introduction?
3 Are the different paragraphs clear and complete? Does each paragraph have its own heading?
4 Are linking words/expressions used in an appropriate way?
5 Does the information sheet *inform* in a clear and readable way?
6 Is the style appropriate for the target readers?

6 Discuss your partner's response to your information sheet. Listen to any suggestions as to how it might be improved. Reread your information sheet. Decide how you will change it.

7 Rewrite your information sheet.

Exam focus

Paper 3 English in Use: Part 3
(error correction – extra word)

About the exam: Paper 3, Part 3 is a correction exercise of which there are two types. In the first type, candidates have to identify additional words which are incorporated into the text. In the second type, errors of spelling and punctuation have to be identified. There are sixteen lines to be corrected and candidates should not expect more than five lines to be correct. In this section we will look at the first type.

Suggested procedure

1 Look at the title and predict what you think the text will be about.
2 Read the text through to get the general idea. (Don't worry about the errors at this point.)
3 Go back and read the text again. Look for typical types of 'extra' words e.g. articles and prepositions.
4 When you have finished, check that no more than five lines are correct.
5 Read the complete text again, checking that each sentence is grammatically correct.

Exam task

In **most** lines of the following text, there is **one** unnecessary word. It is either grammatically incorrect or does not fit in with the sense of the text. For each numbered line 1–16, find this word and underline it. Some lines are correct. Indicate these with a tick (✓). (Spend no more than 15 minutes on this task.) The exercise begins with two examples (**0**) and (**00**).

THE POWER OF PAINT

0	People have <u>been</u> always painted their bodies. The reasons are many: religious,
00 ✓	ceremonial, or simply for decoration. In Brazil, the Kayapo Indians
1	paint to each other's bodies using the blue-black juice of
2	the genipap fruit. An unpainted body can mean so that the person has no one who cares
3	enough to do it. Other Indians regard that an unpainted person as naked. Sometimes
4	body painting can be quite complicated because of every colour and shape has a particular
5	meaning. A popular design among the Thompson Indians in North America was to paint
6	half the face red and the other half black; red did brought the warrior good luck, while
7	black gave his enemy misfortune. In decoration for a religious occasion, the Australian
8	Aborigines use themselves traditional colours and patterns and these are applied
9	by a special person. For instance, when mourning, the mourners they are covered in
10	white paint. Among the Nuba in the Sudan, body painting is art for art's sake: it has
11	no religious meaning, it simply makes the body quite more beautiful. In fact, as a man
12	gets older and less attractive, he replaces paint by clothing. Also a man suffering illness
13	or injury will wear clothes until he recovers. Throughout the world, because people
14	like to decorate themselves according to their own customs. In the Western world
15	there is a multi-million pound cosmetics industry with vast amounts of money which
16	being spent on advertising campaigns to persuade the men and women to buy cosmetics.

1 For questions 1–15, read the text and then decide which word below best fits each space.

When in Britain, you must never complain. Complaining is very un-British. If you are (1) ... waiting half an hour in a shop, if a bus (2) ... is rude to you, if a waiter brings your food ice-cold – you keep your mouth shut. The (3) ... upper lip is the British way. Other nationalities might make a (4) ... , protest loudly or call for the manager, but not the British.

Remember also that British ears are (5) ... not tuned to hear complaints. A friend of mine was a regular (6) ... at a famous and expensive London restaurant. Every day at 2p.m. and 9p.m. the (7) ... manager would come out (as he had been doing for the last 37 years), go from table to table and (8) ... 'Did you enjoy your meal?' For 37 years, hundreds of thousands of properly (9) ... up English people had replied to him: 'Very much indeed.' The man would smile, say 'Thank you very much', and (10) ... to the next table.

One day, however, the lunch was so (11) ... that my friend (Dutch mother, Albanian father) decided to tell him the naked truth. So, when the antiquated manager (12) ... at his table as usual and asked, 'Did you enjoy your meal, sir?' my friend replied: '(13) ... , not at all. It was appalling.' To which the manager gave his (14) ... , obsequious smile, said: 'Thank you very much, sir', and moved on, quite (15) ...

1	**A** made	**B** kept	**C** stayed	**D** held
2	**A** conductor	**B** attendant	**C** assistant	**D** steward
3	**A** hard	**B** inflexible	**C** firm	**D** stiff
4	**A** discussion	**B** argument	**C** quarrel	**D** fuss
5	**A** simply	**B** easily	**C** utterly	**D** modestly
6	**A** supporter	**B** purchaser	**C** customer	**D** guest
7	**A** mature	**B** elderly	**C** outdated	**D** vintage
8	**A** inquire	**B** query	**C** request	**D** probe
9	**A** raised	**B** grown	**C** educated	**D** brought
10	**A** motion	**B** progress	**C** stride	**D** shift
11	**A** offensive	**B** painful	**C** abominable	**D** harrowing
12	**A** appeared	**B** surfaced	**C** descended	**D** joined
13	**A** Sincerely	**B** Largely	**C** Bluntly	**D** Frankly
14	**A** customary	**B** average	**C** commonplace	**D** daily
15	**A** convinced	**B** fulfilled	**C** satisfied	**D** complete

2 Select the correct alternative in each case.

1 Is that your *friend/friend's* car?
2 Do you like watching *horse/horses* races?
3 Could you pass me the *bath's/bath* towel?
4 Would you like some *mint tea/tea of mint*?
5 It was essentially a *lost violin film/ film about a lost violin*.
6 There are lots of *kitchen's/kitchen* cupboards in the new house.
7 Have you got a *timetable of trains/ train timetable*?
8 Look! There's a *bird's nest/nest of birds* in that hedge.
9 This sweater is made of *lamb's wool/ lamb wool*.
10 Has anyone seen a large *matches box/box of matches*?
11 Can you hear a *child's/child* voice?
12 There won't ever be *a tax on educational books/an educational books tax*.

3 Complete each of these sentences with one of the words in the box below.

> drastically   sincerely   abominably
> intimately   patiently   neatly
> intuitively   helplessly

1 He listened .... as she told her long and rather boring story.
2 He .... regretted all the unpleasant things he had said to her.
3 She knew .... that there was something wrong.
4 She's changed .... since she's left home. She's a new person.
5 He always dresses very .... but without much style.
6 He behaved .... at the party. He was rude to several of my friends.
7 He's terribly funny. We were all laughing .... for ages.
8 I wouldn't say I know him .... We're just work colleagues.

The root of all evil?

Listening: a mystery

▶ P4, Pt3 (sentence completion)

1 Look at the pictures above. What do you imagine is the connection between them?

 2 Listen to part of a radio interview with Max Valentin. What is the connection between the pictures? Did you guess correctly?

3 In Paper 4 (Listening), Part 3 you will be asked to listen to a conversation between two or three speakers, for approximately four minutes. You may be required to complete between eight and ten sentences. You will need between one and three words to complete each sentence. The words you need to complete each sentence will be in the conversation that you hear. However, you may have to change these words so they fit grammatically with the rest of the sentence. You will be tested on your understanding of specific information, gist and attitude.

Look at the gaps in these two sentences and discuss with another student how to complete them.

1 Up to now none of the .... has worked out the puzzle and found the prize.
2 For over ten years .... for Max's book lay untouched in his desk.

 4 Now listen to the first part of the interview again for the exact words that are missing.

 5 Think about the gaps in the following statements. Then listen to the whole interview and complete them.

3 Michel Becker .... as the prize for the winner.
4 Because the book offered its readers the chance to become rich it went straight into ....
5 Max told someone he was wrong in order to prevent him from .... a graveyard.
6 The .... clue describes precisely where the prize is buried.
7 Minitel was a kind of .... of the Internet.
8 The number of hours Max was spending at his computer began to have a very bad effect on ....
9 Max feels it would be a kind of .... to reveal the location of the prize.
10 Max thinks that one day he might .... to end the hunt.

i) to be approved
ii) to be too excited
iii) (of a sound) to be able to reach a certain distance
iv) to succeed in doing something
v) to do something too much or for too long
vi) to continue doing something
vii) to be respected and believed by people
viii) to complete a job or put into practice a plan or order
ix) to help someone manage when they are ill or having difficulties

2   Now complete these sentences with one of the expressions in Exercise 1 a)–i).

1 I got a bit .... and bought three pairs of shoes instead of one.
2 A public speaker needs a voice that .... well.
3 Sarah's views .... a lot of .... with the Sales Director.
4 He felt nervous before the speech but he .... it .... well in the end.
5 How long did the party .... for after I left?
6 The bill was finally .... despite strong opposition.
7 I think we should wait until more tests have been ....
8 Despite all the problems they were having, their love for each other .... them ....
9 The joke was quite funny at first but they definitely .... it ....

3   Discuss these questions with other students.

1 How long do you think you will carry on studying English for?
2 Do you know of a situation where a joke was carried too far? What happened?
3 What happens if parents or teachers make threats to children which they don't carry out?
4 Would you be a good public speaker? Does your voice carry well in large spaces?
5 Do you have a friend or is there someone in your family whose views carry a lot of weight? Why is that?
6 Have you ever managed to carry something off that you didn't really think was possible?

6   Discuss with other students.

1 Have you ever been on a 'treasure hunt'? What was it like? Did you enjoy it?
2 Why do you think some people get so obsessed by a 'treasure hunt' like this?
3 Do you think Max Valentin should put a stop to it or should he let it continue until someone finds the owl?

Vocabulary: expressions with *carry*

1   Look at the sentences below containing expressions with *carry*. Match them to the appropriate meanings above right.

EXAMPLE: *a) ii)*

a) People started to get really *carried away*. One man got on the table and started dancing.
b) She's an important person. Her opinions *carry* a lot of *weight*.
c) It's really quite a risky venture. I doubt whether they'll be able to *carry* it *off*.
d) Her great courage *carried* her *through* her illness.
e) The motion was *carried* by 310 votes to 306.
f) It was all quite funny but they really *carried* the joke *too far*.
g) His voice didn't *carry* to the back of the hall. I couldn't hear a word he was saying.
h) Do you think she'll *carry out* her threat to resign?
i) He *carried on* talking despite all the noise.

Reading

▶ P1, Pt1 and Pt4 (multiple matching)

1 Discuss with other students what difficulties young people might have if they became very rich overnight.

2 Read the text quickly to find out in what different ways each of the young people became rich.

3 Read the text again and answer the questions below.

1 For each question you will need to look for a 'parallel expression/sentence' in the text. This might be a phrase /sentence which reflects or illustrates the meaning of the question but uses different words. You will not find exactly the same words in the text as in the question. The parallel expressions /sentences for each question below have been underlined to help you.

2 Choose your answers from the list of people on the right. When more than one answer is required, these may be given in any order.

4 Add two more questions to those in Exercise 3. (Make sure you find parts of the text to justify the answer.) Ask another student to decide which person or people is/are being referred to and which parts of the text justify their answers.

5 Discuss with other students.

How do you feel about each of the four people in the article? Do you think you would like/dislike them? Give examples from the text to support your opinions.

6 Work with another student. Student A look at the rolecard on p.215. Student B look at p.216. Spend a little time thinking about who you are, your attitude and how you will approach the conversation.

Which rich kid(s)

doesn't feel very positive about their new financial situation?	1 ...	
is a little concerned about people who will try to get money from them now they are rich?	2 ...	
believes a conventional school education only prepares children for conventional jobs?	3 ...	A Tom Hartley
is very style conscious?	4 ...	B Simon Cunliffe-Lister
have impressed their parents?	5 ... 6 ...	C Tracey Makin
haven't really adjusted to the idea of having so much money?	7 ... 8 ...	D Karl Crompton
initially thought they had only won a small amount of money?	9 ...	
has good negotiating skills?	10 ...	
haven't changed their lifestyle very much?	11 ... 12 ...	

'Winning the lottery hasn't changed us – we're still here!'

32

RICH KIDS

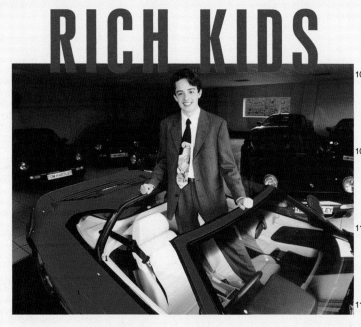

Today there are more and more young people under the age of 25 becoming millionaires. Coming into money at an early age can be tremendously exciting but it can also be fraught with its own dangers and problems. Here are 4 young people who have found themselves in quite extraordinary financial situations very early on.

A TOM HARTLEY

The thoughts of his contemporaries are of football, computer games and the latest designer trainers. Yet Tom Hartley, who struck his first deal selling a Porsche when he was 11, has just become Britain's youngest self-made millionaire at the age of 14.

Hartley has a private chauffeur, mobile phone and wardrobe of designer suits, and in the past year alone he has been responsible for clinching deals worth £8m for his father's luxury used-car business.

Hartley left school at 11 and since then has been educated partly by private tutors but mostly by the so-called 'university of life'. 'I am serving an apprenticeship and I learn something every day,' he said. He admits it's not for him but he certainly doesn't criticise a conventional education for others. 'If someone wants to be a lawyer or a doctor, they should take the normal exams. But for what I want to do, school doesn't suit me,' he said.

His father said of Tom, 'He has been talking with customers on the phone since he was 12 and the thing which really gives him the edge is his ability to know when to close the deal. Tom is a level-headed young man who can keep his cool in all sorts of circumstances. Actually, he's really more like a partner which is why I got him a Ferrari – he'd earned it.'

B SIMON CUNLIFFE-LISTER

At the age of 15 Simon has been left a £10million estate with a manor house, priceless antiques – and a butler. All inherited from a distant bachelor cousin.

Solicitor's son, Simon, who plays the saxophone in a band called Shagwagg, surveyed his new domain yesterday: 'The house would be perfect for a rave – but I suppose that's out of the question.'

Simon will be responsible for the 380-year-old Burton Agnes Hall, near Bridlington, Humberside. Paintings by Renoir and Gauguin, which hang from its oak-panelled walls, and collections of bronzes, porcelain and furniture attract 30,000 visitors a year. However, Simon's untidy bedroom at his current home is covered in pictures of pop stars.

Simon is a pupil at one of the most famous schools in the country, Winchester, which costs a hefty £15,000 a year. His long-term ambition is to become an engineer after completing an appropriate university course. In the short term though he is planning to show his girlfriend, Helen, 15, round the house and its 42 acres. He added: 'I've been told to keep an eye out for gold diggers and I suppose most women would be impressed by all this but I told Helen what to expect and she wasn't overawed at all which is great. Actually, the people at school have teased me quite a bit. They keep asking if I can lend them £10million!'

C TRACEY MAKIN

The National Lottery's youngest millionaire confessed yesterday that she would have been delighted with a mere £53. 16-year-old Tracey Makin thought she would be collecting that modest windfall after matching four numbers in Saturday's draw and it was only the next day, as she was checking her numbers again, that the GCSE student realised she had picked them all – and a win of more than £1million.

Earlier her mother said Tracey seemed to be taking the enormous win in her stride. 'She is being very cool about it, but obviously she is ecstatic,' she said. 'I don't know how she is managing to study for her exams, but she is and she'll be taking her exams in the summer, money or no money.'

Tracey chose her numbers from a combination of friends' birthdays. 'I probably will continue playing the lottery although I was told lightning never strikes twice in the same place,' she laughed. 'It's slowly sinking in but I still haven't really had the chance to think properly about what I'm going to do with the money.'

D KARL CROMPTON

What do you give the man who has everything? Well, in the case of Karl Crompton, something to do wouldn't go amiss. Amazingly, just a fortnight after scooping nearly £11million on the National Lottery, the 23-year-old is – to put it bluntly – becoming bored out of his brain.

Having become one of the richest young men in Britain, you might expect him to be drinking champagne, jet-setting around the Caribbean, or out on the town clubbing to his heart's content every night. Instead, the former electrical store worker dines on fish and chips at home, spends his evenings watching videos and goes out motor cycling with his mates.

Yesterday, unshaven and facing another dreary day of riches beyond the dreams of avarice, Karl admitted: 'I hate sitting around doing nothing. When I was at work it could be repetitive, but at least I kept meeting different people.

'It's hard to comprehend how much money I've got and when I actually stop and think about it, to be honest, it's too much and I haven't got a clue what to do with it. All I've ever wanted is a nice bike, a nice car and a nice house – and it's hard to know what else to get. I suppose I'll buy a house at some stage, but I've lived at home all my life and don't see why I should move out now.'

Grammar plus: verb tenses

1 Name the tenses of the verbs underlined in the box.

- I bought him a Ferrari because he <u>had earned</u> it. *PAST PERF*
- By the time he is 18 he <u>will have become</u> Britain's youngest multi-millionaire. *FU PERF*

- I <u>have been serving</u> an apprenticeship for 2 years. *pres perf cont*
- I <u>have not been watching</u> TV, I <u>have been working</u>. *past perf cont.*
- I <u>had been waiting</u> 3 hours before she arrived.

2 Look at the examples above and match each to one of the uses of the perfect tenses described below.

1 shows the time of an event as being earlier than another time *PAST PERF*
2 shows that the speaker sees the event as ongoing and temporary rather than completed and permanent *PRES PERF CONT*
3 emphasises the activity rather than whether or not it is complete *PRESENT PERF / OR CON*
4 shows the event as being completed by a certain time *fut perf.*

3 The present, past and future continuous tenses are often used to express ideas similar to those expressed by the perfect continuous. Discuss with other students the difference in meaning between the following pairs of sentences.

1 Jim lives with his parents. *perm.*
  Jim is living with his parents. *temp.*
2 I've been painting the living room. *not finished*
  I've painted the living room. *finished in not specific time.*
3 She asks me to help her with homework whenever I'm around. *mutual feeling*
  She's always asking me to help her with homework and I really don't have the time. *our complaint*
4 I won't see her again after what she's done to me.
  I won't be seeing her again now the course has finished.
5 Who banged on the door? *finished, short*
  Who was banging on the door? *long action, finished.*
6 The food is prepared in here. *fact, mutual*
  The food is being prepared in here. *passive*

from Right some move

adverbs of frequency = always

abhor = to hate

v. persive n. persaption

4 Look at the following sentences and decide if the verbs underlined are in a likely and appropriate tense or not. If not, correct them.

1 My neighbours <u>are constantly having</u> wild parties. It's terrible.
2 <u>I had been splitting up</u> with my girlfriend and was feeling terrible. *had walked / walked*
3 Our boss <u>had been walking</u> into the room without us noticing. It was very embarrassing. *cut*
4 I <u>was cutting</u> myself quite badly while shaving this morning.
5 I got to the bus stop and suddenly realised I <u>had left</u> my wallet at home. *CORRECT ok*
6 <u>Will you be working</u> from home tomorrow?
7 <u>Have you been hearing</u> the news today? *heard* *correct*
8 Why do you look so sad? What <u>is worrying</u> you? *CORRECT*
9 <u>I'll have been</u> here for three years in December. *Hom*

5 The following verbs are rarely used in the continuous form.

5 knowledge or mental state
1 emotional state *2 senses and perceptions*

like 5 believe 3 possess 5 know agree
2 smell 4 deny understand 1 love 2 taste
2 belong promise 2 hear 3 own 1 care

4 communication *3 possession*

1 Divide these verbs into five groups according to meaning. There will be three verbs in each group. What is common in meaning between the verbs in each group?
2 Some verbs can be used in the continuous form when they have one meaning but not when they have a different meaning. Decide which of the alternatives below are possible and, in each case, what the meaning of the underlined verb is.

a) <u>I'm thinking</u> you should talk to your bank manager.
b) <u>I'm thinking</u> of spending a week in France in June.
c) <u>I'm seeing</u> Paul tonight.
d) <u>I'm seeing</u> what you mean. *sense perception*
e) <u>I'm tasting</u> the soup to see if it's OK.
f) This soup <u>is tasting</u> fantastic. *sense, fact*
g) <u>She's feeling</u> we should have a long holiday. *opinion, mental state*
h) <u>She's not feeling</u> very well.

caught in the act

How

6 Read the following dialogue between two students. Put the verbs in brackets into one of the following tenses.

> Present Simple, Present Continuous, Past Simple, Past Continuous, Present Perfect Simple, Present Perfect Continuous, Past Perfect Simple, Future Simple, Future Perfect, Future Continuous

A: Hi Julie. How was your summer break?

B: Great! I can't believe it's all gone so fast!

A: So, what (1) _have you been doing_ (you do) since you got back?

B: Well the main thing has been moving all my stuff into the house I (2) _will be sharing_ (share) with four others from next Saturday. It (3) _belongs_ (belong) to the university and it's really nice.

A: Great! Well, while you (4) _were moving_ (move), I was revising for my exams in October.

B: You (5) _are joking_ (joke)! You don't have exams already, do you?

A: Yes, well, you know I (6) _failed_ (fail) a couple of my June exams. So now I have to retake them.

B: Oh yes, I (7) _had completely forgotten_ (completely forget). How awful!

A: At least they (8) _will be_ (be) over soon. Anyway, what's it like in your new place?

B: Well, it's complete chaos at the moment but with luck we (9) _will have unpacked_ (unpack) most of the boxes by the weekend.

A: Listen, if there's anything I can do, just tell me, won't you?

B: Hey thanks but I think we (10) _have done_ (do) all the main things. Anyway, you should be concentrating on your exams!

7 Tell other students:

1 two things you have done in the last year which you are really pleased about

2 two things you hope you will have done by this time next year

8 Imagine you have won a five-day dream holiday. You have unlimited funds. You can go anywhere, use any means of transport and stay in any kind of accommodation.

1 Work with another student. Plan your holiday together. Decide on two main activities for each day of your holiday.

2 Now work with another pair of students. Take it in turns to describe your holidays. Decide who has the best dream holiday. Remember to use the Future Continuous to describe your itinerary.

▶ Grammar reference p.195

Speaking: giving opinions

▶ P5, Pt3 (problem-solving task)

 1 In Paper 5, Part 3 the examiner sets the candidates a problem-solving task which often involves a number of pictures or written prompts. Listen to an examiner setting two candidates a task and look at the pictures below. What three things does he ask the candidates to do?

 2 Now listen to two students doing the following task. What's the main problem with the way they interact during the task?

3 Listen again. Make a note of any expressions you hear under the headings below and then add any other expressions you know.

Asking for opinions	Giving opinions
Agreeing	Disagreeing

4 Now do the task with another student. Remember to give each other plenty of opportunities to express opinions. Use a variety of expressions from the columns in the exercise above.

Vocabulary: compound adjectives

1 Choose the word that collocates best with the compound adjective in each sentence.

1 Of course Jim is a **self-made** .... He didn't inherit a penny.
a) success   b) tycoon   c) millionaire

2 The President of the United States never goes out in public without wearing a **bullet-proof** ....
a) shirt   b) suit   c) vest

3 Jim is very disorganised. He's a bit like an **absent-minded** ....
a) teacher   b) professor   c) scientist

4 I'm afraid we've had to call this **last-minute** .... due to the unexpected resignation of Tony, the Sales Manager.
a) meeting   b) gathering   c) conference

5 Who exactly is this **so-called** .... who is going to tell us all what to do?
a) connoisseur   b) expert   c) professional

6 I hate these modern, **mass-produced** .... I want an old-fashioned one with style!
a) vacuum cleaners   b) TVs   c) sofas

7 Doesn't he look great in that **tight-fitting** .... !
a) cap   b) scarf   c) T-shirt

8 I hate working in **air-conditioned** .... I always catch colds.
a) offices   b) environments   c) spaces

9 I can't come out tonight. I've got a **long-standing** .... to have dinner with my brother.
a) appointment   b) arrangement   c) agreement

10 Sarah is a very **level-headed** .... She never acts impulsively.
a) young woman   b) good friend
c) nice teenager

D **2** Discuss with another student the meaning of each of the compound adjectives above. When you have finished check your dictionary. How are the compound adjectives above pronounced? Where does the main stress fall?

3 Read these sentences. Then match each of the underlined compound adjectives with one of the definitions below.

1 Don't drive fast in <u>built-up</u> areas. It's very dangerous.
2 We were too <u>hard up</u> to afford new clothes.
3 You look quite pale and <u>run-down</u>. Are you eating properly?
4 That's the third <u>broken-down</u> old car I've seen at the side of the road today!
5 Now Sarah's been promoted, we're actually quite <u>well-off</u>.
6 You will receive a <u>one-off</u> payment of £500, but that's all.
7 I feel really <u>burnt out</u>. I've been doing this job for far too long.
8 I hate going shopping on Saturdays. I'm <u>worn-out</u>.

a) when a large machine e.g. a lift, has stopped working
b) your health is ruined because of working too hard
c) very tired, exhausted
d) an area with a lot of buildings and few open spaces
e) having more money than many other people or enough money to have a good standard of living
f) tired and not very healthy
g) happening or done only once, not as part of a regular series
h) not having enough money to buy the things you need, especially for a short period of time

4 Make sentences which show the meaning of seven compound adjectives from Exercise 1 or 3 above. Leave a gap where the compound adjective should go. Show your sentences to other students and see if they can decide which compound adjective is missing.

EXAMPLE: *Clive and Nicola have inherited a lot of money from their grandmother so now they are very ...*

Exam focus

Paper 3 English in Use: Part 6 (gapped text)

About the exam: In Paper 3, Part 6 you will read a text from which a number of phrases/ short sentences have been removed. You will select the appropriate phrase/short sentence for each gap in the text. There will usually be six gaps but nine phrases/short sentences to choose from.

Suggested procedure

1   Read the text through to get the general idea.
2   Read the text again. When you come to each gap, try and predict ways to complete it by reading what comes before and after. Then look carefully at the alternatives suggested below and choose the most appropriate alternative.
3   Read the complete text again with the added phrases/sentences. Make sure that it all makes sense.

Exam task

For questions **1–6**, read the following text and then choose from the list **A–I** the best phrase given below it to fill each of the spaces. Each correct phrase may be used only once. **Some of the suggested answers do not fit at all.** The exercise begins with an example (**0**). Spend no more than 15 minutes on this task.

BLUNDERING BANK 'GIVES' STUDENT £1M

Like most students, Faye Pattison struggles to make ends meet. So, when she checked her bank balance (**0**) ../. .

Barclays explained afterwards that a one-figure error in an international transaction (**1**) ... . A week later, she was even richer – to the tune of £500,000. And by the end of the month, according to her account, she was a millionaire.

Friends began making mischievous suggestions about (**2**) ... . Instead Ms. Pattison, a 21-year-old antiques restoration and conservation student, went to great lengths, helped by her family, (**3**) ... .

After repeated phone calls to Barclays' headquarters in London the tangle was finally sorted out (**4**) ... . She said yesterday: 'The longer it went on, the more my friends began suggesting I should just quietly move the money abroad and take off. But I can honestly say (**5**) ... . It just wouldn't be the right thing to do. It was nice, though, to stare at those figures and dream it was for real.'

Last night, however, Barclays showed some recognition of Faye's honesty by giving her the £300, part of the interest on her fortune. 'What happened was in no way her fault (**6**) ... ,' said a spokesman. 'We have apologised verbally for the inconvenience caused by the mistake and will also be sending her a written apology.'

A   although Ms. Pattison was still left with an unexplained £300
B   that I was never really tempted
C   to ensure the cash reached its proper destination
D   when the bank got in touch with me
E   and we feel she deserves a reward
F   meant the money had gone to her by mistake
G   transferring the money to a Swiss account and disappearing to South America
H   despite having to take out a loan to pay for her tuition fees
I   but I can't say that it didn't cross my mind

J   she was staggered to find it £34,000 in credit

Grammar check: articles

1 Read this text and decide for each gap if you need to add nothing (the zero article)/*a/an/the*.

FUNNY MONEY

In 1642 **(1)** ... General Assembly of Virginia solemnly passed **(2)** ... law declaring tobacco **(3)** ... only valid currency in **(4)** ... colony. **(5)** ... tobacco then remained **(6)** ... basis of Virginian currency for over **(7)** ... century. This was not such **(8)** ... strange aberration as it might seem. **(9)** ... history shows that virtually anything scarce, durable and desirable can become **(10)** ... money.

In more recent times, **(11)** ... most varied objects have functioned as money, from **(12)** ... dogs' teeth in New Guinea to drums on **(13)** ... island of Alor in Indonesia. In **(14)** ... Thailand, most parts of a tiger could be used as **(15)** ... cash, including **(16)** ... claws and **(17)** ... tongue. In **(18)** ... course of time, as in **(19)** ... China, **(20)** ... real thing was replaced by **(21)** ... replica. Pieces of silver in **(22)** ... shape of **(23)** ... tiger's tongue were still changing hands in Thailand only **(24)** ... few years ago.

But **(25)** ... greatest success story among strange currencies was undoubtedly the cowrie shell. For many centuries it was accepted in payment through much of **(26)** ... Africa and Asia. In the French Sudan, cowries remained an acceptable currency for paying taxes until 1907, when they at last succumbed to **(27)** ... relentless advance of paper money and coins.

2 Look at the rules below for the use of articles. Either make up or find from the text above one example for each rule.

EXAMPLE: a) *They sailed across **the** Atlantic Ocean.*

We use the definite article (*the*):
a) with rivers/oceans/seas
b) with superlatives
c) when there is only one thing
d) with particular nouns when it is clear what we are talking about
e) with previously mentioned things.

We use the indefinite article (*a/an*) with:

f) jobs
g) singular countable nouns (mentioned for the first time or when it doesn't matter which one).

We use the zero article with:

h) most streets, towns, countries, mountains etc.
i) uncountable, plural and abstract nouns used in their general sense.

▶ *Exam Maximiser*

Writing: informal/formal letters

1 Look at the expressions below. Decide which would be appropriate in an informal letter to a friend and which would be appropriate in a more formal letter e.g. to a bank. Write I (informal) or F (formal) at the beginning of each sentence.

a) With reference to your letter of 3rd May ...
b) I am writing to express my concern about ...
c) I would therefore be very grateful if ...
d) I'm really sorry for not getting in touch sooner ...
e) I look forward to hearing from you ...
f) It was highly frustrating to discover that ...
g) If this matter is not resolved in the very near future I will ...
h) Do write soon and ...
i) I am writing to enquire whether ...
j) It was lovely to ...
k) This is just a quick note to ...
l) I am sure that you will be aware that ...
m) I just wanted to let you know that ...
n) Please give my love to ...

2 Now complete each sentence above in an appropriately formal or informal manner. Pay careful attention to the grammar of the sentence.

3 Answer the following questions with other students.

1 How do you lay out/organise a letter to a friend/a more formal letter to a company?
2 How do you typically begin and end letters to friends/more formal letters.
3 Where do you typically begin new paragraphs?

4   Read the letter below that Faye Pattison wrote to her bank (see text in Exam focus p.37). There are six parts written in an inappropriate style. Find them and change them into more appropriate language.

Dear Sir/Madam,

Just thought I'd drop you a line to tell you about a series of errors regarding my current account. This all began last week when I checked my account and was over the moon to suddenly find that I was £34,000 the richer!

And this wasn't just a one-off either. Further mistakes meant that by the end of that month I had over £1m in my account.

The bit about this that really got on my nerves was how difficult it was actually to sort this situation out with Barclays' headquarters. I had to make repeated phone calls and was continually being passed from one person to another. This despite the fact that I was actually trying to resolve a problem that Barclays had created.

I can't believe it but everything still seems really up in the air at the moment and consequently I have no idea as to how much should actually be in my account at the moment.

I do hope Barclays will get their act together and sort this mess out pretty soonish!

Faye.

5   Now write the letter that Faye sent to her good friend Laura telling her all about the whole incident. Use appropriately informal language. Begin like this:

Dear Laura,

Really sorry for not having been in touch sooner but things have been really hectic here. You know how it is! Anyway, what I really wanted to tell you about was the most amazing thing that happened with my bank. ...

6   Look at this task and follow the instructions below.

TASK

You recently applied for a credit card. You planned to use the card while travelling around Britain during your summer vacation. Unfortunately, the first time you tried to use it, the cash machine said that the personal identity number you had typed in was incorrect. You typed it in again and the machine kept your card but did not give you any money. When you phoned your bank, they promised to send a replacement card immediately. Two weeks later it had not arrived and you assume that it was sent to the wrong address. Fortunately, your friends in England were able to lend you money to cover your expenses during the rest of your stay.

Now that you are back in your country you have decided to write a letter (200 words) to the head office of the bank complaining about the treatment you received. You are also going to send a cheque to your friends and want to write a note (50 words) to send with it.

---

1   Underline the important information in the task.
2   Write a plan for the letter and note including the main points.
3   Think of ways to express the main points in your own words and linking words to join the points together.
4   Use the formal and informal expressions you practised in Exercises 1, 4 and 5 in your letter and note.
5   Check grammar and spelling and write your letter and note out again if necessary.

Grammar check: relative clauses/ pronouns

1 Read the text below quickly to find out

1 the number of German marks which a dollar would buy at the end of 1923.
2 the country which has had the worst inflation in recent times.

2 Read the text again and complete each gap with one appropriate word.

3 Which of the sentences below is grammatically correct? Where both in a pair are correct, what is the difference in meaning?

1 a) My brother, who is a solicitor, lives in Glasgow.
   b) My brother who is a solicitor lives in Glasgow.
2 a) The man that owns this hotel, is married to my best friend.
   b) The man that owns this hotel is married to my best friend.
3 a) The thief got in through the window which had been left open.
   b) The thief got in through the window, which had been left open.

4 a) The students, who got very good marks, were allowed to go home.
   b) The students who got very good marks were allowed to go home.
5 a) Why don't you tell me which evening is best for you?
   b) Why don't you tell me, which evening is best for you?
6 a) The Eiffel Tower which was built in 1889 was the tallest building of its time.
   b) The Eiffel Tower, which was built in 1889, was the tallest building of its time.

4 Make questions to ask another student. Each question must contain a relative pronoun introducing a relative clause.

EXAMPLE: *What's the name of the American city where there was an earthquake in 1906? (San Francisco)*

► *Exam Maximiser*

THE VANISHING MARK

In the early 1920s, an inhabitant of Berlin went into a local café and ordered a coffee priced at 5,000 marks. By the time he had finished his coffee this unfortunate individual, (1) .... bill had risen by 60 per cent in just one hour, was asked to pay 8,000 marks.

This collapse of the German currency is the world's most famous example of hyperinflation. At the height of the crisis, money was literally not worth the paper it was printed on. At the end of 1922, (2) .... the US dollar was valued at 18,000 marks, Germans thought inflation was bad. But by August 1923 a dollar would buy a million marks, and by November it was even worse, when its value was a staggering 130 thousand million.

In practice, all metal currency, (3) .... had disappeared from circulation, was being hoarded by ordinary people because the metal's value was far higher than the face value of the coin. So the government, (4) .... by this point was getting desperate,

made coins of cheap porcelain instead. Eventually notes were printed on almost any material that was available – shoe leather, cloth, cardboard, even old newsprint.

The problems of living with hyperinflation were enormous. Workers, (5) .... were paid daily with large bundles of notes, were forced to spend their wages immediately. If they didn't they became virtually worthless, and shoppers were seen pushing heaps of money through the streets in wheelbarrows.

Although Germany presents the most famous inflation horror story, it is not the worst. That record belongs to Hungary, (6) .... there were bank notes in circulation in 1946 with a denomination of 100,000,000,000,000,000,000 pengo. However, then a new unit of currency was introduced called the forint, (7) .... was valued at an astronomical 200,000,000,000,000,000,000,000,000,000 pengo.

1 Some of the sentences below contain mistakes in the expressions with *carry*. Find the mistakes and correct them.

1 The sounds of laughter carried off as far as the lake.
2 They are carrying out urgent repairs to the town hall.
3 The motion to ban the sale of guns was carried on by 75 votes.
4 Will you speak to the headmaster? Your views carry a lot of weight.
5 It was hard when she lost her job but her determination to succeed carried her through.
6 Don't you think you're carrying away discipline a bit too far? They're only children!
7 Sorry I shouted. I can get a little carried away at times.
8 It's a demanding role for an actor but I'm sure she'll be able to carry it over.
9 They all carried on reading their newspapers as if nothing was happening.

2 Decide which of the different alternative forms of the verb are possible in each case.

1 What do you think you *are doing/will be doing/will have done* this time next year?
2 I'd been having quite a few problems at work and *was feeling/have felt/have been feeling* quite depressed.
3 She's *talking/had talked/'s been talking* of going abroad for a year. Do you think it's a good idea?
4 They *hadn't/haven't/won't have* been getting on very well recently. Do you know what the problem is?
5 What *have you been doing/are you doing/have you done* all morning? I couldn't find you.
6 Everything *is assembled/is being assembled/is assembling* in these two rooms.
7 By the time I got home, everyone *had gone/was going/had been going* to bed.

3 For questions 1–13, read the following notes written by a bank manager. Use the information in the notes to complete the numbered gaps in the letter to a customer who has made a complaint. Use no more than two words for each gap. The words you need to fill in the gaps do not occur in the notes.

NOTES

Write to Mr. James (letter of complaint 25th March)

– *Sympathise about his long wait to see one of our PBs (Simon Wagstaffe, Tracy Jones, Rachel Green ... all ill that day!). Explain it's really unusual for customers to have to wait so long.*

– *Re: his account going £300 into the red. All bank notices, pamphlets etc. say £200 is all that's allowed, unless you fix up to speak to someone in the bank first. If he wants to do this, we could look at his particular situation.*

– *Say we're sorry for problems he's had. Suggest he gets in touch if necessary.*

LETTER TO BANK CUSTOMER

Dear Mr. James,

Thank you for your recent letter expressing your (**1**) ... with the service of this branch. I can quite (**2**) ... how frustrating it must have been to wait for over an hour for an (**3**) ... with one of our 'personal bankers' but, unfortunately, a number of our (**4**) ... were off sick on that particular day and such a (**5**) ... is, in fact, quite a (**6**) ...

As for the matter of your £300 overdraft. I'm afraid it is clearly expressed in all our (**7**) ... that the (**8**) ... without prior (**9**) ... is £200. Of course, if you would like to make an (**10**) … to discuss your account with us, we could make sure that your (**11**) ... are adequately taken into account.

I do hope that you will accept my (**12**) ... for any inconvenience that you might have been (**13**) ... and trust that you will contact me if you feel that I can be of any further assistance.

Your sincerely,

R. J. Thomas

(Manager)

4 The universal migraine

Love is a universal migraine,
A bright stain on the vision,
Blotting out reason.
(Robert Graves 1895–1985)

Love is like quicksilver in the hand. Leave the fingers
open and it stays. Clutch it, and it darts away.
(Dorothy Parker 1893–1967)

Speaking: what is love?

Read the quotes about 'love' above.

1 Decide which ones are negative about love, which are positive and which are neutral.
2 Discuss with other students what point you think each quote is trying to make and whether you agree with it.

Grammar check: gerund v. infinitive

1 Read the following article and answer these two questions.

1 Is Jin Ye married to the man she loves?
2 Is Lien Hua married?

THE LOST WORLD:
Where women sing to get a husband

JIN YE, 23, sings all the time. She sings to her children, she sings while tending the small vegetable patch behind her house, and singing was
5 a crucial ingredient in the romantic 5-year courtship with her husband.

In the mountains of southern China, home to the ethnic Dong community, people communicate largely in song.
10 Jin Ye tells the story she remembers her parents (1) **tell** her as a child about a young man called Jing Bi (Golden Coin) who introduced songs to the people. 'One day he decided (2) **go on**
15 a long walk. He walked so far that he reached the Kingdom of Heaven. The gates were opened and he saw some young girls who were singing and dancing marvellously. He stayed for
20 seven days and nights and managed (3) **learn** the songs by heart. Then, when he returned home, he tried (4) **teach** his people what he knew. Songs have been important to us ever
25 since.'

'Here,' says Jin Ye, 'we love (5) **sing**

and dance. We enjoy (6) **sing** alone or accompanied by a violin. By singing love songs, we fall in love.' Singing plays such an important part of life
30 that married couples are not allowed (7) **live** together until their families rule that their voices are in perfect harmony. Only then can they hope (8) **have** a long and happy union. Jin
35 Ye and her husband lived apart for five years, meeting each day to sing 'separation' songs until their songs were compatible. 'Song stirs the soul,' says Jin Ye. 'When our voices
40 harmonise well, it proves we will get along.' There is even a Dong proverb – 'Whoever cannot sing cannot expect (9) **marry**.'

Jin Ye laughs as she talks about her
45 husband's singing. 'The first time my husband offered (10) **marry** me I thought he sang really badly. My boyfriend was much better.'

Although some young people do
50 now marry by mutual consent, even independent-minded girls like Jin Ye will agree (11) **abide** by the decision of their elders. 'Every parent wishes an easier life for their children, which is
55 why I listen to them. It was love at first sight with my boyfriend – we met at the evening singing meetings – but he

came from a poor family and my parents wouldn't accept him so I couldn't continue (12) **see** him. They
60 preferred (13) **choose** the man who is now my husband.' Jin Ye doesn't regret (14) **marry** her husband and sees no conflict between the freedom girls enjoy before marriage, when they are
65 allowed (15) **have** different boyfriends, and having a husband chosen for them. 'Love and marriage are two very different things,' she says.

Some couples rarely see each other
70 after their marriage, either because they live a long way apart or, quite simply, because they are not in love. Divorce is rare, but is accepted if a marriage fails. Jin Ye's best friend, Lien Hua, managed
75 (16) **divorce** her husband to marry the man she loved, but it was difficult and expensive. 'She married a man from another village,' Jin Ye explains. 'As they only met rarely she started
80 (17) **see** her old lover. When her husband's family found out, they demanded that the liaison should end, but Lien Hua wanted a divorce. Her husband refused (18) **agree** to the
85 divorce at first, so they had to negotiate and Lien Hua's family had to hand back the entire dowry, and a prized buffalo.'

Love will find a way.
(proverb)

Friendship is a disinterested commerce between equals; love, an abject intercourse between tyrants and slaves.
(Oliver Goldsmith 1728–74)

Say what you will, 'tis better to be left than never to have been loved.
(William Congreve 1670–1729)

2 Read the article again and decide if the numbered verb in each case should be a gerund, an infinitive or if it could be either.

3 Which of the following sentences are grammatically possible? Correct those that aren't.

1 Did you remember to get the soap powder?
2 You shouldn't expect passing your driving test on the first attempt.
3 I started playing the piano when I was six.
4 I wouldn't advise driving tonight.
5 We don't allow to smoke anywhere in these buildings.
6 Have you tried using nicotine patches to help you give up smoking?
7 I regret to leave school when I was only 16.
8 I'm not accustomed speaking in public.
9 I stopped to run and sat down on a nearby bench.
10 He denied to be anywhere near the scene of the crime.
11 They admitted to take the money from their father's wallet.
12 Would you mind to open the window a little?
13 I like to go for a walk before breakfast.
14 He suggested to go back when it was a little less crowded.

4 Choose five of the following sentences and complete them in a way that is true for you.

1 As a child I generally wasn't allowed ...
2 I once tried ... but ...
3 On Sunday mornings, I generally like to ...
4 I'm not really accustomed to ...
5 I generally avoid ...
6 I must admit that I rather regret ...
7 In the future I hope to ...
8 For people who want to give up smoking, I would suggest ...
9 The earliest childhood memory I have is from when I was about ... years old. I remember ...

▶ *Exam Maximiser* M

Vocabulary: similes (*like/as ... as*)

1 Discuss what you think the underlined similes mean.

EXAMPLE: *I miss you like the deserts miss the rain.*
   > **to miss someone very much**

1 Bringing up the subject of the rainforests when he's around is like a red rag to a bull.
2 Keep clear of Tom today. He's like a bear with a sore head.
3 Was the bed in your room OK? – It was great. I slept like a log.
4 I'm afraid it wasn't my kind of party. I was like a fish out of water.
5 He's so insensitive. He just says the first thing he thinks of. He's like a bull in a china shop.

2 Use logic or translation from your language to help you connect the halves of the following similes.

as strong	as a flash
as light	as a sheet
as quick	as a feather
as white	as an ox
as cool	as a cucumber

3 Use similes from Exercises 1 and 2 to describe the following.

EXAMPLE: *Someone who has a bad temper and is in a very bad mood.*
   > **like a bear with a sore head**

1 Someone who doesn't fit in.
2 Someone who shows no sign of nerves.
3 When something is done with great speed.
4 How someone looks if they are suddenly very frightened.
5 When you sleep very deeply and very soundly.
6 Someone who is very insensitive to the situation.
7 When something weighs very little.
8 Something which makes someone very angry.
9 Someone who is physically very powerful.

4 Listen to this song. Which simile do you hear?

5 Now read the lyrics on p.223 and the missing phrases/sentences a)–f). Listen to the song again and decide where a)–f) should go.

▶ *Exam Maximiser* M

Reading

▶ P1, Pt4 (multiple matching)

1 A cliché is an expression that is used too often and has lost most of its meaning. Do you have the cliché in the cartoon in your language? Look at the clichés in bold in the following article. What do you think they mean?

absence makes the heart grow fonder

SWEET NOTHINGS

Stop and listen to a conversation in the bus or in the supermarket and time and time again you will hear conclusions along the lines of: 'Well, you know what they say ... ' And how many times have we all said that 'birds of a feather flock together', or, if it happens
5 to be applicable, 'opposites attract'? Our conversations about life and love are full of clichés that we pull out time and again without really thinking. In fact, they communicate <u>succinct</u>[1] and powerful messages, but that doesn't really explain why we're quite so keen on them.

Dr George Gaskell from the department of psychology at
10 the London School of Economics likens clichés to conspiracy theories – 'hard to disprove and with a grain of truth to them ... so once they're there, they're hard to get rid of. There's something self-reinforcing about them.' Dr Gaskell draws on research evidence which reveals that people are much more affected by something which confirms a hypothesis than something
15 which negates it. So, even if a cliché is disproved ten times more often than it is proved, we'll still fall back on the idea that it must be true every single time.

Clichés, especially those we use when we're in love, are convenient short-cuts, avoiding the need for explanation so that someone gets the
20 general idea immediately. Clichés, say the experts, are rarely challenged and it's their generality that makes them strong. If you're too specific, people have got something to disagree with. Above all, they're familiar.

The big question has got to be whether these pearls of wisdom are true. Should we trust the clichés <u>trotted out</u>[2] about love, or are they just another
25 set of myths?

A Does absence make the heart grow fonder, or B is out of sight, out of mind?

The answer to this, according to Dr Jonathan Potter from the department of sociology at Loughborough University, is that both are features of
30 relationships; people have conflicting feelings and couples can miss each other when separated, yet be quite capable of getting on with their lives. 'You can use either cliché without fear of contradiction,' he says.

Well, not quite without contradiction. Professor Nicholas Emler, from Dundee University, comes down <u>squarely</u>[3] on the side of out of sight, out
35 of mind. 'When people are separated they tend to lose touch – we are very lazy in our personal relationships and forget about them surprisingly easily.'

Of course, the way you felt about the person in the first place might play its part.

40 ## C Does familiarity breed contempt?

Professor Emler says research suggests that we prefer the familiar, that we are happiest when we know what to expect and from whom. Experiments in the States <u>back up</u>[4] Professor Emler's interpretation. In tests, the more people saw new objects, the more they liked them. But if we do prefer the
45 familiar, why do we get bored?

D Is there a seven-year itch?

This proverb did not fare well with the expert. 'There is no evidence to suggest that after any set time couples are likely to break up or have difficulties,' Dr Potter says. 'While it's a good phrase accepting that after
50 people have been together for some time there can be problems, there's nothing magical about the number seven, or any other number.'

But if people do get an <u>itch</u>[5], who are they likely to go for?

E Do birds of a feather flock together, or do F opposites attract?

55 Professor Emler is quite definite on this: one saying is correct, the other a load of rubbish. People are much more attracted to 'their own kind'. Complementary backgrounds, religious, cultural or social, are vital to a happy relationship. 'A lot of research has been done on what draws people together, but the evidence clearly runs contrary to the theory that opposites
60 attract. The fact is that real opposites run a mile from each other,' states Professor Emler.

And what about the theory that the more unobtainable you seem, the more desirable you are to the opposite sex?

G Should you play hard to get?

65 Some psychologists say it's really hit and miss – the theory may work – or it could hopelessly backfire. The experts agree that being nice, considerate, <u>witty</u>[6] and charming is much more likely to win people's hearts.

We do, however, attach status to winning the affections of someone who is seen to be desired by a lot of people, and therefore is necessarily
70 less likely to be obtainable. But ego seems to be the operative word here.

So, why is it that we're sometimes left asking ourselves the question, 'What is it she or he's got that I haven't?'

H Beauty is in the eye of the beholder perhaps?

Research shows that there is some <u>consensus</u>[7] on attractiveness but there is
75 never 100 per cent agreement. According to Professor Emler, 'Cultural stereotypes, cinema and advertising all play their part in shaping our opinion on beauty. While in one group the majority can agree on what they find attractive, it is difficult to say why one person stands out.

'This phrase is a reassurance, it tells people that whatever they look
80 like, there is someone out there who will desire them; that beauty, after all, really is only skin deep. It's also something you can't argue with because people cannot agree entirely on what beauty is.'

2 Paper 1, Part 4 of the exam is a multiple-matching task. You usually have to link each question to a particular section of the text. Answer the following questions by following the procedure below.

Which cliché or clichés do the following statements refer to?

similarity is a key factor in attraction	**1** ...	
there is hope for those of us who aren't supermodels!	**2** ...	
these two opposing clichés might both be true	**3** ... **4** ...	**A** Absence makes the heart grow fonder.
while it makes a good general point, it's wrong to be so specific	**5** ...	**B** Out of sight, out of mind.
the truth of this depends on the particular context	**6** ...	**C** Familiarity breeds contempt.
one expert believes this is complete nonsense	**7** ...	**D** The seven-year itch.
two experts disagree about their validity	**8** ... **9** ...	**E** Birds of a feather flock together.
scientific research contradicts this	**10** ... **11** ...	**F** Opposites attract.
it's true because people are not good at making the necessary effort	**12** ...	**G** Playing hard to get.
any truth in this may be the result of a kind of competitiveness	**13** ...	**H** Beauty is in the eye of the beholder.

3 Explain the meaning of the following numbered words/phrases in the article.

1 succinct (l.7)
2 trotted out (l.24)
3 squarely (l.34)
4 back up (l.43)
5 itch (l.52)
6 witty (l.67)
7 consensus (l.74)

4 Do you agree or disagree with the research and what the experts say about the truth of the different clichés? Where you disagree, say why.

'I wish you'd stop putting me on a pedestal, darling'

Suggested procedure

1 First, skim the whole text to get a general idea of the content. You may wish to highlight parts of each section which you feel are of special significance or interest.

Do this for the text on p.44 and then compare with another student which parts you have highlighted and why.

2 Then, read all of the questions above, highlighting key words. If you are confident of any answers immediately, check them against the relevant part of the text again.

Do this and compare your answers with another student. How many answers did you both get?

3 Go back to the questions you are not sure about. Take each one in turn. Decide which sections they might refer to. Scan those sections carefully. Look for 'parallel expressions' (words or phrases that contain the idea of the key words in the questions).

EXAMPLE:
Question 1: *similarity is a key factor in attraction*
Parallel expression l.56: *People are much more attracted to 'their own kind'.*

Now find 'parallel expressions' in the text for the following:
Question 7: *complete nonsense*
Question 12: *not good at making the necessary effort*

4 At the end, check all the different sections are included in the answers. Also check you have answered all the questions.

Compare all your answers with another student. Where there are any differences go back to the text to justify your ideas.

Speaking: language of speculation

1   Look at the three photos above. Discuss with another student what you think the relationships between the people in each photo might be. Their body language and facial expressions might give you some clues about this. How long do you think they've known each other? Do you think they get on well or not in general? Are they …?

- strangers
- casual acquaintances
- siblings
- friends
- boyfriend/girlfriend etc.

2   Listen to these people discussing their ideas. Did they have the same ideas as you?

3   Listen again and complete the following expressions of speculation you hear used.

EXAMPLE: 1 *Well,* **it looks to me like** *the young couple are probably …*

1   Well, ... the young couple are probably boyfriend and girlfriend.
2   My .... it's quite a new relationship.
3   I .... she is about to do something stupid …
4   I .... it's pretty up and down …
5   On second thoughts I .... they are only work colleagues.
6   I .... they were in some kind of serious relationship …
7   I .... but, to be honest …

4   Now describe what you can see in the three photos on p.223, saying what you think is the relationship between the people in the photos and why. Try and use some of the expressions for speculating that you have just heard.

Exam focus

Paper 4 Listening: Part 3 (sentence completion)

About the exam: In Part 3 of Paper 4 you will hear a conversation between two or three speakers, of approximately four minutes, which you will hear twice. It could be a radio broadcast, a meeting, an interview etc. You will either have to complete sentences with missing information (a maximum of three words) or answer multiple-choice questions. There will be between six and twelve questions – each question is worth one mark. You will be tested on your understanding of specific information, general meaning and the attitude of the speakers.

Suggested procedure

1   You will have 45–60 seconds to look at the questions before the conversation begins. Read all the sentences and, for the sentence completion task, predict what the missing words might be. Remember there will be no more than three words missing.

2   Listen and make a note of the missing words. You will hear the words you need in the text. Remember, you may have to make changes to the words you hear in the text so that they fit grammatically with the rest of the sentence.

3   When you listen for the second time, check the answers you already have are correct and listen carefully for any answers you still need.

4   Finally, read through all your answers, checking the spelling and grammar are correct.

Exam task

You will hear part of an interview with two people who are both interested in encouraging young people to enjoy Shakespeare. For questions 1–9, complete the sentences. You will hear the recording twice. Follow the procedure outlined above as you attempt the task below:

According to the programme, a major problem is that young people find Shakespeare's work [1]

The main characteristics of DiCaprio's portrayal of Romeo are his [2]

Angela thinks the most significant feature of the film is that the [3] isn't simplified or changed.

Angela is sure that the film has been successful in convincing [4] that Shakespeare's work is still relevant and exciting.

Simon and Angela agree that the new Shakespeare craze is partly a result of an ongoing [5] in the way teachers approach his plays.

In teaching Shakespeare, Simon, like Luhrmann, divided the text into [6]

Simon believes that Shakespeare can have a powerful effect on [7]

One way of bringing the text to life is to get pupils to [8] events which take place off stage.

14-year-old pupils can now be asked exam questions in which they have to describe how they would [9] a certain part of a play.

Grammar plus: modals (advanced features)

1 Match each of the following sentences to the idea they express.

1 Couples *can* miss each other when separated.
2 She *could* read before she started school.
3 I've *got to* finish this work before I go to bed.
4 You *can't* smoke in here.
5 You *ought to* take better care of your dog.
6 You *must have* had a great holiday. You look so well.
7 You *needn't* come to the airport with me.
8 *Can* I use your car to pick up some shelves?

- permission
- theoretical possibility
- weak obligation
- strong obligation
- lack of obligation
- prohibition
- deduction
- ability

2 Look again at Exercise 1. What other modals can be used to express the ideas below? Give examples.

EXAMPLE: *permission – can, may*

3 Go back to the 'Sweet Nothings' article on p.44. Find three examples of modals. What ideas/meanings do they express?

4 Some of the sentences below are incorrect or don't make sense. Change them as necessary.

1 You don't have to bring a calculator into the exam room. If you do, you will automatically fail.
2 They might not have known that the main road was closed.
3 Do I may leave early today? I'll come in at 8a.m. tomorrow.
4 You would better shut the window before you catch cold.
5 Can't you to play any musical instrument?
6 You might as well go home now. There's nothing more you can do here.
7 You could stay up until 11p.m. tonight as it's your birthday but then you must go to bed.
8 Do we have to visit our cousins on Sunday?
9 Try as I might, I couldn't make him understand my point of view.

10 The gift is beautiful but I couldn't possibly accept it.
11 She can have misunderstood what you were trying to say. Why else would she react so strangely?
12 Oughtn't we to have invited Pete and Sarah to the party?
13 By the end of this month I hope I can use this new computer programme without any difficulty.

5 Beginning with the words given, make the second sentence in each case below mean approximately the same as the first sentence.

1 It's not a good idea to drink coffee just before you go to bed.
   You …
2 I am as happy as it is possible for me to be.
   I couldn't …
3 It's possible for it to get very cold here in winter.
   It …
4 It's impossible that they took the car without asking me.
   They …
5 It's essential for all students to register by Wednesday at 11a.m.
   All students …
6 It really wasn't necessary for you to put up those shelves. But I'm glad you did.
   You …
7 Perhaps they didn't realise how late it was.
   They …
8 It would be inadvisable to book the flight until you are sure you can go.
   You'd …
9 Isn't it necessary to switch the heating on manually? It doesn't have a timer.
   Don't …
10 It wouldn't have been right for me to let you pay for everything.
   I …
11 It was wrong of her to call me all those names.
   She …

6 Read the following advice given about 'first dates' in a teenage magazine. Decide which of the alternative modals in each case is possible. More than one may be correct.

FIRST DATES

Imagine you've met someone you really like but you don't know them very well. You have finally decided that you want to ring them up and ask them out but are feeling pretty nervous about it all.

5   Actually, there are a number of things you (**1**) *can/ should/may* do to make the whole process a little less painful than it sometimes is.

First of all, you really (**2**) *ought/must/can* have some definite suggestions as to where you (**3**) *must/could/might*
10 go etc. There's nothing worse than getting into a conversation like this and then spending ages trying to work out what you would both like to do.

If they would like to go out with you, then you (**4**) *must/ must have/might* make sure that you agree an easy place to
15 meet up. Standing, waiting at different exits to a tube station for hours (**5**) *could/must/can* be a bit of a passion killer on a first date!

Next, when you're getting ready for the evening, don't try too hard. You definitely (**6**) *haven't to/didn't have*
20 *to/shouldn't* go out and get new clothes for the occasion. Wear clothes you know and like and feel comfortable in.

If he or she is a bit late, don't get anxious. They (**7**) *must/ can/might* have been held up unavoidably. Alternatively they (**8**) *should/need/might* be trying to make some kind of
25 point but either way, just relax. If you're feeling nervous about what you (**9**) *could/can/might* talk about, try thinking of a few topics which you think will be of interest to the other person.

During the evening, whatever you do, show interest in
30 the other person. Don't spend ages talking about yourself. You (**10**) *have got to/should/could*, for example, ask them about their family, their work/studies, their interests etc.

Check if they (**11**) *have to/need to/ought to* be home at a certain time. Try and make sure that you do both get home
35 on time. There's nothing worse than upset parents to ruin a great evening!

If you follow this advice you (**12**) *can/should/may* find that you (**13**) *can't have/shouldn't have/needn't have* worried after all ... and you (**14**) *have to/can/might* even manage to
40 fix up a second date!

---

7   Now write your own short article giving advice about what to do when you are invited round for dinner at your girl/boyfriend's house to meet their parents for the first time. Include as many modals as possible.

▶ Grammar reference p.194

Watch Out!   *didn't need to/needn't have*

Which sentence means

1   it wasn't necessary but it happened?
2   it wasn't necessary and it probably didn't happen?

a)   *I needn't have* cleaned the house today. My parents have been delayed and aren't coming until the weekend.
b)   I *didn't need to* clean the house after all. Joe had already done it.

English in Use

▶ P3, Pt3 (error correction, spelling and punctuation)

1 In Paper 3, Part 3 of the exam you may be asked to identify and correct spelling and punctuation mistakes in a short text. Look out for:

Typical spelling mistakes
- 'silent' letters being missed e.g. *debt*
- wrong suffixes e.g. *independant, conducter* etc.
- words which sound the same but are spelt differently e.g. *bored – board*
- words which double or don't double the final consonant e.g. *cutting* v. *printing*

Typical punctuation mistakes
- capital letters
- commas and full stops
- apostrophes
- brackets

2 Read the text quickly to find out how one married couple showed their gratitude to Lufthansa airline.

3 Read the text again. There are five correct lines, five spelling mistakes and six punctuation mistakes. (You will not be told this in the exam!) Look at each numbered line (1–16). If there is no mistake, put a tick (✓) at the end of the line. If there is a mistake, underline it and correct it. (Try reading the text sentence by sentence. This can help to identify if there has been a punctuation mistake.) The exercise begins with three examples (0), (00), and (000).

THE HEIGHT OF WEDDED BLISS

marriage

0	One of the most unusual <u>marrige</u> ceremonies ever held
00 ✓	must surely be the mass wedding that took place in
000	midair <u>between/</u> Tokyo and Bangkok in 1972. This was
1	a publicity stunt organised by the german airline
2	Lufthansa to launtch the first commercial jumbo jet
3	fliht of a European airline. Inviting Japanese couples
4	to take part in a jumbo wedding the airline found itself
5	beseaged by eager applicants. Twenty couples were selected
6	and on the appointed day headed across the tarmac of Tokyo
7	airport, led by a Shinto priest). The event was a curious
8	mixture of ancient custom and commercial enterprise. After
9	take-off, the couples were married; one by one in full
10	traditionall dress before a Shinto shrine erected inside the
11	cabin. At the wedding feast, the ritual drink of rice wine was
12	served. After a stop in Bangkok, where the Wedding party was
13	blessed by a Buddhist monk, the newlyweds' took off for
14	a free honeymoon in the Black Forest. One couple,
15	it seems, were espesialy grateful to their hosts, naming
16	the baby boy who arrived nine months later 'Lufthansa'.

D **4** Now correct all the mistakes you have found including the two examples. Compare your answers with another student. If you disagree, either check a dictionary or go back and look at the text again.

5 Look back at a recent piece of written work. Did you make any mistakes of punctuation or spelling? Do you understand why? Make a list of the common punctuation and spelling mistakes that you make and refer to this when you check through future written work.

6 Here are some commonly misspelt words in English. In each case decide if the word is correctly or incorrectly spelt. Where it is incorrect, correct it.

EXAMPLE: 1 *definately* > **incorrect**. *It should be* **definitely**.

1 We've <u>definately</u> taken the wrong turning.
2 You're <u>completely</u> wrong!
3 I'm not sure <u>wether</u> to take the job or not.
4 That's <u>quiet</u> an interesting idea.
5 Could you <u>recommend</u> a good restaurant near here?
6 That's a rather <u>incovienient</u> time for the meeting.
7 You'll <u>loose</u> a lot of money if you invest in that company.
8 What are you going to have for <u>dessert</u>?
9 We stayed in this <u>wonderfull</u> hotel on the first night.
10 I'm afraid we don't have enough <u>accommodation</u> for all our students.

▶ *Editing checklist p.214*

'So it wasn't a mis-spelling, then'

Vocabulary: noun collocations (with *of*)

1 Connect a noun from the left with a noun from the right to create well-known phrases.

a grain		opinion
pearls		endearment
a load		gold
a slip		truth
a difference	of	rubbish
a heart		contradiction
a lapse		concentration
a term		wisdom
the price		the tongue
(without) fear		time
a question		failure

2 Listen to the phrases above in context.

1 Check your answers.
2 Decide where the main stress falls.

3 Listen again and decide on the appropriate definition below for each phrase.

1   be very kind
2   a small amount of truth
3   the consequence of not succeeding
4   a slight disagreement
5   when it is necessary to wait for something
6   something you say when you mean to say something else
7   a way you address someone you love
8   sure that no one else will say you are wrong
9   a short time when someone is careless or forgetful
10 to say something is complete nonsense or stupid (spoken informal)
11 wise remarks (often used jokingly to mean slightly stupid remarks)

4 Take it in turns to describe to another student a situation which illustrates one of the phrases in Exercise 1. They must respond with the appropriate phrase.

EXAMPLE: Student A: *I remember when I was beginning to learn English I once said 'Where is the chicken?' instead of 'Where is the kitchen?'. I knew immediately what I'd said but it was really funny.*
Student B: *It was a* **slip of the tongue.**

Listening: messages

1 Discuss with other students. How do you feel about

• leaving messages on answerphones?
• receiving answerphone messages?

2 You will hear five short telephone messages. Decide on the correct alternative in each case below.

Message 1: The caller
a) is confused about something.
b) gets slightly embarrassed.
c) tries to apologise for her behaviour.

Message 2: The patient
a) will need to see a new doctor.
b) must wait at least a week for a new appointment.
c) has a choice to make.

Message 3: The main purpose of the phone call is
a) to reassure.
b) to make a request.
c) to pass on a message.

Message 4: The caller
a) definitely wants to buy.
b) may be interested in buying.
c) isn't sure exactly what is being sold.

Message 5: The caller
a) is upset by some unexpected news.
b) makes a suggestion as a result of some unexpected news.
c) is annoyed that no one is answering the phone.

3 Listen again to the messages. Imagine these messages are not for you, they are for a friend. Make a note of the main points of each message.

Writing: notes/messages

1 Read the following notes and messages.
Discuss with another student:

- the purpose/context of each one.
- who you imagine is writing to whom.

1
> You are blocking my driveway.
> Please move asap!
> J. Simondson (53 Acacia Ave.)

2
> SORRY – NO HOT CHOCOLATE.
> COFFEE STILL OK BUT HOT
> WATER NOT VERY HOT!
> ENGINEER CALLED.

3
> Hope the party was good. Should
> be home by 6pm. Why don't we
> get a take-away + video????
>
> xxx

2 Make a list of typical differences between the language in
notes and messages and other types of writing.

EXAMPLE: 1 *You don't always need to write complete sentences.*

3 Abbreviations are often used in notes/messages. What do
you think the following abbreviations in bold stand for?

1
> please ask John for all
> the details **e.g.** time,
> place, dress code **etc.**

2
> so after we left the party
> pto

3
> *Everyone must arrive by 7pm.*
> ***NB*** *jackets and ties are obligatory.*

4
> Could you let him have
> all the relevant **info.**
> **i.e.** all monthly reports
> going back to Jan. 99
> (**incl.** appendices).

4 Put the following information into concise messages.

1
- *Sandra is married to Mark.*
- *locked herself out*
- *having coffee with Julie (next door)*
- *waiting for Mark*

Write the note that Sandra leaves for Mark on the
front door of their house.

2
- *Sarah is Brian's boss.*
- *not feeling well, going home early*
- *wants copy of finished report left on desk*
- *will read through first thing tomorrow morning*

Write the note that Sarah leaves on Brian's desk.

1 Use the words in the right-hand column to form one word that fits into the same numbered space in the text.

WEDDING OF STRANGERS

A wedding between two strangers who met for the first time when they exchanged marital vows during a peak-time radio broadcast has come in for widespread (**1**) ... . Carla Germaine and Greg Cordell were married after winning each other in a 'lonely hearts' competition organized by BRMB radio station. The service, perhaps (**2**) ... , attracted the highest ratings figures of the year.

The model and the salesman were (**3**) ... of their critics and say they have made a serious (**4**) ... to make their marriage work. 'Everyone seems to have the (**5**) ... that we will split up, but we're going to prove them wrong,' Cordell said (**6**) ... .

The couple were selected from 200 (**7**) ... candidates by a panel including (**8**) ... counsellors and an astrologer. As well as each other, they won a free honeymoon in the Bahamas, a sports car and a luxury two-bedroom apartment.

1 CRITIC

2 SURPRISE

3 DISMISS

4 COMMIT

5 EXPECT

6 DEFY

7 HOPE

8 RELATE

2 Complete each of the following sentences with one appropriate word. (Contractions count as one word.)

1 We had .... leave now before it gets dark.
2 Surely they .... have known that you were going to take us home.
3 I .... possibly tell you where Gemma is. She made me promise to keep it a secret.
4 You should have seen Petra's face when she spilt that wine on the carpet. She .... have been more embarrassed.
5 You .... have told me that you'd already had dinner. I wouldn't have cooked if I'd known.
6 You know you .... have paid in cash. They have credit card facilities.
7 They .... ever have to work again now they have won the lottery.
8 .... you need to ask your parents' permission to have a party at your house?

3 Unjumble the words in italics in the following sentences.

1 I keep having these strange *sslepa* of concentration. I just can't explain it.
2 It was just a slip of the *gnoteu*. I didn't mean anything by it.
3 It may be intended as a term of *nmdnreteea* but to be honest I don't like it all.
4 There isn't a *ginar* of truth in these accusations.
5 The price of *lirfuea* is just too awful to contemplate.
6 What he considers to be his *rsealp* of wisdom are in fact just outdated clichés!
7 I think I am without fear of *rnnccttooiida* when I describe this as the best year we have ever had.
8 We had a slight difference of *nniooip* but it was certainly no more than that.

4 Write sentences containing a simile, referring to each of the words in the box below.

bull   fish   log   feather   cucumber   ox   sheet

EXAMPLE: *bull > Don't mention the government to him.*
It's like a red rag to a bull.

5   Where will it end?

Listening: cryonics

1   Discuss with other students:

- What is *cryonics*? (If you don't know, look at the dictionary definition on p.215.)
- What do you think about this?

 2   Listen to this extract from a radio programme. Make a note of what the Michaels family are doing and why.

3   Listen again and complete the following sentences appropriately.

1   The headquarters of The Cryonics Institute is in ....

2   Paul and Maureen believe that after they die they will still ....

3   The reason for being sent to America is so that they can be kept in cold storage in ....

4   Paul doesn't mind if his son, Alex, ...

5   Paul's attitude to what he is doing is totally ....

6   Paul thinks that spending money to be frozen is like having ....

7   Famous people who are interested in cryonics include ....

8   Paul has hated the thought of death since he was ....

9   Mrs Michaels compares what they are planning to do with ....

4   What do you think of what the Michaels are doing? Do you think it is a sensible use of their money?

Speaking

▶ P5, Pt3 + Pt4

1   In Part 3 of this paper you will be given some kind of problem-solving task usually involving pictures. You and your partner will carry out the task together for three to four minutes (with no participation by the examiner).

After this, you may be asked to report the decisions you have reached and then in Part 4 you will be asked questions of a more general nature related to the topic of Part 3 for another three to four minutes.

 2   Look at the magazine cover designs below and on page 55 and listen to the task. Look at Exercises 3, 4 and 5 before you do it.

The end of the desktop computer

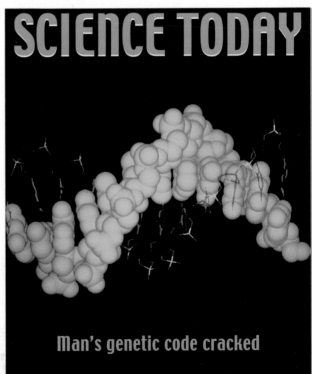

Man's genetic code cracked

3   Before you do the task, look at the following phrases and decide why we use them.

1   *So, what you really mean by that is* that you feel that the WAP mobile phone is too specific an image to have on a general science magazine?
2   *If I understand you correctly, then* you think that having a picture of a strand of DNA would make it feel too technical for the average reader?
3   *What I understand by that is* that you feel that focusing on a current issue like destruction of the environment could attract a lot of younger readers.

4   Listen to the sentences above on the recording. Pay particular attention to the stress and intonation given to the phrases in *italics* and then practise saying them.

5   Now listen to the task again and do it. Use the phrases in Exercise 3 if and when appropriate.

6   Read the following questions and think about how you would answer them.

1   Do you think it is important for children to study science at school? Why/why not?
2   How do you think we can encourage more young people to take up science as a career?
3   Do you think there are any problems about scientific research being left more to private companies than being funded by government?

4   What areas do you think scientists should be researching into with most urgency?
5   Do you think that science has helped to improve the quality of our lives or not?
6   If you had to nominate one thing as the most important scientific discovery, what would it be and why?

7   Now listen to some people discussing three of these questions. Did they have similar views to you?

8   Now listen again and make a note of the phrases that the speakers use when they add comments to what their partner has already said.

1   Just .... that, I would also say that ...
2   Whilst .... point, I must say that ...
3   Adding .... said, I also feel ...

9   Work in groups of three. One student will be the examiner, the other two will be the exam candidates. The examiner should ask one of the candidates to respond to one of the questions in Exercise 6. When that candidate has had a chance to respond, the examiner should pass the question to the second candidate for further comment. (This will not always happen in the real exam.) Take it in turns to be the 'examiner'!

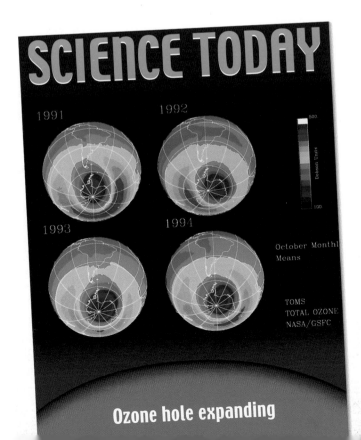

Ozone hole expanding

Are robots the future?

55

Writing: review

1 Discuss with other students:

- What different things are reviewed in newspapers/magazines?
- To what extent do you feel you are influenced by reviews?

2 Look at this information about writing reviews. Then read the review on the right. Does it contain the different elements referred to? Is it a good review? Why/why not?

In Part 2 of Paper 2, you may have the option of writing a review. You could be asked to review any of the following: films, television programmes, books, exhibitions, concerts or other performances.

You will generally be asked to review from a particular perspective e.g. why the film or book would/would not be interesting for people of your own age. You may be asked to compare and contrast two similar events or two different things e.g. a book with a film.

Reviews usually include the following elements*:

1 Background information about the author of the book/the director of the film/the theatre company e.g. *'Women are from Mars too' is director Alex Hernández's second film.*
2 A brief account of the plot of the film/book/play or a brief description of the performance or exhibition e.g. *The action takes place in Chicago in the late 1980s. Three young people sharing an apartment find themselves taking care of a friend's pet puma.*
3 Critical comment (either positive or negative) about what you saw or read e.g. *The author successfully creates an atmosphere of suspense.*
4 Your personal opinion and recommendation e.g. *This is a wonderful adaptation of a famous novel. I recommend the film to anyone interested in Russia.*

*Reviews of more than one book, play etc. may recycle the elements (1234, 1234.)

BLADE RUNNER (1982)

Director Ridley Scott, noted for his elaborate production design on 'Alien', again brings to the screen a brilliantly conceived view of the future. Based on Philip K. Dick's story, 'Do Androids
5 Dream of Electric Sheep?', the film stars Harrison Ford as Deckard, a dogeared cop recently retired from his position as a 'blade runner', a sort of officially authorised bounty hunter.

Thanks to some amazing special effects, 'Blade
10 Runner' is a mesmerising peek into the near future. Set in a horribly polluted Los Angeles teeming with street urchins, the story explores Ridley Scott's neon nightmare vision of things to come. As a 'blade runner', Deckard must hunt down androids called
15 'replicants', genetically-pioneered robots with human appearance and superhuman abilities who have been designed to explore other worlds and build colonies in space. A group of replicants have rebelled against their four-year lifespan and fled to Earth to find the
20 key to immortality. Deckard's mission is to hunt the escapees down.

This is a hugely influential movie which time has neither dimmed nor diluted. In the war between human and non-human, both sides pose the same
25 global questions; who am I, where am I going, how long have I got to live? In fact, Ridley Scott's vision looks as fresh today as it did in 1982. The foundation of this is the film's look, its atmosphere and attention to detail; this is where the film scores
30 so highly. Quite simply Blade Runner is one of the most stunning examples of pure cinema ever made. If you haven't seen it yet, you just don't know what you've been missing.

3 In the review there were a number of adverb + adjective/participle collocations e.g. *brilliantly conceived, horribly polluted, hugely influential*. Look at the table below and decide which of the adverbs on the left can collocate with the words on the right.

highly	successful
profoundly	amusing
utterly	moving
excruciatingly	ridiculous
hugely	disappointing
amazingly	tedious
	impressive
	entertaining

4 Look at this task. Decide what you are going to review. Look through the review on p.56, the model review on p.206 Writing reference and the useful language box on p.207. Make a note of any words or phrases you think you might be able to use in your review.

TASK

An international magazine for young people is doing a series of reviews of books/films called *I had to see/read it again!* You have been asked to contribute a 250-word review of a book or film that you have read or seen more than once and which made a deep impression. Give some background information to the book or film, briefly describe the contents and then summarise your feelings about it and why it made such an impact on you.

5 Now write your review, taking care to:

- respond to all the parts of the question
- organise your review into paragraphs (Check the elements of a good review in Exercise 2 above.)
- begin your review in a way that captures the reader's interest
- use a wide range of interesting vocabulary

Listening: song

1 Who were Dr Jekyll and Mr Hyde? What do you think is meant by a 'Jekyll and Hyde' personality?

2 Read the words to the song below and predict the missing words. They all rhyme with the last word of a previous line.

Dr Heckyll And Mr Jive

Dr Heckyll works late at the laboratory
Where things are not as they seem
Dr Heckyll wishes nothing more desperately
Than to fulfill all of his (1) ...
5 Letting loose with a scream in the dead of night
As he's breaking new ground
Trying his best to unlock all the secrets
But he's not sure what he's (2) ...

Dr Heckyll is his own little guinea pig
10 'Cos they all think he's mad
Sets his sights on the search of a lifetime
And he's never, never (3) ...

Whoa oh, it's off to work he goes
In the name of science and all its wonders

Chorus
15 *This is the story of Dr Heckyll and Mr Jive*
They are a person who feels good to be (4) ...
This is the story of Dr Heckyll and Mr Jive
Believes the underdog will eventually (5) ...

Not long now till the ultimate experiment
20 He's breaking all the rules
He wants to cure all matter of imbalance
In this world of (6) ...

He locks the door and he looks around nervously
He knows there's no one there
25 He drinks it down and waits for some reaction
To all his work and (7) ...

Hey, hey he fumbles for what to say
He loves the world except for all the people

Chorus

 3 Now listen to the song and check your answers.

4 Discuss with another student the answers to these questions.

1 Why do you think 'things are not as they seem'? (l. 2)
2 Why does he 'scream'? (l. 5) What does 'to break new ground' mean? (l. 6)
3 In what way is he 'his own little guinea pig'? (l. 9)
4 What does 'to set your sights (on something)' mean? (l. 11)
5 What is 'the underdog'? (l. 18)
6 What is 'the ultimate experiment'? (l. 19)

5 Now look at the extract on p.222 from Mary Shelley's famous novel *Frankenstein* about another overambitious scientist who creates a monster. Answer these questions:

- What has the narrator done?
- How does he feel about this?

6 Sometimes students agree to test new drugs for money, to show what side effects there might be on humans. Would you ever consider doing this?

Grammar check: conditionals

1 Put the verbs in brackets into the correct tense in the sentences below.

1 You .....won't pass..... (*not pass*) your science test unless you do some serious revision this weekend.
2 If he'd known what was going to happen, he ..wouldn't have started.. (*not start*) the experiment.
3 I ..would have gone.. (*go*) to the Sheryl Crow concert if I wasn't going to be away on holiday next week.
4 If you ..say.. (*say*) the word 'walk', our dog runs to the front door! — general truth
5 If you ..did.. (*do*) a bit more exercise you would feel a lot better.
6 You should read the new Michael Crichton thriller if you ..get.. (*get*) the chance.
7 If you press this button, the machine ..adds.. (*add*) extra sugar to your coffee.
8 Can I borrow your car, if I ..promise.. (*promise*) to take good care of it? → request
9 If you ..had come.. (*come*) to the party, you would have met my sister. — 3 cond.
10 Tell Tom to ring me if he ..has.. (*have*) the chance. — request

2 Refer back to the examples in Exercise 1 and complete these rules with the missing tenses.

1 To talk about something that is always true we can use this structure:
If + Present Simple, + ...
2 To talk about something that is possible we can use this structure:
If + ... , + *will*
3 To talk about something that is not true in the present and unlikely or impossible in the future we can use this structure:
If + ... , + *would*
4 To talk about something that is imaginary in the past we can use this structure:
If + ... , + *would have*

3 Complete the following sentences in a way that is true for you. Then find the student in the class who has completed their sentences in the most similar way to you.

1 If I have some free time tonight I will ...
2 If I become completely fluent in English, I will ...
3 If I won £1,000 on the lottery, I would ...
4 If I had the chance to visit anywhere in the world, I would ...
5 When I was younger, if I had ...

▶ *Exam Maximiser* M

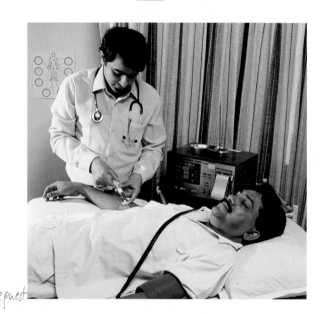

Vocabulary: science and medicine

1 Match the following words to the definitions below.

1 to clone
2 a cell
3 reproduction
4 an organ
5 (skin) tissue
6 an embryo
7 genetic engineering
8 fertilisation
9 a technique
10 a physicist
11 ethics
12 DNA

a) a part of the body, such as the heart or lungs, that has a particular purpose
b) an animal or human in the early stages of development before birth
c) a special skill or way of doing something, especially one that has to be learned
d) moral rules or principles of behaviour for deciding what is right and wrong
e) to make sperm join an egg so that a young baby or animal develops
f) the act or process of producing young animals or plants
g) an acid that carries genetic information in a cell
h) to make an exact copy of a plant or animal by taking a cell from it and developing it artificially
i) the material forming animal or plant cells
j) someone who works in the science concerned with the study of physical objects and substances, and of natural forces such as light, heat and movement
k) the science of changing the genetic structure of an animal, plant or human in order to affect the way it develops
l) the smallest part of a living thing that can exist independently

2 Check you can pronounce all the words in Exercise 1, numbers 1–12, correctly.

D **3** Use your dictionary to find the following parts of speech.

1 A noun from *to clone*.
2 A verb and adjective from *reproduction*.
3 An adjective from *embryo*.
4 A noun from *genetic*.
5 A verb from *fertilisation*.
6 A noun from *physicist*.
7 An adjective from *ethics*.

4 Discuss with other students.

1 What is involved in 'cloning' and 'genetic engineering'? What purposes could they be used for? Are there any ethical issues? If so, what are they?

 2 Listen to these comments about cloning. Which of these views do you particularly sympathise with? Why?

3 Is the role of the 'scientist' simply to discover new things? Or are scientists at all responsible for what uses their discoveries are put to?

Reading

▶ P1, Pt2 (gapped text)

1 Look at the title of the article below and discuss.

What do you think the article will be about and what ideas/views might be discussed?

2 Read the article, ignoring the gaps. Decide what the writer's attitude to Richard Seed is.

3 Next to the article are paragraphs which are missing from the main text. They are in jumbled order and there is one more than is required. To help you decide where each one should go, follow these instructions.

1 Look at Paragraph G. You will see the words *The second cloning method* ... have been underlined. What does this phrase tell us about what comes directly before this paragraph? Find the appropriate gap in the main text where this paragraph should go.
2 Look at Paragraph C. The words *this* and *he* are underlined. What/who do they each refer to? Find the gap in the main text where this paragraph should go.
3 Look at the other extracted paragraphs. Pay particular attention to the underlined words. Decide who or what they refer to. Allocate one paragraph to each of the gaps.

4 When you have decided on one paragraph for each gap, read the complete article from beginning to end to be sure that it makes sense.

5 Discuss with other students.

How does your view of Richard Seed compare with that of the journalist who wrote the article?

Cellmates

Had Richard Seed been your typical scientist – prone to caution and qualifying statements – he would never have become famous. If he'd even looked different, more mousy and cerebral, he might not have got the huge exposure on American television that he did. But as it was, his habit of uttering alarming far-fetched statements, his didactic manner and forbidding appearance ensured him his time in the media spotlight. For several days at the beginning of 1998, he became a household name as the first person who was going to clone human beings.

(1 ———)

There are, in fact, two ways of cloning animals and, potentially, humans. The first is by embryo splitting, which already happens naturally in the case of identical twins. From time to time a very early-stage embryo will divide to form two separate individuals who are genetically identical. It's possible to repeat this process artificially, but because only a very few cells are available at the stage where they divide, this method can only result in a few clones.

(2 ———)

Neither the increased legislation nor the public condemnation has caused Seed to question the validity of his plan to clone human beings. A Harvard-trained physicist who started working in reproductive sciences 20 years ago, he co-founded a company in the 1970s that developed a technique for transferring embryos in cattle. Later, he used the same technique on humans, attempting to transfer embryos from fertile to infertile women.

(3 ———)

If the idea of human cloning makes most of us feel uncomfortable, why don't governments simply ban it outright? The problem is that we risk throwing the (cloned) baby out with the bath water. The technology could be enormously useful. Following the outrage over Seed's announcement, American biotech companies and scientists were fearful that hasty, badly worded legislation would restrict valuable, ethically acceptable research.

(4 ———)

Nevertheless, the idea of cloning
70 is terrifying to many because it
seems to diminish us and at the
same time to give us enormous
power, a power we don't think we
are ready for. But Steve Jones,
75 professor of genetics at University
College, London, says we probably
shouldn't worry so much.

(5 ———)

A human clone, it is said, would
be a person's identical twin born 20
80 or 30 years later. A clone might
look like a younger version of its
parent and have many of the same
predispositions and inclinations but,
'You're going to get someone who is
85 raised by different parents, in a
different time, who will fall in love
with different people,' says Thomas
Murray, director of the Center for
Biomedical Ethics, Cleveland, Ohio.

(6 ———)

90 The issue of human cloning
raises a hundred questions to which
there are few clear answers. What
about the situation where a mother
wants to 'replace' a daughter who
95 has died in a car crash? Supposing a
couple had a child with kidney
failure: would it be right for them to
clone a sibling to be a compatible
organ donor?

(7 ———)

100 'If I look at some of my deepest
fears,' says Steve Jones, 'they're not
about cloning. But I do have fears
about genetics. I'm often shocked
that my own students don't think
105 there are ethical problems. Many
have the feeling that, if you can do
it, then you should.'

It's a pity science can't be made
to stop, back up a bit. We haven't
110 had time to fully absorb the ideas
surrounding human cloning, and
already we're moving into even
more ethically murky waters. Until
we get the issues about cloning
115 sorted out, what chance do we have
with an even more complicated
matter — our ability to make
offspring who are far superior to us
genetically? Or whatever happens
120 then to pass as being superior.

Extracted paragraphs

A He claims the procedure led to the birth of three healthy babies. 'Clones are fun,' he booms. 'They're so much fun, I plan to make five of my own.' It's an alarming thought. The vision of five more Richard Seeds looming over me is so distracting that I can't think of much to say in response.

B 'My mother is an identical twin, so I'm used to the idea of human clones. She and my aunt are clearly different people who happen to look remarkably the same. People who say clones aren't natural are effectively saying that people are simply the sum of their genes. They're not. People are people.'

C This was not going to be some time far into the future, but within months. It was a relatively simple matter, he airily claimed. No matter that other scientists said it couldn't be done, or ethicists that it shouldn't be done. He insisted he was going to go ahead.

D Having said this, geneticists currently appear to be less interested in issues of human cloning than the ethical and practical implications of genetic engineering. This is the kind of technology that could one day allow us to preselect a whole range of desirable traits for our children.

E Despite such criticisms, his relative lack of experience in the field doesn't seem to concern him. 'It's true that there are probably 40 or 50 people in the US who are better qualified to do this than I am, but, in the sense of project organisation, I am definitely number one.'

F 'They may be utterly uninterested in their parents' line of work. If you were to find some DNA of Shakespeare's, for example, and create ten embryos from it, it's very unlikely any of them would grow up to be a great poet.'

G The second cloning method – the one that Seed says he is going to use – is nuclear replacement. Genetic material taken from a foetal or adult cell is introduced into an unfertilised egg that has had its own genetic material removed.

H This could, amongst other things, give us an insight into the origins of cancer and information about how and why we age. It could lead to huge advances in organ replacement and, for example, a way of creating new skin for burn victims.

'George was DNA tested last week but they couldn't find any'

61

Grammar plus: conditionals (advanced forms)

1 Compare the following sentences in each pair. Then decide if the statements below are true or false.

1 a) Had he been a typical scientist, b) If he had been a typical scientist,	he would never have become famous.
2 a) If you happen to/should see Dr Powell, b) If you see Dr Powell,	please ask him about the results of my test.
3 a) Supposing/Imagine a couple had a child with kidney failure, b) If a couple had a child with kidney failure,	would it be right for them to clone a sibling to be a compatible organ donor?
4 a) If you were to find some DNA of Shakespeare's, b) If you found some DNA of Shakespeare's,	it's very unlikely that you could use it to create a great poet.
5 a) If you'll wait here, b) If you wait here,	I'll see if the doctor is free.

1 Inversion (leaving out *if*): This is more formal style.
2 *If + happen to/should*: This form emphasises that something is more unlikely or just a chance possibility.
3 *Supposing/Imagine* (in place of *if*): This is a more polite form.
4 *If + was/were to*: This form makes an event seem more hypothetical. (It is not used with 'state' verbs.)
5 *If + will/would*: This form is used to make requests more polite.

▶ Grammar reference p.192

2 One word is missing in each of the following sentences. What is it?

1 If I were say that I had always loved you, what would you say?
2 We spent more time with her, she might have told us what was happening.
3 If you just be patient, I'm sure the doctor will see you soon.
4 Supposing you had twins, that be a problem?
5 If you happen see Mr Parker before I do, can you explain why we were late.
6 You to go through with legal action, it could become very expensive.

3 Complete the second sentence in each case so it has approximately the same meaning as the first sentence.

EXAMPLE: *Please come this way and I'll show you to the director's office.*
***If you'll** come this way, I'll show you to the director's office.*

1 Would you go to college if you got all the necessary grades?
Supposing ...
2 Why don't you do the shopping and I'll make dinner?
If you'll ...
3 You wouldn't be in this situation if you'd listened to my advice.
Had you ...
4 Imagine they discovered a cure for the common cold, they would make a fortune.
If they were ...
5 Could you tell me if, by any chance, you see my address book?
If you happen ...

4 Work with another student to write a short interesting dialogue which must include the following sentence.

So, if you happen to see Leslie, could you please tell him that it was all a terrible mistake.

5 Think of a 'dilemma' to ask other students in your class. Write your dilemma using one of the new conditional forms from Exercise 1.

EXAMPLE:
• *Imagine you found £20 in the street, what would you do with it?*
• *If you were to see a teenager shoplifting in a supermarket, what would you do?*

Vocabulary: collocations (body)

1 Decide which of the phrases on the left below you can see illustrated.

2 Now match the phrases on the left with appropriate situations on the right.

EXAMPLE: *a) viii)*

a)	hold your breath	i)	when you are annoyed
b)	drum your fingers	ii)	when something is tasty
c)	shrug your shoulders	iii)	in disbelief
d)	wrinkle your nose	iv)	to show disagreement
e)	crack your knuckles	v)	when you are angry
f)	purse your lips	vi)	when something smells bad
g)	clench your fist	vii)	when you don't care
h)	twist your ankle	viii)	when you are feeling anxious
i)	pull a muscle	ix)	while playing a sport e.g. football
j)	raise your eyebrows	x)	to annoy other people
k)	shake your head	xi)	when you are impatient
l)	lick your lips	xii)	if you step awkwardly while walking on rough ground

3 Take it in turns to mime each of the actions in Exercise 2 a)–l)
to your partner. They must say what you are doing/have done.

EXAMPLE: *You're raising your eyebrows!*

4 Now respond to your partner miming the actions by asking for a
reason. Your partner should explain why/how.

EXAMPLE: Student A: *(licking her lips)*
Student B: *Why are you licking your lips?*
Student A: *I'm thinking about the meal that my boyfriend
is going to cook for me this evening.*

Grammar check: future

1 Read the following dialogue and decide if neither, one or both of the alternative future forms are definitely possible.

> **A:** So, what (**1**) *are you doing/do you do* at the weekend?
>
> **B:** Nothing much. How about you?
>
> **A:** Well, Steve and I (**2**) *will probably have gone/will probably go* to the Science Museum. They've got this great new section on genetic engineering which might be useful for the course I'm doing. By the way, I've been meaning to ask you. Are you still thinking of moving out of your flat?
>
> **B:** Yes. I really do want a place of my own. I hope I (**3**) *'ll be saving/'ll have saved* enough by the end of the year, so I (**4**) *'ll begin/'m beginning* looking seriously then.
>
> **A:** That sounds good. And when (**5**) *do you start/are you going to start* that course in computer science you keep talking about?
>
> **B:** October. I can't wait!

2 Now write down when we use each of the following forms to talk about the future. Give an example of each form in a sentence.

EXAMPLE: *Present Continuous* e.g. ***I'm playing tennis tomorrow evening.*** *We use the Present Continuous to talk about arrangements that have already been made.*

1 Present Continuous
2 Present Simple
3 *will*
4 *going to*
5 Future Continuous
6 Future Perfect

▶ *Exam Maximiser* [M]

Exam focus

Paper 3 English in Use: Part 3 (error correction – spelling and punctuation)

About the exam: Paper 3, Part 3 is a correction exercise of which there are two types. In the second type, errors of spelling and punctuation have to be identified. There are sixteen lines to be corrected and candidates should not expect more than five lines to be correct.

Suggested procedure

1 Read the text through to get the general idea.
2 Read the text again. Read sentence by sentence to help you identify punctuation mistakes. Look at each word in turn to help you identify spelling mistakes. Cross out the mistakes as you find them and write the correction. If a line is correct tick (✓) it.
3 When you have finished, check that no more than five lines are correct.

Exam task

In **most** lines of the following text, there is either a spelling or punctuation mistake. For each numbered line **1–16**, find the errors and correct them. Some lines are correct. Indicate these with a tick (✓). The exercise begins with three examples (**0**), (**00**) and (**000**).

THE POWER OF THOUGHT

0 ✓ A completely paralysed man has been given the ability
00 to communicate/ with the outside world through
000 electronic implants which were fused with his brain ͨɟells.
1 A pear of implants have enabled the man to control a
2 cursor on a computer screen just by thinking about moveing
3 his body. By pointing the cursor at diferent symbols he
4 can make the computer say phrases such as, 'I'm thirsty,
5 or his favourite, 'See you later. Nice talking to you.'
6 Researchers at Emory University hope the tecnology
7 will eventually allow paralysed people to operate artificial
8 limbs and New Scientist magazine notes that its the first
9 time such a connection has been made directly in the
10 brain rather than with nerves, in the spine or limbs. Each
11 implant is a hollow glass cone and contains a tiny electrode
12 'The trick is teaching the patiente to control the strength and
13 pattern of the electric impulses' being produced in the brain,'
14 says dr Bakay, the leader of the Emory team. 'After some
15 trainning they are able to "will" a cursor to move and
16 then stop on a specific point on the computer screen.'

Paper 3 English in Use: Part 6 (gapped text)

1 Read the following text and then choose from the list **A–J** the best phrase to fill each of the spaces. The exercise begins with an example (**0**).

GIFTS ARE FULL OF MEANING FOR GIVER AND RECEIVER

Millions of the Christmas, anniversary and birthday presents (**0**) ....*J*.......... are dismissed, disdained and returned. At the same time, unkind thoughts occur about whoever chose the gift. What really matters is not the gift itself, (**1**) .... Recipients evaluate the gift and place it in a category: from affirming an already good relationship to contributing the last straw to a teetering one. What we all want, of course, (**2**) .... : something that signals that the other person knows what our wants and needs are. An affirming present does not have to be expensive or personal, just something that proves the giver was paying attention. A close marriage or friendship is most likely to produce these kinds of gifts, although in relationships that are already strong a poor choice does not normally cause serious rifts. In relationships that are good, a present is considered strengthening (**3**) .... An engagement ring is the classic example, but it could be anything that symbolises greater commitment and understanding. Many gifts have no real impact either way. This is often the case with family members, for example, a sister who gives bath oil to a sibling (**4**) .... Nobody says anything because it is not worth a scene or hurting feelings. A weakening present is one (**5**) .... It signals the giver was going through the motions or, worse still, insults the recipient. An example of this is the husband (**6**) .... on a romantic anniversary. The severing gift is the last, ugly proof that things have reached the point of no return. For instance, the ex-lover who gives a membership to a dating service.

A is something we would not buy for ourselves

B that damages the relationship

C when you already have one

D but the symbolism

E when it takes things to the next level

F that you have chosen particularly carefully

G who gives a vacuum cleaner

H is an affirming present

I who always has showers

J that we select so carefully each year

---

2 Match the word stems in the left hand column to the suffixes in the right hand column. You can use some of the suffixes with more than one stem.

a)	indecis-	1 -ness
b)	resent-	2 -ion
c)	hospital-	3 -ism
d)	hero-	4 -al
e)	kind-	5 -ment
f)	intellig-	6 -ish
g)	child-	7 -ity
h)	privat-	8 -ious
i)	develop-	9 -ent
j)	spac-	10 -ful
k)	loy-	11 -ise

3 Eight of these sentences contain errors. Find them and correct them.

1 They've risen the life expectancy of people living in the developed world by more than 25 years.
2 I'm sure our team can win the other team if they really try.
3 I feel myself rather unwell.
4 She asked me to call her when I was in Rome but I forgot it.
5 He paid me a ticket to Madrid.
6 I know she's got a very irritating voice but she can't help it.
7 He promised he'd write but I'm still expecting.
8 Before you close, check that you've got your keys with you.
9 Thank you so much for the perfume. I love!
10 My grandfather tells wonderful stories about life when he was a boy.

4 In each sentence circle the correct alternative to complete the sentence.

1 He seemed to know *intuitively/attentively* that she felt shy and uncomfortable.
2 When I do my shopping my dog Spot waits *neatly/patiently* outside the supermarket for me.
3 She cried *drastically/bitterly* when he left.
4 I want to apologise most *sincerely/attentively* for the mix up about your order.
5 His hand moved almost *imperceptibly/intimately* until it was touching hers.

Paper 3 English in Use: Part 3 (error correction – extra word)

5 In **most** lines in the following text, there is **one** unnecessary word. It is either grammatically incorrect or does not fit in with the sense of the text. For each numbered line **1–16** find this word and underline it. Some lines are correct. Indicate these lines with a (✓) at the end of the line. The exercise begins with two examples (**0**) and (**00**).

CUPID'S TARGET

0 ✓	Why is the heart the organ that represents love? In some ancient religions
00	it was regarded as the place where the spirit dwelled <u>on</u> and in the West it
1	has always been associated with the moral courage. In medieval Europe the
2	hearts of monarchs were often buried in the lands they had conquered
3	and their bodies returned them to the places they had come from. A flaming
4	heart was a frequent symbol in Western art of religious intensity and saints'
5	hearts have become revered relics. Strangely, until the seventeenth century
6	no one knew what the anatomical function of the heart really was being. It
7	was the English surgeon William Harvey, who after years of research into,
8	he discovered that it was a rather simple pump. Even after Harvey announced
9	his discovery in 1628 the romantic mystery surrounding the heart grew up
10	rather than diminished it. Poets like Shakespeare were increasingly inclined
11	to use it as a metaphor for love. In the second half of the nineteenth century
12	it became so fashionable to put stylised images of the heart as a symbol of
13	romantic love on cards. Today modern medical science can mimic the
14	mechanics of the heart to save some lives. It is, after all, just a pumping
15	muscle. But try telling that to the broken hearted. They know where does
16	love lies.

Paper 3 English in Use: Part 2 (open cloze)

6 Complete the following article by writing each missing word in the spaces. **Use only one word for each space.** The exercise begins with an example (**0**).

MAKING THE MOST OF CARNIVAL

Carnival is definitely (**0**) _not_ a spectator sport. It's very difficult to really get (**1**) ... away by the atmosphere (**2**) ... you are taking part yourself and by that I mean (**3**) ... a disguise of some kind, even if it's nothing (**4**) ... than a mask or a funny hat. In fact, the (**5**) ... of people who do not bother to dress up is usually fairly small, so you (**6**) ... almost certainly be conspicuous out of fancy dress. You are bound to regret not (**7**) ... gone to a bit of trouble when you see everybody else having the time (**8**) ... their lives. Ask a friend to lend (**9**) ... a costume if you do not have (**10**) ... . You (**11**) ... even find that they are available for hire somewhere. If all else fails, you (**12**) ... always improvise with old sheets and clothes. After all, you don't (**13**) ... to look spectacular, elegant or beautiful, but you (**14**) ... try to enter into the spirit of the festivities if you want to enjoy (**15**) ... .

7 Make noun phrases for the following.

1 wool taken from lambs
2 the entrance where artists enter a theatre
3 a show where boats are displayed
4 a degree that takes three years to finish
5 a sauce made with cheese
6 a ceiling in a living-room
7 a choir for children
8 the tail on a rabbit
9 the national monuments found in Poland
10 a door on a cupboard

8 Complete these noun phrases in as many ways as you can think of.

1 a bowl of ...
2 a carton of ...
3 a herd of ...
4 a set of ...
5 a bunch of ...
6 a clove of ...
7 a packet of ...
8 a litter of ...

9 Complete the sentences by choosing the most appropriate option **A, B, C** or **D** to fill in the gap.

1 Negotiators are attempting to .... the peace treaty that was signed last month.
   A assure **B** safeguard **C** ensure **D** endanger
2 The artist Magritte apparently .... great pleasure from simple things like walking his dog.
   A derived **B** developed **C** evolved **D** decayed
3 They are hoping to .... a magazine devoted to e-commerce early in the new year.
   A land **B** launch **C** propel **D** eject
4 Exposed wires represent a potential fire ....
   A certainty **B** peril **C** jeopardy **D** hazard
5 You must come to the meeting. Your input is absolutely ....
   A crucial **B** serious **C** trivia **D** significant

Paper 3 English in Use: Part 3 (error correction – punctuation and spelling)

10 In **most** lines of the text below there is a spelling or punctuation error. Find the errors and correct them. Some lines are correct. Indicate these with a tick (✓).

STUDY FINDS TWINS ARE ALSO 'MIRROR IMAGES'

relatives

0 Even rellatives have trouble and others don't even try to tell them apart
00 but an Australian study has revealed many twins are not just identical they ,
000 ✓ are 'mirror images' of each other. Adelaide University researchers found many
1 identical twins were the reverse of each other one right-handed and the other
2 left-handed, for example. The study also found some identical twins with finger
3 prints that coresponded on opposite hands and birth marks that were mirrored.
4 The findings have called into question the tradicional belief that identical twins
5 tend to be carbon copies of each other. Researchers stumbled upon the discovery
6 when examining the symmetry of twins' finger prints and teeth. The study suggests
7 that twinning may ocur as the body is working out what is right and left. Twins
8 Patrick and Michael Gilbey, aged four, are the spiting image of each other. Yet
9 they are not exactly the same. Michael, the older of the duo, is right-handed,
10 while Patrick is left-handed. Their mother, Sally Gilbey, said the twins mirror
11 tendancies started to show when they began pre-school last year. When they
12 were born, doctor's were unsure if they were even identical because Michael
13 had a lower birth wait, but he has since caught up. Ms Gilbey said she has
14 herd of cases where mirror-image twins have their appendix located on the
15 opposite side of the body. People always ask me how I can tell the boys apart,
16 but I don't have a problem unless they are on their own', she said.

11 Eight of these expressions are wrong. Correct them.

1 like a horse in a china shop
2 as white as paper
3 to sleep like a cat
4 like a fish out of water
5 as cool as a courgette
6 like a red cloth to a bull
7 like a bear with a sore paw
8 as quick as a cheetah
9 as strong as an ox
10 as light as a hair

The sporting life

Listening

▶ P4, Pt2 (note taking)

1 How do you imagine the world of sport will change over the next 50 years? Consider these areas:

- new sports
- income and status of sports stars
- existing athletics records

 2 Listen to the following extract and make brief notes of Mary Fitzroy's answers to the above questions.

3 Listen to the extract again and complete the notes for questions 1–9. Before you do this, try and predict what kinds of words might be missing from each gap.

4 Play *Twenty Questions* with other students. Student A thinks of a sport. The other student(s) have to try and find out what sport it is in the fewest number of questions. The questions must be answerable by *Yes* or *No*.

EXAMPLE: Student A: *OK, ready.*
Student B: *Do you play this sport in teams?*
Student A: *Yes.*
Student C: *Does it help to be tall to play this sport?*
Student A: *No.*

FUTURE OF SPORT

Main reason why Cup Final is a 'great' event: [_____ 1]

Location of majority of population in 2050: [_____ 2]

Games that will continue: [_____ 3] *and five-a-side football*

Games that will decline: *cricket and* [_____ 4]

New sports: *Bar Fly Flying, Bungee Running and* [_____ 5]

Sport of the poor: [_____ 6]

Situation of sports stars: *more pay,* [_____ 7]

1936 world record for 100 metres: [_____ 8]

Unattainable world record for 100 metres: [_____ 9]

Grammar plus: future (advanced features)

1 Each underlined structure below has a description of its use. Two of the descriptions are untrue. Find them and correct them. (If necessary, see p.193 Grammar reference for help.)

1   *They <u>will be measuring</u> in thousandths of seconds in 2050.*
    to say something will be in progress at a particular time in the future
2   *<u>Will you be going</u> to the weekend training session?*
    to make a polite enquiry
3   *By 2050 the sporting elite <u>will have been elevated</u> further ...*
    to say something will be completed at a particular time in the near future
4   *You <u>won't have heard</u> the results of the match yet.*
    to express an assumption
5   *They're <u>about to begin</u> the opening ceremony. He's <u>on the point of doing</u> his first ever bungee jump.*
    to refer to the next moment
6   *All competitors for the 100m <u>are to assemble</u> on the track at precisely 2.45p.m.*
    to indicate an informal arrangement
7   *The race <u>is due to</u> start at 11a.m.*
    to indicate a previously scheduled time

2 Five of the following sentences contain grammatical mistakes. Find the mistakes and correct them.

1   I've never smoked and I'm not about to starting now!
2   I hope we be sitting by the pool in our new house this time next month.
3   Work on the new bridge due to start on September 1st.
4   Do you think you'll be staying for the whole afternoon?
5   They won't have been realised that everything has been delayed by an hour.
6   We were on the point of leave when it all started to get quite exciting.
7   We are to get a 10% pay rise next month.
8   There's no chance they'll have finished putting in the new kitchen by the end of the week.

3 Tell another student if you are on the point of doing anything significant in your life.

EXAMPLE: *I'm **on the point of moving out** of my parents' house and into a place of my own.*

4 Ask someone politely about the following things using the Future Continuous.

EXAMPLE: *What **will you be doing** this summer?*

1   their plans for the weekend
2   the location of their summer holiday
3   the method of returning home today
4   the time they will next see their best friend
5   the length of time they will continue to learn English

5 Work in pairs. Student A look at the notice below. Student B look at the notice on p.215. There are five differences between the information on the notices. Say what time the various events are *due to* take place and find the differences.

EXAMPLE: *The evening is **due to** start at 7p.m. with a welcome by the director.*

CAMBRIDGE SCHOOL		
	7p.m.	Welcome by director
	7.15p.m.	Open buffet
	8.20p.m.	Live band 'DeLuxe'
	9p.m.	Disco
	10p.m.	Results of charity raffle
	10.15p.m.	Surprise entertainment!
	10.50p.m.	Live band 'RJE'
	11.30p.m.	Karaoke competition
	midnight swim!	

Summer Party

6 Tell another student one thing you hope you will have done in:

1   three months' time
2   six months' time
3   one year's time
4   five years' time

▶ Grammar reference p.193

Speaking

1 Choose someone you would like to nominate for the title of world's greatest sportsperson. Write down five facts about them.

2 Tell the other students the facts about your sportsperson and see who can guess their identity first.

EXAMPLE:
Student A:

1 He was born in Brooklyn, New York in 1963.
2 He starred in the hit movie 'Space Jam'.
3 He is 2m3cm tall.
4 He is well-known for his endorsement of many consumer products.
5 He retired from playing basketball in 1999.

Student B:
Michael Jordan?

Exam focus

Paper 1 Reading: Part 1 (multiple matching)

About the exam: Paper 1 Part 1 is a multiple-matching task. The text is generally on one topic but is sometimes divided into different sections. You are usually required to link each of 12–18 questions with a particular section of the text.

> *Suggested procedure*
> 1 Read the instructions carefully.
> 2 Read the whole text to get an idea of the content of each section.
> 3 Read all of the questions, highlighting key words/phrases. Make a note of any answers you are confident about.
> 4 Go back to the questions you are not sure about. Take each one in turn. Decide which sections they might refer to. Scan those sections carefully for 'parallel expressions'.
> 5 Check you have answered all the questions.

Exam task

Answer questions **1–14** by referring to the article about athletes. For questions **1–14**, answer by choosing from the list (**A–D**) on the right below. Some of the choices may be required more than once.

Which athlete

ran two long distance events in one Olympics?	**1** ...	
nearly died between winning their first and second Olympic Games?	**2** ...	
won one competition despite intense suffering?	**3** ...	
would consciously do badly on certain occasions?	**4** ...	**A** Daley Thompson
suffered physical injury due to the lack of a common household item?	**5** ...	
had a third Olympic victory which seemed almost miraculous?	**6** ...	**B** Al Oerter
has impressed the writer by their courage as much as by their continuing athletic achievement?	**7** ...	
won his Olympic event more than three times?	**8** ...	**C** Ron Clarke
ignored their doctor's advice?	**9** ...	
was believed to be too badly injured to return to competitive athletics?	**10** ...	**D** Ana Quirot
ran in conditions that they were quite unused to?	**11** ...	
in one competition thought everything depended on the first attempt?	**12** ...	
suffered physical injury during an opening ceremony?	**13** ...	
deliberately trained at an unusual time?	**14** ...	

THE BRAVEST ATHLETES IN THE WORLD

PAT BUTCHER PAYS TRIBUTE TO THOSE SPORTSMEN AND WOMEN WHO HAVE VENTURED FAR BEYOND THE PAIN BARRIER IN PURSUIT OF THEIR DREAM.

There is some intangible element that separates the champion from the also-ran. Doubtless the geneticists will be able to isolate it one day and implant it, but for the time being, we can only marvel at the men and
5 women who win whatever the odds. Like double Olympic decathlon champion **Daley Thompson**, who would train on Christmas Day, strengthened, he said, by the knowledge that none of his competitors would be doing the same. Thompson would also try to reproduce the pressure of competition by
10 deliberately doing poorly in the first two attempts at one of his disciplines (the shot put, for example) in order to force himself to throw the best on the third attempt, since that's how many chances he would get in proper
15 competition. And indeed, Thompson would regularly pull out a winner in exactly those circumstances, when all seemed lost.

20 But more remarkable still are those champions who overcome injury, tragedy, war and oppression to get to the top. **Al Oerter** stands in the front
25 rank. On the face of it, Oerter's four successive Olympic gold medals in the discus mark him out as a man who transcended competition. Yet Oerter had to
30 face setbacks which would have defied any ordinary athlete to even get to two of those Games.

Oerter lived on the East Coast of the USA, a continent away from the Californian sunshine under which the majority of his competitors trained. But that was a minor inconvenience
35 compared with the almost fatal car crash he survived between his 'surprise' Olympic gold at the age of 20 in Melbourne 1956 and his incredible triumph in Rome four years later, where he won again.

But his victory in Tokyo in 1964 after a series of grave physical injuries was the sort of comeback which is normally associated
40 with a visit to Lourdes*. After Rome, Oerter began to suffer from a chronic cervical disc injury, which required him to wear a neck brace. Undaunted, he continued to train and compete. If that wasn't bad enough, a week before Tokyo he tore a cartilage in his lower rib.

45 Doctors advised six weeks' rest, but after a shot of Novocaine, and with an ice pack taped to his side (and his neck brace on), Oerter went out and set an Olympic record in qualifying. But in the final, he faced Ludvik Danek, who hadn't lost in 45
50 competitions. Oerter told a colleague, 'If I don't do it on the first throw, I won't be able to do it all.' He didn't do it on his first throw. Out of the medals after four attempts, he gave it everything he'd got on his fifth. Oerter was probably the only person in the
55 stadium not watching the discus as it winged its way to another Olympic record – he was doubled up with pain. But he had won again as he did, albeit in less heroic circumstances, in the next Olympics.

Multiple world record holder **Ron Clarke** of
60 Australia was another great athlete who suffered excruciating pain in the pursuit of his goal in the Olympic 10,000 metres in Mexico in 1968. Athletes had been warned that the thin air at altitude could affect them badly; there were even fears for their lives. The
65 Australian team doctor was moved to agree when Clarke collapsed in his arms after finishing as first non-altitude runner in fifth place, and had to be administered oxygen while unconscious for ten minutes.

It wasn't the first time that Clarke had been forced to
70 withstand extreme pain in the pursuit of glory. When the Olympics were in Melbourne in 1956, Clarke, then the world's leading junior miler, was chosen to light the Olympic flame. But the torch had been overloaded with magnesium, and inextinguishable burning matter fell on the youngster's arm as he
75 mounted the steps. Uncomplaining, he continued and duly lit the cauldron. He spent the rest of the ceremony having medical treatment.

In Mexico, Clarke returned later in the week to contest his other distance, the 5,000 metres. But the Aussie is convinced that the
80 heart condition which he now suffers so badly that he can barely jog three kilometres without stopping is a direct result of pushing himself to the limit.

But the Grand Prix for courage in the face of overwhelming adversity must go to **Ana Quirot**. World 800 metres silver
85 medallist in 1991 and Olympic bronze medallist the following year, Quirot was at home in Cuba a few months later, preparing to give birth to her first child when she was victim of a horrific domestic accident.

Because soap powder can be difficult to get, clothes are often
90 boiled in an alcoholic spirit. Quirot's wash literally exploded on the stove and into her face and body. She suffered third degree burns to much of her skin, lost her child and almost died. She spent months in hospital, followed by years of skin grafts, and the odds against her returning to athletics, let alone winning
95 anything, seemed astronomical.

There was surprise when she resumed her training in early 1994, amazement when she turned out for the Pan-American Games later that year, and incredulity when she won the silver medal.

100 We ran out of superlatives the following year when Quirot not only returned to the highest level of competition, but won the World 800 metres title in Goteborg, in the fastest time of the year. Quirot was already a much admired athlete. But she has won many more fans, not simply by her comeback after such adversity,
105 nor for her victories, but by the manner in which she has comported herself. Her willingness to face up to the camera with pride and defiance has been a source of inspiration to everyone who has encountered her.

* Lourdes: a small town in SW France considered by Roman Catholics to be a holy place. Many sick people go there to be cured.

Vocabulary: competitive sports

1 Match the following words and phrases to the appropriate definitions.

1 an also-ran
2 the decathlon
3 the shot put
4 to pull out a winner
5 the discus
6 a setback
7 a comeback
8 set a record
9 the pursuit of glory
10 a bronze medallist
11 to resume training

a) something that delays or prevents progress, or makes things worse than they were
b) a competition including ten different sports
c) someone who has come third in a competition e.g. the Olympics
d) to run a race faster, jump further etc. than anyone else
e) an event where you try and throw a heavy metal ball as far as possible
f) someone who has failed to win a competition
g) to start practising your event or sport after a period of absence
h) to produce the throw, score the goal etc., often unexpectedly, which results in victory
i) doing well again after being absent or unsuccessful for a period of time
j) the act of trying to achieve fame and honour in a determined way
k) an event where you try and throw a heavy plate-shaped object as far as possible

D **2** Do you know how to pronounce the words and phrases correctly? If not, check in a dictionary.

3 Work in groups with three or four other students and discuss these questions.

1 If a bronze medal is for third place, what are for first and second places?
2 There are 'track' events and 'field' events. Apart from the discus and shot put, what other field events do you know?
3 What different events are involved in the decathlon?
4 Do you know any matches or sporting occasions when a team or player has pulled out a winner at the last moment?
5 a) Name a sportsperson who has had a number of setbacks in their career.
    b) Name a sportsperson who has made a comeback after a period of absence.
6 Why do you think some athletes are so driven by the 'pursuit of glory'?

Speaking

▶ P5, Pt3 (problem-solving task)

1 Work with another student. Imagine you are considering ways to encourage people to do more sport or exercise. Below are some ideas for you to consider. Talk to each other about the different ideas and try and decide which two would be the most effective.

2 Now listen to two people doing Exercise 1. As you listen, make a note of:

- three expressions used to make an additional point
- three expressions used to indicate lack of complete agreement

3 Discuss the following questions with another student. Where appropriate, use the expressions you made a note of in Exercise 2.

1 How important do you think it is that ordinary people take regular exercise?
2 Do you think the way some people become dedicated fans of a particular team is healthy or unhealthy? Why?
3 Is there any real difference, do you think, between watching sport on TV and actually going to the event?
4 What are the potential problems for child athletes who dedicate themselves to their sport?
5 Do you think there is any problem with the role of business and advertising in sport today?
6 Do you think the Olympic Games is more than just a big sports competition?

Listening: no football for girls

1 Discuss with other students.

Do you think it is right that girls and boys should be separated to play sports? If so, from what age should they be separated?

2 Listen to this extract from a radio programme about Harriet Slynn, a young sportswoman. Answer these questions.

1 Which of the following sports are not referred to?

> cycling football cricket rugby golf
> skiing basketball horseriding athletics
> gymnastics swimming

2 How would you describe Harriet's parents' attitude to their daughter?

3 Listen again and write down the significance of these words/phrases.

EXAMPLE: *Nine – The age that Harriet had to quit her football career.*

1 148th
2 1m30cm
3 three
4 midfield
5 a cauliflower ear
6 six out of seven
7 Fridays
8 a woman referee

4 Do you think opportunities for boys and girls in general are equal these days? If not, why not?

Vocabulary: language of gender

D

1 The words in the box below are gradually being replaced by other words which do not indicate if the person is male or female. What are the replacement words? (Check your ideas with the extract on p.215 from the *Longman Dictionary of Contemporary English*.)

EXAMPLE: *chairman* > ***chairperson***

> chairman   air hostess   headmaster
> policeman   spokeswoman   fireman
> saleswoman

2 Here are some words and phrases in everyday use. Check you understand what they mean. Then decide if you think they are acceptable or should be replaced with alternative expressions.

1   What do you think the <u>man in the street</u> thinks about this issue?
2   Paul is <u>a man of his word</u>. He'll never let you down.
3   It's important to <u>be your own man</u> and not be overly influenced by the opinions of others.
4   The audience rose and applauded <u>as one man</u>. The show had been a great success.
5   The helpline is <u>manned</u> 24 hours a day, seven days a week.
6   The destruction of the environment is the most serious threat facing <u>mankind</u>.
7   I'm afraid I can't help you. It's <u>every man for himself</u>.
8   He's a real <u>man of the people</u> even though he holds such a position of power and influence.

3 Discuss with other students.

1   Many women today prefer the title Ms to Miss or Mrs. Why do you think this is?
2   In many books (see the example below) a choice is made to use *he* when referring to unknown individuals. Is this acceptable? Alternatives include using *she* or *he/she* or even *they*. What would you recommend?

EXAMPLE: *At the beginning of a new course, the teacher should always attempt to make **his** students feel relaxed and welcome in their new class. **He** should introduce **himself** and then introduce the students to one another.*

Grammar check: modifiers/intensifiers

1 Read the text below and decide if you can use one or both of the alternatives in each case.

BASKETBALL FAVOURITE

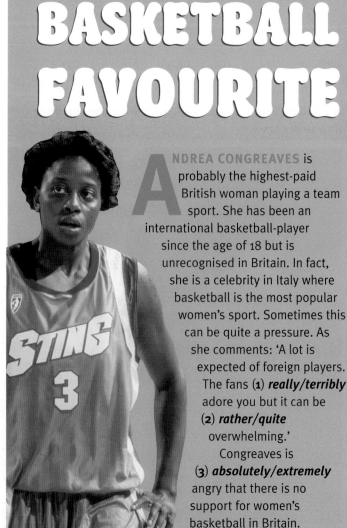

ANDREA CONGREAVES is probably the highest-paid British woman playing a team sport. She has been an international basketball-player since the age of 18 but is unrecognised in Britain. In fact, she is a celebrity in Italy where basketball is the most popular women's sport. Sometimes this can be quite a pressure. As she comments: 'A lot is expected of foreign players. The fans (**1**) *really/terribly* adore you but it can be (**2**) *rather/quite* overwhelming.' Congreaves is (**3**) *absolutely/extremely* angry that there is no support for women's basketball in Britain.

2 Look at the modifiers/intensifiers in the box below. Using the text below decide which are typically used with gradable adjectives (e.g. *interesting*) and which with non-gradable adjectives (e.g. *impossible*). Write G or NG next to each adjective.

very   absolutely   rather   extremely
fairly   terribly   really   completely
quite   pretty   totally

▶ *Exam Maximiser*   M

3 Tell another student about the last time that you were:

- really cold
- quite pleased with yourself
- totally amazed
- extremely grateful
- pretty annoyed
- absolutely exhausted

Watch Out!   *quite* ◀

What's the meaning of *quite* in these two sentences?

1 I think the match on Saturday is going to be *quite* hard.
2 I think it's *quite* ridiculous of you to play in a match when you are feeling so ill!

'It (**4**) *completely/really* annoys me that basketball isn't recognised in this country. The media could do more and the Sports Council should give more money to the sport.' As the England women's team manager comments, 'Andrea is (**5**) *terribly/very* modest, but she is (**6**) *extremely/really* important to England. She is one of the best players in Europe.'

Andrea is not (**7**) *particularly/terribly* optimistic about the future for British basketball. 'Even if we do (**8**) *quite/ reasonably* well in future major championships, I don't believe things will change. It's a shame because there are a lot of (**9**) *extremely/totally* talented players in this country who just aren't getting the support they deserve.'

English in Use

▶ P3, Pt4 (word formation)

1 Read the text below. Is it written by someone who:

1 doesn't like football fans?   3 is a completely dedicated fan?
2 can't understand football fans?   4 wishes he wasn't a fan?

THE LIFE OF A FOOTBALL FAN		
Being a fan is not a vicarious pleasure, despite all appearances to the contrary. Our fun is not a (**1**) ...-down version of the team's fun, even though they are the ones that get to score the goals. The (**2**) ... we feel on occasions like this is not a (**3**) ... of others' good fortune, but it is truly our own. And when there is a (**4**) ... defeat the sorrow that engulfs us is, in effect, self-pity. The players are merely our (**5**) ... . I am a part of the club, just as the club is part of me; and I say this with total (**6**) ... that the club (**7**) ... my views, and treats me (**8**) ... on occasions.	1	WATER
	2	EXCITE
	3	CELEBRATE
	4	DISASTER
	5	REPRESENT
	6	AWARE
	7	REGARD
	8	APPALLING

2 Read the text again.

1 What part of speech e.g. noun, adjective etc. should go in each space?
2 Should the missing word be in a positive or negative form?

D **3** Now use the words in the box to the right of the text to form one word that fits in the same numbered space in the text. Compare your ideas with other students. Decide on your final set of correct answers. Then check in a dictionary.

4 Now try another word-formation task.

THE ART OF FENCING		
Fencing is a popular sport that demands (**1**) ... and quick reflexes. It is, (**2**) ... , the modern version of the (**3**) ... duel and the weapons that are used are the modern (**4**) ... of the everyday swords of the past. The 'foil' is the weapon distinguished by its (**5**) ..... and hits are made only on the trunk of the body, not the limbs or head. The 'epée' is most like the old duelling sword and is stiffer and more solid. It is (**6**) ... with this to make hits anywhere on the body, head or limbs. The 'sabre' is like the old cavalry sword and has proved its (**7**) ... in cutting as well as thrusting. Fencers wear masks and thick waistcoats for (**8**) ... from injuries which can occur during matches.	1	AGILE
	2	BASIC
	3	TRADITION
	4	EQUIVALENCE
	5	LIGHT
	6	PERMIT
	7	EFFECTIVE
	8	PROTECT

Writing: formal letter/informal note

▶ P2, Pt1 (compulsory)

1 Look at the task and read the model answer on pp.200–202 Writing reference. Decide which of following pieces of advice for this task are valid.

- Never use any words that come from the task or input texts.
- Avoid copying long phrases from the task or input texts. Paraphrase them instead.
- Use as many words and phrases from the input texts as possible.
- Mainly use your own ideas with some ideas from the information you are given.
- Use the ideas and information provided. Avoid inventing new information.
- Be as imaginative as you can and invent freely.

2 Read the task at the top of the next column and answer these questions:

1 What are the key words/phrases in the task? The first few important parts have been highlighted for you.
2 Look again at the task and model answer on pp.200–202 Writing reference.
   a) In what ways are the style of the letter to the Campsite Director and the covering note to Sophie different? Give examples.

EXAMPLE: *The letter begins* **Dear Mr McNamara;**
The note begins **Hi Sophie**

   b) To what extent will the above differences in style apply to the letter and note you are going to write?
3 Now look again at the task on this page. What is the purpose of the letter to the Director of LangSports Co. and of the note to Tina?

Get Fit, Have Fun AND Improve your English!

In two weeks, on one of our specially designed sports breaks, you'll

- ▶ **speak better English**
- ▶ **develop your sports skills and**
- ▶ **get to make lots of new friends from around the world!**

Our comprehensive package includes

- **language tuition from trained and experienced teachers**
- **local accommodation with friendly, welcoming host families**
- **a wide range of sports to choose between**
- **all sports instruction from professional coaches**
- **all inclusive price**
- **additional full evening and weekend social programme**

All enquiries to: LangSports Co.
191 Beaconsfield Road,
Enfield, London N19 3OL
Tel: 0208 993 8689

... It really sounds like the holiday didn't match up to all the things they promised in the ad. What a shame! I do think they ought to do something to make up for your bad experience, especially as you'd been looking forward to the holiday so much. If I were you I'd complain to the Director.

By the way, my brother went on a similar kind of holiday this summer and he had a great time! So, if you want to know more about who he went with and so on – just let me know, OK?

Anyway, good luck with it all and let me know what happens!

love,

Tina.

3   Look at this paragraph plan for the letter to the Director of LangSports Co. Then complete the letter which has been started for you below in approximately 200 words.

Paragraph plan
1   Say who you are and give your reason for writing.
2   Group your complaints logically e.g. organisation of course, sports training, social events (you may not be able to refer to all of them in the number of words available).
3   State what you want done as a result of your complaint.
4   Close.

NOT REALLY 'TWO WEEKS' WITH LOSING A DAY AT BEGINNING AND END ARRIVING AND DEPARTING

NEARLY ALL THE OTHER STUDENTS WERE FROM GERMANY!

SOME 'TEACHERS' WERE LOCAL UNIVERSITY STUDENTS

FAMILY QUITE NICE BUT LONG WAY FROM COLLEGE

FOOTBALL, TENNIS AND BASKETBALL ONLY REGULAR SPORTS ON OFFER

SOME OF THE STUDENTS COULD PLAY BETTER THAN THE COACHES

HAD TO PAY FOR MANY EVENING SOCIAL EVENTS

NOTHING ORGANISED FOR FIRST WEEKEND

Dear Sir/Madam,

I am writing as the result of my recent 2-week stay in Brighton on a LangSports Co. 'sports break'. Unfortunately the holiday was ...

To begin with ...

As a result of this experience, I think it is only fair if you ...

I look forward to hearing from you in due course.

Yours faithfully,

J. Judice

Fabiana Judice

4   Prepare a plan for the note to your friend Tina. Then write the note.

English in Use

▶ P3, Pt5 (register transfer)

1 In Paper 3 English in Use, Part 5 you are required to read two texts and transfer information from one to the other. The second text will have gaps in and it will be written in a different 'register' from the first i.e. more formal/informal. You must complete the gaps with no more than two words and *not* use words from the first text.

2 Read the first text below (School Report) and summarise the main points to another student.

3 Imagine you are one of Rob's parents chatting to a friend about how Rob is getting on at school. Have the conversation, communicating the main points but in more informal language. (Do not refer to the second text yet.)

EXTRACT FROM A SCHOOL REPORT

```
Physical Education

I am delighted to say that Rob has
participated fully and enthusiastically
throughout this year. He is a strong
athlete who has shown significant
improvement in his strength, stamina
and ability. He has been in school
teams for football and swimming, making
a major contribution to both teams,
which came first in the local schools'
championships. In addition, he was
given the captaincy for 3 important
football matches and was excellent at
fostering a strong team spirit.

There are, however, areas of concern.
First of all, his attendance at
practice sessions has been very
inconsistent. He is often late and in
inappropriate kit. And, there have been
occasions when he has been unable to
control his temper during competitions
which has put the position of the
entire team in jeopardy.

If Rob is unable to deal with these
issues, then next term he will, very
regretfully, be dropped from the teams
concerned.
```

4 Now, read the second text and complete the gaps following the suggested procedure.

Suggested procedure

1 Read the complete text once before you start attempting to complete the gaps.
2 Make sure you understand the meaning of each sentence including gaps.
3 Refer to the equivalent part of the first text to check exactly the meaning of the missing part.
4 Decide on the part of speech of the missing word(s).
5 Complete the gaps, paying careful attention to the form and spelling of the words you insert.
6 Do not use words which appear in the first text.

EXTRACT FROM AN INFORMAL LETTER

... You asked how Rob's getting on at school. Well, we've just had his report and the teachers, generally, seem pretty happy. His PE teacher is particularly (0) *pleased* with how (1) ... he's been in the PE classes. He also said that Rob's made good all-round (2) ... and that he's done (3) ... to help the school (4) ... the recent championships. They even (5) ... him captain for a (6) ... matches and, apparently, he was great at getting everyone to (7) ... as a team.

Typically, though, Rob hasn't been (8) ... to practice sessions (9) ... AND he's been (10) ... the wrong kind of sports clothes! That's bad enough but it seems he's also (11) ... his temper in matches, meaning that the team could have been (12) ... .

I must talk to him about this otherwise they probably won't (13) ... him play for the school teams any more ... .

1

Complete the gaps in the following sentences with one of the words from the box in the correct form.

> glory decathlon setback pull resume put
> competitor bronze comeback set

1 It was amazing. They .... out a winner by scoring in the last minute.
2 After being 3–0 down they made an amazing .... and finally drew 3–3.
3 Jack Reeves has .... a new world record for the second time this year.
4 I will .... training as soon as my ankle injury has healed up.
5 After many .... she will be entering her first major competition for some time in the summer.
6 I'm afraid he was not very happy about being the .... medallist. He could only think of gold.
7 Do you know the ten different events that make up the .... ?
8 It's the never-ending pursuit of .... which keeps these athletes training month after month.
9 Don't you have to be pretty big to be good at the shot .... ?
10 Two of the .... failed to turn up for the race.

2

There is one missing word in each of these sentences. Decide what it is and where it should go.

1 You won't seen the notice saying that all tomorrow's events have been cancelled.
2 She's about buy a new flat and move out of her parents'.
3 Will you taking the binoculars with you to the match?
4 What time is the match due kick off?
5 It's impossible to know how fast people be running in a hundred years' time.
6 They're on point of buying that empty land next to our house to turn into tennis courts.
7 All students are assemble in front of the school for the awards ceremony.

3

The underlined words have incorrect endings. Replace them with the correct endings.

1 The flightperson came back and asked if I would like some more coffee.
2 Policepeople seem to be getting younger and younger these days.

3 David will make a very good chairofficer for the meeting, I think.
4 I could never be a fire attendant. I would be scared to death!
5 The spokesofficer for the company denied that there would be any further redundancies.
6 She's not a very good headmistress. She finds it difficult to keep the children interested in her lessons.

4

Complete each of these sentences in a logical way.

1 I thought Tim's parents were very hard on him. First they said he couldn't go out with his friends for a whole week and on top of that ...
2 It's true that, on the whole, Kylie is a lovely person. Having said that though ...
3 This government has reduced both inflation and unemployment. At the same time, we do need to remember that ...
4 You know that Derek broke the record despite appalling weather conditions. What's more ...
5 Did you know that Mr Deacon said he would come and give us all extra lessons just before the exam? Not only that ...

5

For questions 1–15, complete the following text with one missing word for each gap.

BIRTH OF THE OLYMPICS

It all began in 776 BC, with a simple foot race of about 200m held at Olympia in Greece. (1) ... four years from then, athletes as well (2) ... poets and artists met there for a festival in honour of the god Zeus. (3) ... from foot racing, the event came (4) ... include wrestling, boxing and the pentathlon. Winners became overnight heroes and (5) ... festival merited a permanent place in the Greek calendar to mark a span of four years (6) ... they called the Olympiad.

The games (7) ... for nearly 1200 years, until AD 393, (8) ... the Christian Roman Emperor Theodosius 1 banned all such 'pagan' celebrations. A millennium and a half later, a French baron began a campaign to recreate that spirit (9) ... good-natured but serious competition. Baron Pierre de Coubertin's family wanted (10) ... to become an officer in the French Army. But de Coubertin believed that the cause of peace (11) ... be better served (12) ... a regular meeting of amateur, world-class athletes and dedicated his energy (13) ... realising his dream. During the 1890s he (14) ... speech after speech to international sports associations, and (15) ... last persuaded them to revive the name and spirit of the ancient Olympic Games.

UNIT
7
The ties that bind us

Speaking: family dynamics

 1 Read and listen to the quotations below. Work in small groups. Discuss with other students.

1 What do you think each one means?
2 Which do you agree with? Which do you disagree with? Why?

2 Choose two of the quotations you found most interesting. In your group check you know the correct pronunciation of each word and make a note of the words which should receive more stress.

3 Work with a student from another group. Read your quotations out loud to them. Ask them what opinions their group had about these quotations.

Our children will hate us too.

John Lennon, singer/songwriter (1940–80)

Without a family, man, alone in the world, trembles with the cold.

André Malraux (1901–97), French novelist and politician

In the healthiest families, the power is shared by agreement. In the others, one parent or the other is usually more powerful.

Actor John Cleese and psychologist Robin Skinner in *Families and How to Survive Them*

Parents are sometimes a bit of a disappointment to their children. They don't fulfil the promise of their early years.

Anthony Powell, writer

The family is the place where the most ridiculous and the least respectable things in the world go on.

Ugo Betti (1882–1953), Italian playwright

No matter how old a mother is, she watches her middle-aged children for signs of improvement.

Florida Scott-Maxwell, US psychologist

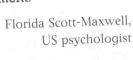

God gives us our relatives: thank God we can choose our friends.

Ethel Watts Mumford (1878–1940), humorous writer

Exam focus

Paper 4 Listening: Part 2 (note taking)

About the exam: In Part 2 of Paper 4 you will hear a monologue of approximately two minutes ONCE only. It could be an announcement, a radio broadcast, a talk, a telephone message or a speech. You will either have to complete sentences with missing information or take notes (a maximum of three words). You will have 30–45 seconds preparation time to read the notes before you hear the text.

The young Chris Chaplin (on the right) with his parents and sister.

Suggested procedure

1 Read the instructions which will usually give you:
   a) the main idea of the text you are about to hear e.g. whales
   b) some information about the speaker e.g. an author
   c) some information about where the text comes from e.g. a radio interview
2 Think about the possible content of what you will listen to and typical words that you might expect to hear.
3 Read the notes you are given and try and predict the kind of information that is missing e.g. a date or a name.
4 Write down the missing information as you hear it. If you miss an answer don't get distracted – concentrate on getting the next piece of information. (Remember that some of the information may be repeated.)
5 Look through and check your answers are spelt correctly at the end.

Exam task

You will hear a talk about Chris Chaplin, the son of Charlie Chaplin. As you listen, complete the notes for questions **1–8. Listen very carefully as you will hear the recording ONCE only.**

CHRIS CHAPLIN

Physical similarities to father: a) [_____] **1**

b) *smile*

Number of Chaplin children: [_____] **2**

Occupation: [_____] **3**

Similar characteristics to mother: a) [_____] **4**

b) *self-effacing*

Father's financial situation in youth: [_____] **5**

Value of father's estate at death: [_____] **6**

People responsible for running Chaplin estate: a) *Chris*

b) [_____] **7**

Quality inherited from father: [_____] **8**

Reading

▶ P1, Pt3 (multiple choice)

1 Discuss the questions below with other students.

1 How much difference does having one, two, three or more children in a family make to the children?
2 Do you think there is an 'ideal' number of children in a family?
3 Do you think the position (i.e. oldest/youngest) can affect the personality of a child? If so, how?

2 Read the article below. Does the article suggest that there is an ideal number of children in a family or not? (Ignore the ▲s and the underlined words for now.)

How the family pecking order affects you

Are you the eldest in your family? Do you strive for perfection but ▲ are never quite satisfied with what you do? Perhaps you are the middle child and
5 feel a compulsion towards attention-seeking behaviour, or the youngest ▲ who needs other people to sort out your problems. Countless academic studies say your place in the family is such a strong factor in developing your personality
10 that <u>it</u> can have a major influence on the rest of your life.

Joy Berthoud, ▲ author of a new book, *Pecking Order*, has been convinced by research confirming <u>this</u>. But she is quick to point out that there are
15 many variables, dictated most notably by age gap and the gender of the children. 'A girl with a sister two years her senior will be closer to the model of the second child than a girl with a brother 10 years older, who might well display more of the
20 characteristics of a first or only child.'

As a first child, according to Berthoud, you will probably adopt some of your parents' behaviour and generally be quite 'grown-up'. You receive all their attention, but all their expectations are also
25 heaped on you. 'When child number two arrives,' she explains, 'there will be fear of the withdrawal of your parents' love and, more than likely, a noticeable reduction in the amount of attention they give you. <u>This</u> is when you will start to try to
30 please adults, to become even more like them – conservative and responsible – in an effort to win back what you've lost. As you grow up, <u>this</u> can lead to feelings of never being good enough, but with or without this insecurity, you'll probably be a
35 high achiever because you're trying so hard.'

'I have one clear memory of my sister Jane arriving on the scene,' says Julie, 31, a civil servant. 'I was two and a half, and I climbed into her carry-cot when she wasn't in it and lay down. I
40 think I must have wanted to be a baby again, and get all the attention she was getting. I was quite like my mum and dad – they're both teachers with a strong art bias, and I became quite arty, too,' says Julie. 'I went on to study graphic design. But
45 Jane was into numbers and computers. She was also far more outgoing than me, with an active social life. I was less confident and much more level-headed and sensible.'

The second child is most commonly identified as
50 taking the opposite line to their older sibling. Feelings of inferiority can inspire the second to outdo the first in academic areas, but they will usually find something else to be good at. This position in the pecking order will also give you less

55 respect for the established order, unlike the older sibling trying to be like the adults. There will be nothing to be gained from it. The behaviour of these children will, in short, generally lean towards that which attracts attention, and they
60 will more than likely have a more relaxed attitude to life. Sibling rivalry is also common.

Karen Gunn, 29, a writer and assistant on a magazine, has a brother, Douglas, seven years her junior. She also has a sister, Fiona, who is 31.
65 Middle children are often left feeling like the odd one out, not having the attachment to their parents that their older sibling has but also not being the baby of the family, with the consequent attention heaped on it. This often provokes
70 attention-seeking behaviour.

Karen admits she has always striven to be noticed. 'I was always the crash-bang wallop one of the family. Fiona was much more reserved and thoughtful when we visited relatives. I'd always
75 be saying, "Look at me, I can do a hand stand."'

The youngest child doesn't have to worry about dethronement and can consequently focus on the road ahead with no distractions. But equally, being pampered might undermine his or
80 her ambition. Only children are similar in many ways to first children, but their behaviour is not modified by dethronement. Constant interaction with adults gives them social maturity but emotional immaturity. The strong parental
85 relationship can be supportive and encourage self-confidence, but it can also be claustrophobic. Only children may well leave home early.

3 Read the article again and answer questions (1–6) below. Give only one answer to each question.

1 Joy Berthoud feels that academic research regarding position in the family

 A should be treated with scepticism.

 B is still in its early stages.

 C needs to take complicating factors into account.

 D has made good progress in recent years.

2 Joy Berthoud believes that the effect of the arrival of the second child on the first is

 A largely negative.

 B largely positive.

 C equally positive and negative.

 D never the same.

3 Julie's comments about her sister

 A contradict Berthoud's theory.

 B only partially support Berthoud's theory.

 C support Berthoud's theory to a large extent.

 D raise issues not referred to by Berthoud.

4 Berthoud believes the second child's attitude to the first child will

 A lack respect.

 B be competitive.

 C be quite relaxed.

 D be resentful.

5 Middle children

 A are quite reserved.

 B get the most attention.

 C are often rather clumsy.

 D can feel disregarded.

6 Only children

 A have the same personality characteristics as first children.

 B may feel a strong need to break away from their parents.

 C will only benefit from the amount of contact with adults.

 D can experience a sense of general insecurity.

4 Discuss with other students. To what extent do the points in the article reflect your experience?

Grammar plus: substitution/ellipsis

1 Look at the first three paragraphs of the text on p.82.

1 There are three places marked with a ▲. In each of these places a different word is understood by the reader but left out of the text by the writer. Can you identify what word is missed out in each case?

▲ ....

▲ ....

▲ ....

2 There are are four words/phrases underlined. In each case, can you identify what the underlined word refers back to?
   a) line 10 *it* ....
   b) line 14 *this* ....
   c) line 29 *This* ....
   d) line 32 *this* ....

2 Look at the box below and decide which substitute word should be used in each sentence 1–6.

Substitution

We often try to avoid repeating a word or expression that has already been used. To do this, we can use other words as substitutes e.g. *it, one, do, there, that, so, neither, not.* This has the effect of tying together or 'connecting' phrases and sentences.

1 Ann: *Do you think Mary will come to the film?*
   Petra: *She might* ....
2 James: *I'll be at the restaurant by 8p.m.*
   Kevin: *OK, I'll see you* ....
3 Tina: *Are you going to go out with Sam?*
   Laura: *I think* ....
4 John: *I can't decide whether to buy a new car or a second-hand* ....
5 Joe: *Are you going to do this essay tonight or* .... *?*
6 Mary: *Sarah lost her job on Friday.* .... *came as an enormous shock.*

3 Look at the box below and decide which words/phrases are being missed out in each sentence 1–9.

Ellipsis

We often leave out words in order to avoid repetition. This is called ellipsis.

1 They feel tired but .... very pleased with themselves.
2 She was thinking of taking some holiday next week but now she can't ....
3 Eat as many as you want ....
4 Jim is leaving on Friday. He will ring you later to explain why ....
5 I haven't got any blue towels. Only green ....
6 Those are Melanie's trainers. These .... are mine.
7 She promised she'd come and visit me but she hasn't ....
8 If you can .... , phone me when you get to the hotel.
9 I'm sorry I got so angry. I didn't mean to ....

4 Look at 1–10 below. Find the mistake in each one and correct it.

1 **A:** Will Mike pass his exams?
   B: I certainly hope.
2 **A:** Are you going to have the living-room redecorated?
   B: No, I'm afraid I can't afford.
3 We don't want a new music system. Our old is still perfectly OK.
4 **A:** We won't have a proper holiday this year.
   B: So will we.
5 **A:** Sandra should be at home after 9p.m.
   B: OK, I'll drop by so after work.
6 They said they'd give us a ring when they arrived but they hadn't.
7 **A:** Tell Julie I want a word with her!
   B: Don't worry. I do.
8 **A:** Who does this wallet belong to?
   B: Oh, I think it's Joan's one.
9 **A:** Do you think Paul's been delayed by traffic?
   B: I expect it.
10 We seem to have more free time now than we used.

▶ Grammar reference pp.196–197

▶ *Exam Maximiser* M

5 Work with another student. Decide how the following paragraphs can be improved in style by using substitution or ellipsis.

It is well-known that relationships between children and their parents fundamentally affect adult behaviour. But now the importance of the relationships between children and their parents is being challenged as new research shows that a child's relationship with its siblings may have a more important effect on future adult behaviour.

Psychologist Francine Klagsbrun says 'Our relationship with our siblings is unmatchable. We have our siblings whether we like our siblings or whether we don't like them. As parents die, friends drift away, marriages dissolve, that relationship with our siblings continues and the memories of life that has been shared with them remain with us for a long time after childhood has ended.'

6 Check a piece of written work that you have done recently. Could you have used substitution or ellipsis to improve your style? Show another student your ideas.

Vocabulary: word + prepositions (1)

1 The following sentences come from the text on pp.82–83. Without referring back, can you complete them with the missing preposition?

1 Do you strive .... perfection?
2 ... but are never quite satisfied .... what you do.
3 ... it can have a major influence .... the rest of your life.
4 Joy Berthoud has been convinced .... research ...
5 ... there are many variables, dictated .... age gap and gender ...
6 As a first child, according .... Berthoud, you will ...
7 ... there will be fear of the withdrawal .... your parents' love ...
8 ... a noticeable reduction .... the amount of attention they give you ...
9 ... this can lead .... feelings of never being good enough.
10 This position will also give you less respect .... the established order ...

2 Now put the following verbs in the correct columns according to the prepositions they are usually followed by.

refer congratulate pay apologise plead
benefit coincide refrain result concentrate
suffer specialise insist confide confess
react apply

in	for	with	from	on	to

3 Choose six of the verb and preposition combinations above that you are less confident about using correctly. Make one sentence for each to demonstrate you understand their meaning. Try and make the sentences true about yourself where possible.

EXAMPLE: *I hope to **specialise in** veterinary science after I leave school.*

Speaking: talking about families

1 Listen to Tony describing his family. Complete the family tree started below and make notes of any special information about the different family members or relationships between them.

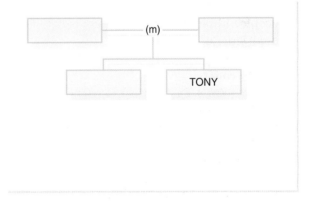

2 Work with another student.

1 Speak for two to three minutes without interruption. Your partner should draw a tree diagram of your family and make notes of any special information about the different family members and relationship between them.
2 After you have finished, your partner should tell you what they have understood about your family by referring to their notes. See how much they remembered.

Grammar check: hypothetical meaning

1 Look at the following sentences and decide if they are correct or not. If they are not, correct them as necessary.

1 I wish my dad couldn't always be so cross with me.
2 I wish I had an older brother.
3 If only I would spend more time with my family!
4 I'd rather we don't spend the whole evening with your parents.
5 I wish my sister would come and see us more often.
6 If only grandfather were here today!
7 Don't you wish you had revised more for the exam?
8 David and Sarah really wish they could be there for Sam's birthday.
9 Would you rather I came back a bit later?
10 It's time the children go to bed.
11 I wish I could stop biting my nails!
12 Suppose somebody will see us taking the money?

2 Now match one of the (corrected) examples above to each of the rules below. Some of the rules may be used more than once.

EXAMPLE: *a) 2*

> a) We use **wish + Past Simple** to express a wish that is not true in the present. We also use it to express wishes that might come true in the future.
> b) We use **wish + would** to talk about other people's irritating habits. This form is not often used with *I* or *we*.
> c) To talk about our own irritating habits we use **wish + could**.
> d) We use **wish + Past Perfect** to refer to things we are sorry about in the past.
> e) **If only** is used with the same verb forms as *wish* but is often used when your feelings are stronger.
> f) **It's time** is used with the Past Simple to talk about the present or future. We mean that the action should have been done before.
> g) **I'd rather** is used with the Past Simple when we want to say what we want to happen in the present or future
> h) **Suppose** means *What if?* We use it to describe something that may possibly happen or that may have happened.

► *Exam Maximiser*

3 Complete the following sentences in a way that is true for you. Tell another student. They must decide which one you feel most strongly about.

1 I wish I was ...
2 I wish I hadn't ...
3 I wish *(name of someone close to you)* wouldn't ...
4 I wish I could ...
5 It's definitely time I ...

Vocabulary: commonly confused words

1 Work with other students. Choose one of the groups of words A–D below. Use your dictionary to find the differences in meaning between the words in each pair. Check the pronunciation, part of speech and meaning of each word.

A: childish/childlike; effect/affect; lose/loose; specially/especially

B: stationery/stationary; principle/principal; lonely/alone; memory/souvenir

C: lie/lay; raise/rise; practice/practise; ensure/insure

D: channel/canal; worthless/priceless; imply/infer; hard/hardly

2 Work with students who have studied different groups of words. Explain to them the difference between the words in the pairs in your group.

3 Now complete the sentences below with one of the words from Exercise 1 in the correct form.

1 This painting is .... We know that it is a fake.
2 You'll find more paper and pens in the .... cupboard.
3 Could you .... the table while I finish off getting the food ready.
4 Are you .... that I haven't been working very hard this term?
5 I've got .... any cash. I must go to the bank this morning.
6 The film had a very powerful .... on me. I can't stop thinking about it.
7 Can you .... that your mother remembers to take her pills?
8 If we .... this match, we will be out of the championship.
9 He has no .... He'll do anything for a profit.
10 It can be .... difficult for drivers to see cyclists at night.

Listening: song

1 Discuss with other students. Do you think there is something special about:

1 a father's relationship with his son?
2 a father's relationship with his daughter?
3 a mother's relationship with her son?
4 a mother's relationship with her daughter?

2 Read the words to this song and predict the missing words. Think about the likely rhymes with previous lines.

 3 Listen to the song and check your ideas.

4 Tell another student about a dream you remember. Do you think it had some kind of special meaning?

When You Dream

With life just begun,
my sleeping new son
has (1)..................... that roll back in his head
They flutter and dart,
he slows down his heart
and pictures a world past his (2).....................
It's hard to believe
As I watch you (3).....................
Your mind drifts and weaves

When you dream
What do you dream about?
When you dream
What do you dream about?
Do you dream about
music or mathematics
or planets too far for the (4).....................?
Do you dream about
Jesus or quantum mechanics
or (5)..................... who sing lullabies?

His fontanelle pulses with lives that he's lived
With memories he'll learn to ignore
And when it is closed, he already knows
he's forgotten all he knew (6).....................
But when sleep sets in
History begins
But the (7)..................... will win

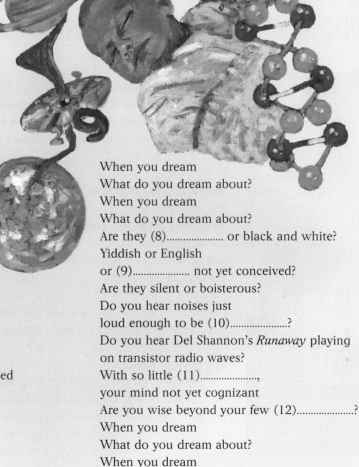

When you dream
What do you dream about?
When you dream
What do you dream about?
Are they (8)..................... or black and white?
Yiddish or English
or (9)..................... not yet conceived?
Are they silent or boisterous?
Do you hear noises just
loud enough to be (10).....................?
Do you hear Del Shannon's *Runaway* playing
on transistor radio waves?
With so little (11).....................,
your mind not yet cognizant
Are you wise beyond your few (12).....................?
When you dream
What do you dream about?
When you dream
What do you dream about?

87

Writing: leaflet

1 What is a 'leaflet'? What are the usual purposes of a leaflet? Can you give any examples of leaflets you have seen or been given recently?

2 Read the leaflet below and decide what its aim is.

3 Read the leaflet again. Do you think it is effective? Why/why not?

1 What do you think of
   - the title
   - the headings
   - the style (appropriately informal/neutral/formal?)
   - the amount of information given
   - the tone (is it selling itself too hard?)
2 Would you consider going on the London Eye as a result of reading it? Why/why not?

4 Read this task and the answer on p.89. Do you think the answer is very good/quite good/not very good? Why?

> **TASK**
>
> An increasing number of tourists are coming to visit your country. Your national tourist office is producing a series of leaflets about tourist attractions in your area and around the country. You have been asked to write a leaflet about one attraction that you know.
>
> Write the **leaflet** (in approximately 250 words), highlighting why visitors should come to this attraction and any useful practical information they should know.

The London Eye
On top of the world!

The British Airways London Eye has been launched! See London like you've never seen it before. This stunning attraction is now open to the public. Amazing views across the whole of London. An event the whole family will love! To book tickets call 0870 500 0600.

Part of a great tradition
The London Eye is one of the most imaginative Millennium projects to have been conceived of for London. In its inspiration and in its design it has drawn on the great tradition of celebratory structures such as the Ferris Wheel built for Chicago's World's Columbia Exposition in 1893 and the Eiffel Tower built for the Paris Exposition in 1889.

The perfect symbol
The architects on the project came up with the concept of a wheel as the ideal symbol for the Millennium. It represents the turning of the century, is a universally recognisable symbol of regeneration and time, and introduces a new shape into a rectilinear city. Research into the history of Ferris wheels has been drawn on to assist the design of a wheel on which people can ride, see breathtaking views of London, and which is itself an object of beauty.

> **How to get there:**
> *Tube* > *Embankment, Waterloo, Charing Cross*
> *Train* > *Waterloo East, Charing Cross*
>
> **Opening hours:** *10.00–18.00*
>
> **Prices:** *Adults £7.45*
> *Children £4.95*
> *Senior Citizens £5.95*

THE MILLENNIUM DOME

This is a leaflet for the increasing numbers of tourists coming to this country. It is produced by the National Tourist Office. It tells you about one important attraction in this country – The Millennium Dome. The Millennium Dome was builded specifically to give off the new Millennium and it has all sorts of expositions inside about different things like Body, Mind, Work, Faith, Communication, and so on. It tells many exciting informations about the past, present and future and points the way forward for a better tomorrow.

There are lots of interactive things for kids to do so they won't get boring which is a lucky thing for parents! And there are many different shops and cafés to look around and have a bite to eat in.

Also, you mustn't miss the Millennium Show which is showing everyday in the Central Arena. This is terrific and there is an huge combination of dance, sound, lights and acrobatics to keep you biting your nails.

The Millennium Dome is a tremendous success and thousands of people have visited it still. (All my friends and family have been.) So don't miss out, it's the luck of a lifetime! And it's only £20.

The easiest way of getting there is by underground on the Jubilee line to North Greenwich. The trains are often and comfortable and not too much expensive. From the tube station it is only a short walk to the Dome place.

I am recommending that you have a walk around the outside of the Dome itself if you can tear yourself away from the exhibits inside! It is very pleasant to watch the River Thames and there is also a building which shows how the Dome was building and a marvellous little model of it.

5 In fact, on the CAE marking scale for Paper 2 (p.211 Writing reference) this answer would be classed as Band 2. Read the description of a Band 2 answer below and then find specific examples of how the leaflet matches the Band 2 description.

EXAMPLE: *A Band 2 answer it says will contain 'notable irrelevancies'. In the answer the student writes* **(All my friends and family have been.)**

Band 2	Some attempt at task but lack of expansion and/or notable omissions/irrelevancies. Noticeable lifting of language from the input, often inappropriately. Errors sometimes obscure communication and/or language is too elementary for this level. Content not clearly organised. Would have a negative effect on target reader.

6 Read another student's answer to a similar task on p.212 of the Writing reference. Look at the teacher's comments and advice on pp.212–213. Then read the improved answer that comes after it. Has it followed all the advice?

7 Now rewrite the leaflet about the Millennium Dome. Improve it so that it would achieve a higher band result. Invent any further details about the Dome and its contents that you would like to add to the leaflet.

8 Prepare to write your own answer to the task in Exercise 4. Work with another student. Decide which tourist attraction you will write your leaflet about.

Suggested procedure

1 Write a paragraph plan e.g.
   Paragraph 1: Introduction: explaining what the attraction is and 'selling' it to the reader.
   Paragraph 2: Some background history about the attraction.
   Paragraph 3: Information about what there is to do at the attraction.
   Paragraph 4: Practical information for visitors.
2 Brainstorm possible ideas to include in the different sections of your leaflet. You can make up information if necessary.
3 Decide which ideas to include and what order they will go in.
4 Choose an eye-catching title for your leaflet.
5 Think about who you expect to read the leaflet. What will be the most suitable style to write the text in?
6 Write the text in about 250 words. You may wish to use bullet points and/or sub-headings to make the leaflet easy and interesting to read.
7 Refer to the Editing checklist on p.214 Writing reference. Make sure you haven't made any mistakes.

9 Show your leaflet to other students. Do they think your leaflet is attractive, easy to read, informative and persuasive?

English in Use

▶ P3, Pt1 (multiple-choice cloze)

1 Discuss with other students what you think young people today want most out of life.

2 Read the text below to see if your ideas were the same as in the study.

3 Read the text again without looking at the words below. Decide what words might fit each space. Look at the context around each space. The missing word may be part of a fixed phrase/expression.

4 For questions **1–15** below, decide which word best fits each space. Think about the precise meaning of each of the options. Make sure your choice best fits the meaning of the sentence in the text.

	A	B	C	D
1	drive	eagerness	ambition	yearning
2	putting	keeping	having	wanting
3	drop	fall	slip	jump
4	made	aimed	looked	set
5	youth	young	juniors	juveniles
6	loose	relaxed	generous	liberal
7	oaths	vows	pledges	promises
8	pressures	weights	burdens	loads
9	proceeded	revealed	emerged	rose
10	site	place	situation	location
11	bedtime	goodnight	pyjama	dream
12	organised	managed	controlled	disciplined
13	system	respect	way	method
14	have	make	get	take
15	determined	firm	persistent	stubborn

5 Discuss with other students how true these views are of young people that you know.

BORN TO CONFORM

The coolest kids in Europe share a single (**1**) ... : they want to get married, have children and live happily ever after. They know it means (**2**) ... their children first and sticking with their spouses even if they (**3**) ... out of love. This news comes from the report of a new study that (**4**) ... out to find the answer to the modern riddle: What will today's (**5**) ... really, really want tomorrow?

Poignantly, one of the clearest answers is that they want to have happy families. Even in the most (**6**) ... countries there was condemnation for divorce, demands that parents should keep their marriage (**7**) ... , and admiration for stable couples.

It appears that among the middle classes, the quality of our children's lives has suffered from the (**8**) ... on parents in high-stress professions. In the days when the concept of 'quality time' first (**9**) ... , I remember seeing a TV producer on (**10**) ... dial home on her mobile phone to read her son a (**11**) ... story. This is just not good enough.

Quality time cannot be time-(**12**) ... . Children need unconditional time in the same (**13**) ... that they need unconditional love. This study found a generation that had given up trying to (**14**) ... its parents' attention but was (**15**) ... to do better by its own children.

'The funny thing is, I don't feel any different now than I did when I was your age.'

1 Remove part or all of the underlined word or phrase to avoid repetition or insert a short substitute word/phrase in its place.

1 **A:** Have you been to that new art gallery yet?
   B: Yes, I went <u>to the gallery</u> just last weekend.
2 **A:** Do you reckon that Simon and Julie will get married?
   B: No, I don't think <u>they'll get married</u>. They're too young anyway!
3 **A:** Please don't forget to pick up some more butter from the shops!
   B: Of course I <u>won't forget to get some</u>. It's on my list.
4 **A:** I haven't sent her a birthday card yet.
   B: Don't worry. <u>I also haven't sent her a birthday card.</u>
5 **A:** I'm probably going to buy that camera we saw yesterday.
   B: Which <u>camera</u>? We looked at hundreds!
6 **A:** Do you imagine they'll ever forgive me for what I did?
   B: Yes, I think they will <u>forgive you for what you did</u> eventually.

2 Delete any words in the following sentences that do not need to be there.

1 Take as much time as you need to take.
2 I'm sorry Sir. We don't have any silk sheets left. Just cotton sheets.
3 I don't know whose that car is. This car is mine.
4 I'm surprised that he forgot to ring you. I'm sure that he had intended to ring you.
5 I thought she would have got me a present but she hasn't got me one.
6 She is excited by the new job but she is also a little apprehensive about it.

3 For questions **1–6**, read the following text and then choose from the list **A–J** the best phrase to fill each of the spaces. Each correct phrase may only be used once. **Some of the suggested answers do not fit at all.** The exercise begins with an example (**0**).

ANIMAL FAMILIES

Hissing and grunting loudly, a 'mute swan' belies its name (**0**) *J* . Should a suspected foe approach too closely, this great white bird can deliver a knockout blow with its powerful wings, (**1**) ... .

Many animals protect their young, though not all so aggressively. Some birds, such as plovers, (**2**) ... . Either parent may feign injury, careering across the ground with one wing held out as if broken, to lure the predator, such as a fox or stoat, away from their young. Some birds fly off (**3**) ... : a rail will carry them, one at a time, in its bill, while a woodcock carries them between its feet.

Mother crocodiles too, carry their young. After hatching from the eggs laid on the river bank, the young crocodiles are vulnerable to predators such as marabou storks and hornbills. The mother picks her young up with remarkable tenderness in her great toothed jaws, (**4**) ... . Few other reptiles show such gentle care.

Fish generally leave their eggs and young to fend for themselves. The mouthbrooders are an exception. The female or male, or both, depending on the species, take the eggs into their mouths. Protected from predatory fish and from fungi and bacteria, the eggs hatch in the mouth and the baby fish swim out, (**5**) ... .

Even some insects show a surprising degree of parental care. Earwigs remain with their eggs until they have hatched. Among bees, wasps, ants and termites, a queen does all the laying of eggs, and then the workers (sterile females) care for the eggs and the larvae (**6**) ... .

A with their chicks from the danger area
B and takes them down to a safe stretch of quiet water
C until they turn into adults
D although they do learn from their mistakes
E capable of breaking a person's arm
F teaching them various hunting techniques
G try instead to outwit a predator
H not needing to sleep more than two hours at a time
I though they will rush back in should danger threaten

J in defence of its young against an intruder

91

As luck would have it

Speaking: merely superstition?

Discuss the following questions with other students.

1 The objects above are considered by some people to be symbols of good luck. What other things do you know that are supposed to bring good luck?
2 Do you believe in luck? Some people say that 'you make your own luck'. Do you agree with that? When was the last time you had some good or bad luck?
3 What is a coincidence? Have you ever heard of or experienced any strange coincidences?

Reading

▶ P1, Pt3 (multiple choice)

1 Read the article below quickly. Is the main point of the article to say that:

1 there are more coincidences in life than we imagine?
2 scientists don't take coincidences seriously enough?
3 there are normally reasons behind coincidences?
4 it's surprising that we don't experience coincidences more often?

The laws of freak chance

Sue Hamilton was working alone in her office when the fax machine broke down. Unable to fix it, she decided to call her colleague Jason Pegler, who
5 had set off home a little earlier. Finding his home number pinned up on a notice board, she called him and began to explain the problem. But Jason quickly
10 stopped her saying any more: 'I'm not at home,' he explained. 'I just happened to be walking past this phone box when it rang, and I answered it!'

The number Sue found on the notice
15 board was not Jason's home number at all. It was his employee number – which was the same as the number of the phone box he was walking past when she called. It was a bizarre coincidence, one of those
20 that fascinate and perplex us. From a chance meeting with a long-lost friend to weird parallels between world events, coincidences hint at 'spooky' laws in our universe.

25 Last year an amazing set of coincidences put Paula Dixon in the headlines – and saved her life. On a flight from Hong Kong to London, she began to feel ill. A call went out to any doctors
30 on board the plane, and two – Professor Angus Wallace and Dr Tom Wong – duly emerged. The presence of two doctors was fortunate but not so unusual. However, Paula had a potentially fatal
35 collapsed lung – Professor Wallace was not only an expert in accident surgery but had just finished doing a course specifically dealing with precisely this type of crisis. Dr Wong turned out to
40 have with him the one textbook needed to help them carry out the surgery. They saved Paula's life and won world-wide acclaim.

But scientists claim coincidences are
45 simply the result of people remembering a few 'amazing' confluences of events, but conveniently forgetting all the times when nothing amazing happens. A classic example is the 'small world' effect, where
50 two strangers at a party discover they have a friend in common.

People at parties tend to be from the same social class, level of education, income bracket and the same area. So, the
55 likelihood of meeting someone with whom you share a trait is higher than it might seem.

Sociologists have found that individuals typically have around 150
60 people whom they regard as 'close'. Therefore each of us typically has an entourage of around 23,000 'friends of a friend'. Say we have about five acquaintances for each close friend, the
65 number swells to 600,000. The chances of meeting someone on a train with whom you share an acquaintance are therefore surprisingly high: for the UK population, it's around one in a 100. If you also
70 include socio-economic factors that boost the numbers of people from particular backgrounds travelling by train to particular destinations, the chances rise even higher.

75 There is another effect at work behind some coincidences. They often seem surprising because we mix up two different probabilities: one – the chances of something interesting happening, and
80 two – the chances of something interesting happening after it has been given many opportunities to occur.

2 Read the article again and choose the correct alternative in each case.

1   The first coincidence in the text is surprising because of the
   A   time that Jason left the office.
   B   fact that Jason wasn't at home.
   C   number that Sue phoned.
   D   position of the phone box.

2   The second coincidence is surprising because
   A   both doctors were experts in the particular area.
   B   one of the doctors had written a textbook about this kind of problem.
   C   there were so many doctors on the flight.
   D   of the combination of fortunate factors.

3   Which attitude do scientists have towards the significance of 'strange coincidences' in everyday life?
   A   disbelief
   B   respect
   C   curiosity
   D   confusion

4   Mendeleev made his discovery because
   A   of his desire for fame.
   B   he took a seeming 'coincidence' seriously.
   C   of his obsession with organisation.
   D   no one else took the behaviour of electrons into account.

5   Crick and Watson won the Nobel Prize because they
   A   discovered a new chemical.
   B   noticed how DNA reacted under certain conditions.
   C   built on someone else's discovery of a coincidence.
   D   learnt new things about certain chemicals.

For example, the chances of getting a 'double six' in a single throw of two dice is one in 36. But the probability of getting at
85 least one from 25 attempts is 50:50. The more you try, the better your chances – but it's easy to forget the number of 'tries' involved in real-life coincidences. How many millions of people walk past phone boxes each day, but never find a friend on the other end of the line if it happens to ring?
90   Although scientists have little time for everyday coincidences, they treat them seriously when they occur in science. Apparent coincidences in nature have often led to major scientific breakthroughs.
   When the chemical elements are arranged according to
95 their atomic weight, for instance, they seem to fall into groups with similar properties. Coincidence? The Russian chemist Dmitri Mendeleev didn't think so – and in 1871 published his Periodic Table[1], now found on the walls of countless laboratories. It emerged that the 'coincidence' was the result of
100 a deep principle controlling the behaviour of electrons in atoms.
   The famous discovery of the double helix of DNA[2] also benefited from a coincidence. In the early 1950s, an Austrian biochemist noted that the amounts of key chemicals in DNA –
105 codenamed A, T, G and C – seemed to follow a rule. If the amounts of A and T were combined, they always equalled the levels of G and C. Cambridge scientists Crick and Watson thought this was a clue, and used it to find the structure of DNA. This 'coincidence' won them a Nobel Prize and
110 launched the whole field of modern genetics.

[1] Periodic Table = a list of elements (simple chemical substances) arranged according to their atomic structure
[2] DNA = an acid that carries genetic information in a cell

3 Tell another student your reaction to the article. Do you agree that coincidences usually have a rational explanation?

4 Read the text again and make questions for the following answers.

EXAMPLE: *Because she couldn't repair the office fax machine.* – ***Why did she call Jason?***
1   Jason's home telephone number.
2   London.
3   Because they managed to save Paula's life under very difficult circumstances.
4   Because people who go to the same parties will generally have a lot in common anyway.
5   150.
6   50:50.
7   1871.
8   Crick and Watson's discovery of the double helix of DNA.

5 Talk to another student about things you have in common. You have five minutes. Give yourselves

• half a point for an easy similarity e.g. you both have blue eyes.
• one point for a medium similarity e.g. you are both 22.
• two points for an unlikely similarity e.g. you both have a father called Antonio.

See which pair of students can score the most points!

Grammar plus: verb patterns (2)

1 Find examples of the following verbs in the 'Laws of Freak Chance' text on pp.92–93. Which are followed by the *-ing* form? Which are followed by the infinitive form? Which can be followed by both?

> decide begin stop happen seem
> finish need

2 Six of the following sentences are incorrect. Find the mistakes and correct them.

1 She doesn't remember to learn to ride the bicycle.
2 I couldn't imagine to live in a big city.
3 Do you miss having contact with colleagues now you work from home?
4 I like to get up an hour before I have to leave for work.
5 What do you intend doing after you leave school?
6 Surely you are not allowed to know the exam questions in advance?
7 I'm sorry but they made me to tell them where I had hidden the money.
8 Why don't you try memorising new vocabulary just before you go to sleep?
9 They encouraged me starting playing the piano from a very early age.
10 Don't forget to phone your grandmother this evening.
11 We didn't expect you being home so soon.
12 He went on to say how much he had enjoyed the evening.
13 They begged to lend them the money they needed.
14 We intend to start work on the new concert hall as soon as planning permission has been received.
15 John tried hard to open the window but it was stuck.

3 Give the appropriate heading to each set of verbs in the box below by numbering each column.

1 verbs followed by *-ing* or infinitive (with *to*) with different meanings
2 verbs followed by *-ing* or infinitive (with *to*) with small or no difference in meaning
3 verbs normally followed by infinitive (with *to*)
4 verbs normally followed by *-ing*
5 verbs normally followed by object and infinitive (without *to*)
6 verbs followed by an object and infinitive (with *to*)

□	□	□
avoid, detest, imagine, keep on, mind, miss, put off, risk	beg, dare, encourage, invite, persuade, urge	allow, attempt, deserve, expect, fail, manage, neglect, threaten

□	□	□
forget, go on, like, regret, remember, stop, try	make, let, help	begin, continue, intend, propose, start

4 Choose the correct alternative in the brackets in each case below to finish the rule correctly.

1 Verbs followed by an infinitive e.g. *I **expect to see** him tonight* often refer (back to the past) (forward to the future).
2 Verbs followed by *-ing* e.g. *I **remember locking** the front door when I left this morning* often refer to an action or state (before the main verb) (after the main verb).

5 Complete these sentences using the verbs in the box in the correct form. (You may need to add an object.)

1 She (*persuade/ask*) my boss if I could have some extra time off.
2 Do you (*regret/leave*) school at 16?
3 Will you (*let/help*) you cook dinner?
4 Apparently they (*expect/work*) every evening until this deal is signed.
5 How did you (*avoid/have*) to do military service?
6 You should (*try/see*) a hypnotherapist. It really helped me give up smoking.
7 We (*intend/be*) home before midnight but we missed the last train.
8 We (*urge/reconsider*) our proposal.
9 You don't (*deserve/treat*) so badly by your so-called friends.
10 I'm afraid (*neglect/keep*) in contact with many of our friends.
11 I (*threaten/tell*) Sarah if he doesn't stop seeing Melanie.
12 They (*dare/do*) a bungee jump and I did!
13 You shouldn't (*attempt/lift*) that box by yourself.
14 We had to (*stop/check*) the oil level several times.
15 Do you (*miss/talk*) to your brother now he's left home?

6 Take it in turns to ask another student questions using the verbs from Exercise 3 on p.94. The other student should answer truthfully. Use a different verb each time.

EXAMPLE: Student A: *Is there anything that you really* ***regret doing*** *recently?*
Student B: *Yes. I really* ***regret not having*** *studied English harder at school!*

► Grammar reference pp.197–198

Vocabulary: synonyms

1 Look at the words in the left hand column of the table below and tick the column which contains an approximate synonym (a word with the same meaning).

	A chance	B many	C normally	D unlikely	E increase
boost					
far-fetched					
typically					
countless					
maximise					
coincidence					
inconceivable					
generally					
luck					
numerous					

2 Now listen to the words used in context and check your ideas.

D **3** Work in groups.

1 Each group should take one group of synonyms from Exercise 1. Refer to dictionaries and find out what, if any, differences exist between the meaning of each word in the group.
2 Explain your findings to students from other groups.

4 Complete each sentence with an appropriate word in the correct form from the table in Exercise 1.

1 In order to .... available power, solar panels are placed on the highest part of the building.
2 She stared up at the great glaring moon and the .... stars.
3 It is .... British behaviour to suffer in silence rather than complain.
4 It's .... that the missing children could have survived so long without food.
5 Many of the factory workers signed up for overtime to .... their meagre wages.
6 There's no skill in a game like roulette. It's all ....
7 The cars are .... tested for safety and reliability before leaving the factory.
8 .... scholars before Copernicus had suggested that the earth went round the sun.
9 The idea of travelling to other solar systems may sound .... but scientists now see it as a real possibility.
10 You're going to Bermuda? What an amazing .... So am I!

D **5** Now find one approximate synonym for each of the following words. (Refer to a thesaurus or a dictionary such as the *Longman Language Activator*.) Make a note of any differences in meaning with the original word. Then compare your synonyms with other students.

- a meeting
- to remember
- interesting
- a problem
- quickly

6 Record in your vocabulary notebook all the new words you have learnt. Take care to note the exact meaning and context when particular words can be used.

Listening: five bizarre tales

▶ P4, Pt4

 1 You will hear five short extracts in which various people are talking about their experiences of strange coincidences.

First, match the extracts as you hear them with the people, listed **A–H**, who are speaking. Remember, there are five extracts and eight speakers to choose from.

TASK ONE

A a father

B a hospital worker

C a boss

D a wife

E a friend

F a grandchild

G a guest

H an aunt

	1
	2
	3
	4
	5

2 Listen to the extracts again and this time match them with the correct topics **A–H** below. Make a note of any key words or phrases that help to justify your choices.

TASK TWO

A photographic evidence

B an old boyfriend

C homework research

D encounter with a stranger

E a weird premonition

F fire brigade rescue

G a family reunion

H an illness reveals all

	6
	7
	8
	9
	10

3 Listen to these sentences from the extracts. Complete the missing part.

1 Who .... but when he eventually called back ... .
2 Well, ... when we discovered that they were his first cousins.
3 and then, ... , it turned out that our brothers were both born on July 5, 1960.
4 Would .... ? She was standing right next to me.
5 Well, ... In a passageway were two large tea chests filled with very old, torn magazines.

4 Listen again and repeat the extracts with similar intonation.

5 Prepare to recount a surprising incident to another student. Use something that has happened to you or invent an incident based on one of these situations.

- You met someone today at your school/college/ work who you have just discovered was born and brought up in the house next door to yours, where you lived for the first ten years of your life.
- You stood behind a famous TV personality at the supermarket today and had a short conversation with them.

6 Now tell your story to another student. Include at least one of the expressions you learnt above. Begin like this:

You'll never guess what happened to me today ...

Grammar check: reported speech

1 Put the following into reported speech.

1 *It was the most amazing coincidence!*

2 *I'll never forget the day I had a premonition that I should phone my dad.*

3 *I've often wanted to find out what happened to my cousins.*

4 *Are you married to a Cancerian?*

5 *I couldn't believe my eyes when I realised who it was.*

6 *I don't know why but I must go to this address tomorrow morning.*

EXAMPLE: 1 *He said it had been the most amazing coincidence.*

2 Complete each of the following sentences with one of the prepositions from the box.

of	for	on	with	from

1 Tom apologised .... being late.
2 They congratulated her .... doing so well in her exams.
3 Sam pleaded .... her not to leave.
4 Mike reminded Jane .... the last time they went away on holiday together.
5 They tried to discourage her .... leaving school early.
6 He blamed himself .... what happened at the party.
7 Simon accused his best friend .... lying to him.
8 Sarah insisted .... going round to her boyfriend's flat to see if he was in.

3 Use the reporting verbs in the box to report the following sentences.

admit   suggest   warn   accuse   remind
apologise   promise   deny   agree

EXAMPLE: 1 *She reminded him to get his father a*
birthday card.

1 Don't forget to get your father a birthday card.
2 You really shouldn't hang around with those boys.
3 Why don't we go out to that new Italian restaurant?
4 I'm sorry I borrowed your car without telling you.
5 I will help you with your essay tomorrow, honestly.
6 I didn't steal any money from the till.
7 It was you who took my CD, wasn't it?
8 Yes, it's true, I have been seeing a lot of Debbie.
9 Yes, OK, I'll come and help you with the shopping if you really want me to.

▶ *Exam Maximiser*

4 Think of a) an interesting conversation you had recently or b) part of an interesting dialogue you heard on a TV programme or film recently. Report it to another student.

EXAMPLE: *I met a friend from school last weekend. I*
hadn't seen her for nearly five years. She told
me that she had given up her teaching job and
had decided to travel around South America. I
asked her how long she was thinking of going
for and she said that ...

Vocabulary: word formation (prefixes)

*My brother is the **unluckiest** person I know!*

D   **1** Use a dictionary if necessary and write down two words whose negative can be begun by:

un-	dis-	im-	il-	ir-

2 Contradict each of the following statements using the word in brackets with one of the prefixes above.

EXAMPLE: *This chair is quite (comfortable). **Actually,***
I think it's quite uncomfortable!

1 What you're saying is completely (*relevant*).
2 That dog is always (*obedient*).
3 I found his story quite (*believable*).
4 This argument is completely (*logical*).
5 He's very (*mature*) for his age.

3 Look at the prefixes in bold in each of these sentences. Match them to their meanings below.

1 I'm sure you **mis**understood her. She definitely wants to go to university.
2 He says that astrology is just a **pseudo**science.
3 I'm afraid you'll have to **re**type this letter. It's full of mistakes.
4 You wouldn't think from his behaviour that he was an **ex**-Prime Minister.
5 I hope you won't think I'm **anti**social but I don't feel like coming out tonight.
6 The **post**-mortem revealed very little about the way that Mills had died.
7 They live in a small **semi**-detached house in the suburbs.
8 The garden is getting terribly **over**grown.
9 It's probably the best political **auto**biography I've ever read.
10 Have you got a **mono**lingual dictionary?

a) former	f) not real/false
b) too much	g) against
c) again	h) one/single
d) of or by yourself	i) after
e) half	j) badly/wrongly

4 Now decide which of the prefixes in Exercise 3 can be added to each of these words.

circle   graduate   syllable   pilot   build
clockwise   estimate   pronounce   intellectual
husband

Speaking

▶ P5, Pt2 (comparing and contrasting)

1 Discuss with another student. What are the four parts of Paper 5 Speaking? What usually happens in Part 2? How long does each candidate have to speak? (If you need help look back at the Speaking Section in Unit 2.)

2 Tell another student about the last time you had a piece of really good news. What was it? How did you feel?

3 Work with another student. Look at Pictures 1 and 2. Decide which of the sentences (1–3) might be appropriate to use in comparing and contrasting these pictures.

1 In the first picture I can see a man wearing glasses, boots and a heavy winter coat. He's got brown hair and he could be in his forties or fifties. The same man is on the left in the second picture.
2 In the first picture, there's a man staring at the ground and holding some kind of machine. I think he's probably looking for something as he's concentrating hard, so the machine might be a metal detector. The second picture seems to suggest his efforts have paid off.
3 The first picture looks as if it might be in England. It's a very muddy field with a few trees and houses in the background. It looks quite cold and cloudy. I can see the same field in the second picture but here there is also a tractor in the background.

4 Decide who will be Candidate A (Pictures 1 and 2) and Candidate B (Pictures 3 and 4). In turn:

1 Compare and contrast your pictures. Say what is happening in each picture and how people are feeling.
2 Say whether you found the task easy or difficult and how you could have done it better.

1

2

English in Use

▶ P3, Pt5 (register transfer)

An English student wants to get a summer job working for the magazine *Would You Believe It?* For questions 1–13, complete the formal letter to the editor of the magazine, using the advice given in the informal letter from a friend who is a journalist for the same magazine. **Use no more than two words for each gap.** The words you need do not occur in the notes.

LETTER FROM A FRIEND

Dear Sally,

This is just to let you know what I've found out about possible summer jobs here at the magazine.

Firstly, you ought to write a letter to the Editor (Susan Renshaw) explaining that you are looking for work over the university holiday period. It's probably a good idea to mention my name and mention that I said you should write to her. Tell her about your university course and also that you do the sports bit for the student newspaper.

Do explain that you're really interested in getting into this area after university and that this would give you a great chance to learn. Emphasise you can work almost any hours they want and that you don't mind doing any kind of job.

Make sure you tell her how to get hold of you and suggest she gets in touch if there is anything else she needs to know. Really hope this helps and that it all works out!

Love,
Renzo.

LETTER TO MAGAZINE EDITOR

Dear Ms. Renshaw,

I am writing to (**0**) **enquire** whether you might have any (**1**) … for temporary employment at *Would You Believe It?* magazine over the summer period? I'm actually writing at the (**2**) … of Renzo Crace (an old family friend).

I am currently doing a (**3**) … in English at Manchester University and I also write a regular sports (**4**) … for the student newspaper.

I should say that I am seriously (**5**) … doing a course in (**6**) … after my B.A. and I feel this would (**7**) … me with some very valuable (**8**) … . I would be extremely (**9**) … in terms of my hours of availability and I am quite (**10**) … to take on any type of work that you might be able to offer.

I can be (**11**) … at the above address for the next 4 weeks. Please (**12**) … me know if you require any further (**13**) … .

Yours sincerely,

Sally Braithwaite

Sally Braithwaite

Writing: competition entry

1 In Paper 2, Part 2 you may be asked to write an entry to a competition of some kind. 'Competition entries' are not a separate text type but can involve writing a description, an article, a review or a narrative. It is important to make what you write as interesting and engaging for the reader as possible.

2 Look at these different examples of 'Competition entry' tasks. Discuss with another student which one you would prefer to do and why.

Adverts & competitions

A

A FUNNY THING HAPPENED TO ME THE OTHER DAY!

Have you had a strange or funny experience recently? Has there been an odd coincidence in your life or an unexpected piece of luck? If there has, why not tell us what happened?
We are offering a prize for the 3 most interesting, well-written 250-word accounts. The best entries will be included in the June edition of The COMPETITION magazine.

B

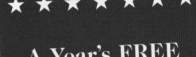

A Year's FREE Fitness Centre Membership!

Fitness For All magazine wants you to share your experiences of getting fit. If you've had some success at getting and staying fit, we want you to tell others about it. In about 250 words tell us what you do to stay fit and how you keep motivated.

The writers of the best accounts will receive a year's free membership of the fitness centre of their choice.

C

Get away from it all!

Is there somewhere you've always dreamed about travelling to but have never had the chance? Tell us where and why you would like to go and you could win a week's, all-expenses paid holiday to the destination of your choice.

If you are interested in taking up this opportunity, write to:

Explore The World, PO Box 412, Newcastle Upon Tyne.

3 Read this entry to A in Exercise 2. Answer these questions about it.

- Does it include varied and interesting vocabulary? Give some examples.
- How is the writing organised? What is the purpose of the first and last paragraphs?
- What linking words/phrases are used? Find examples.
- What effect does the entry have on the target reader? Do you think it would have a chance of winning the competition? If so, why?
- Is the entry written in a relatively formal or informal style? Do you feel this is appropriate?

A FUNNY THING HAPPENED TO ME THE OTHER DAY!

I have always been an addict of soap operas. In fact, my favourite is 'EastEnders' which I have been watching avidly now for over 10 years.

As it happens, a few weeks ago, I was watching an episode where Michelle (my favourite character) had just been shot in the leg. It was very dramatic and I was glued to the set. After it had finished I was absolutely exhausted from the stress of it all. Nevertheless, I'd promised my friend Jo that I'd go out with her to see a movie that she's been wanting to see for ages. 'Come on or we'll be late' she pleaded in exasperation.

It was pouring with rain and we splashed through the puddles until finally we arrived at the cinema. To our intense annoyance there was an extremely long queue and we had to wait in line for over 20 minutes. Finally, we got in, bought an enormous box of popcorn and stumbled through the darkness until we gratefully discovered two seats together.

After a minute though I suddenly thought that I was hallucinating. I could quite definitely hear Michelle from EastEnders talking. The hairs on the back of my neck stood up. I listened harder. It was definitely her. Slowly I looked around and there she was, sitting right behind me. At first I just couldn't understand why she wasn't in hospital having her leg seen to and then it dawned on me ...

4 Now write your own entry for one of the competitions in Exercise 2.

1 Make sure you read the question carefully. Highlight key words/phrases.
2 Brainstorm all possible ideas for what you might include in your answer.
3 Select the best ideas. Then try to organise them into possible paragraphs. Make sure your answer has a clear structure.
4 Write your draft. Include linking words within and between paragraphs as appropriate.

5 Show your draft to another student. Ask them if they think the text is engaging. Does it capture the reader's attention? Discuss places in the text where you could make the language more varied and interesting.

6 Write your final version of the competition entry. Make your handwriting as clear and easy to read as possible. Make sure you avoid basic mistakes of grammar, spelling and punctuation.

Exam focus

Paper 3 English in Use: Part 1 (multiple-choice cloze)

About the exam: Paper 3, Part 1 is a multiple-choice cloze task. There is a short text with 15 gaps followed by 15 four-option multiple-choice questions. This question tests phrases and collocations, as well as idioms and phrasal verbs.

Suggested procedure

1 Read the complete text quickly to get the general idea.

2 Read the text again. Stop and try to predict the possible missing word *without looking at the four alternatives*.

3 Look and see if the word you predicted is one of the alternatives. If so, choose it. If not try and eliminate the alternatives which are definitely wrong. They may be wrong because they don't fit with the following preposition or they are the wrong word for the phrase.

4 If you are left with more than one alternative that you think might be correct – guess! You don't lose marks for a wrong answer.

Exam task

For questions **1–15**, read the text below and then decide which word best fits each space. The exercise begins with an example (**0**).

HIGH STAKES

Few people in the world of high (**0**) *C* had heard of Marc Colombo. There was no (**1**) ... why they should have done. He was a mere foreign-exchange (**2**) ... , at the Lloyds Bank in Lugano, Switzerland. But in 1974, Colombo (**3**) ... the headlines around the world leaving (**4**) ... money experts open-mouthed in amazement. Lloyds (**5**) ... that 'irregularities' had cost the bank a (**6**) ... £32 million. What had the 28-year-old Colombo been (**7**) ... to? And how had he got (**8**) ... with it?

Colombo had been watching the world's leading (**9**) ... change their values on the foreign exchange markets. He decided to buy 34 million US dollars with Swiss francs in three months' time. If, as he (**10**) ... , it turned out that the dollar was (**11**) ... less when the time came to settle, he would make a handsome profit. But the dollar's value did not (**12**) ... . It went up. And Colombo lost £1 million.

Consequently he increased his stake, and went for (**13**) ... or nothing. Without Lloyds (**14**) ... a thing, he set up transactions totalling £4,580 million in just nine months. At first, he was betting that the dollar would lose value. It did not. (**15**) ... he switched to gambling that it would go on rising. It did not.

0	**A** money	**B** investment	**C** finance	**D** banking
1	**A** cause	**B** purpose	**C** basis	**D** reason
2	**A** dealer	**B** salesman	**C** merchant	**D** retailer
3	**A** knocked	**B** struck	**C** hit	**D** beat
4	**A** hard-hearted	**B** hard-headed	**C** hard-pressed	**D** hard-hitting
5	**A** announced	**B** publicised	**C** broadcasted	**D** divulged
6	**A** swaying	**B** shaking	**C** staggering	**D** wobbling
7	**A** down	**B** off	**C** up	**D** on
8	**A** away	**B** on	**C** through	**D** by
9	**A** monies	**B** rates	**C** accounts	**D** currencies
10	**A** expected	**B** contemplated	**C** wondered	**D** considered
11	**A** value	**B** cost	**C** worth	**D** charge
12	**A** tumble	**B** trip	**C** spill	**D** topple
13	**A** twice	**B** pair	**C** twofold	**D** double
14	**A** considering	**B** speculating	**C** suspecting	**D** believing
15	**A** So	**B** Moreover	**C** Despite	**D** However

1 Rewrite the sentences below, using the verb given and keeping the meaning of the original sentence.

1 Simon finally talked me into applying for that job at the post office.
persuade

2 My teacher wouldn't allow me to leave the class before the bell went.
let

3 I'm really sorry that I didn't revise more for my exams.
regret

4 You should have won the competition. Your poem was by far the best.
deserve

5 When are you thinking of leaving?
intend

6 Do you think he'll be able to move all that rubble by himself?
manage

7 He gave me no option but to promise never to see them again.
make

8 It really doesn't bother me if I can't smoke in the office.
mind

9 They don't eat meat if at all possible.
avoid

10 I can't believe that he owned up to stealing that car.
admit

2 Choose the correct alternative in each case.

1 The company launched a publicity campaign to *boost/maximise* the newspaper's circulation.

2 Twenty years later he was still trying to get over Marcia's death. It seems almost *far-fetched/inconceivable*, doesn't it?

3 *Generally/Typically*, these small stores do not keep fresh meat or vegetables.

4 I want to thank all the people, too *numerous/countless* to mention, who have helped me win this election.

5 Well, isn't that a *luck/coincidence*. I never expected to meet you here!

3 Rephrase these sentences, keeping the same meaning, by adding a prefix to the underlined words. You may need to change some of the other words in the sentence.

EXAMPLE: *Could you type this letter again?*
> ***Could you retype this letter?***

1 I'm sorry. I've cooked this meat for too long.
2 John's former wife rang me at home last night.
3 Sarah is not always loyal to her friends.
4 They kept raising issues which weren't relevant.
5 He lives by himself and is not at all social.
6 We estimated the work would take longer than it did.
7 We didn't understand what she meant.
8 Concealing this information is not legal.

4 Use the words in the column to the right of the text to form one word that fits in the same numbered space in the text.

HARD TO BELIEVE!		
Albert and Betty Cheetham hit the headlines recently thanks to an astonishing list of coincidences. On holiday in Tunisia, the (**1**) ... couple found themselves dining opposite another retired couple – Albert and Betty Rivers. And, also (**2**) ... , Mr Cheetham and Mr Rivers had both previously worked for a railway company, while Mrs Cheetham and Mrs Rivers had both worked for the post office. The two couples also made the (**3**) ... that they both had two sons and five grandchildren and, to their (**4**) ... , that the date and time of their (**5**) ... was exactly the same i.e. 2p.m. August 15th, 1942.	1	RETIRE
	2	COINCIDENCE
	3	DISCOVER
	4	AMAZING
	5	MARRY
A more sustained coincidence is that seven of the eight US Presidents who died in office were elected at exactly 20-year intervals between 1840 and 1960. It was eventually Ronald Reagan, beginning his (**6**) ... in 1980, 20 years after John F. Kennedy, who broke the cycle after surviving an (**7**) ... attempt and finishing his last term (**8**)	6	PRESIDENT
	7	ASSASSINATE
	8	LIVE

Where there's a will …

Jodie Foster

Marie Curie

Reading

▶ P1, Pt2 (gapped text)

1 What do you think the people in these photos have in common?

2 Read the article quite quickly and decide which of the following areas are mentioned:

1 the causes of high levels of motivation
2 problems with getting promoted at work
3 ways that parents affect their children's attitudes to sports

4 strategies for achieving your goals
5 ways that people cheat in sports

MOTIVATION
The Key To Success

Have you ever wondered why you have such trouble keeping your New Year's resolutions, or why you can't get
5 that promotion[1] you want? In fact, it could all be down to a problem of motivation[2].

(1 ———)

So, what are the causes of <u>these differences</u>? Cary Cooper, a psychology[3] professor, has written several books about people
10 who have really pushed themselves to make it to the top in business – one pretty reliable[4] indicator of high motivation levels. 'We found that for quite a few people who've achieved success[5], <u>the motivation comes from some adverse life event early in childhood</u>.' Cooper concludes that this motivation is
15 not to achieve power[6] over others, but to gain control over events – something most of the people surveyed lacked when they were younger.

(2 ———)

<u>Another area</u> where good motivation can make the difference between triumphant success and abject failure[7] is
20 sport. Dr Stuart Biddle, of the University of Exeter, is a sports psychology expert. He's found that athletes have two main types of motivation: a motivation to win regardless of whether they've played well; and a motivation to play well regardless of whether they win or lose.

(3 ———)

25 Like Cooper, Biddle has also found that these two kinds of motivational style develop[8] at a young age. '**It could be a socialisation thing,**' he says. 'Kids come home from school after sport and some parents will say, "How did you enjoy it?"

or "Did you improve[9]?" It's an attitude which is going to 30 enforce that what's important is taking part. Others might say, "Did you win?" and may even give their children a hard time if they didn't. That tells the kid there's nothing valuable in 35 playing sport unless they win and they get socialised into that mentality.'

(4 ———)

Take New Year's resolutions. While most people make them, hardly anyone actually sees them through. Marie Mosely, a freelance psychologist, suggests that <u>what you need to do to be</u> 40 <u>successful is to focus on the outcome of what you want and how that will affect your life</u>. In other words, instead of obsessing about all that chocolate and ice-cream you resolved to give up, try thinking about how good you'll look a few months after you've given them up. 45

(5 ———)

Another important factor as to whether you succeed or not is to do with determination[10]. Do you *really* want to lose weight, or learn that language? This may sound obvious, but sometimes it can be hard to know your own motives. 'People who don't achieve their resolutions often don't because they 50 feel pushed into it by others or feel that they "should" do it for some reason or other.'

(6 ———)

Use anything that works, no matter how strange. But above all, keep focused on your future success. Imagining it can really help, so picture what you want and who knows, one day, it 55 might actually become reality!

Richard Branson

4   Check your answers with other students. Say how the underlined parts of the text relate to the previous or following paragraphs.

5   Read the text again with the paragraphs in the correct order and answer the following questions.

1   Why are some people so highly motivated to achieve success according to Cary Cooper?
2   What kinds of motivation do athletes have?
3   When Biddle says 'It could be a socialisation thing', what does he mean?
4   What different ideas are given in the text to help you achieve success in your goals?

6   Discuss these questions with other students.

1   Do you agree that motivation levels are fundamentally affected by childhood experiences?
2   What things are you highly motivated to do/not highly motivated to do? What do you think are the reasons for this?
3   Which (if any) advice in the article did you think was useful for helping to improve motivation levels?

3   Now read the article again (in not more than 15 minutes) and insert the missing paragraphs below in the correct place. Parts of the text and missing paragraphs are underlined. These parts give clues as to where each paragraph goes.

A   Other ways to improve your motivation levels include improving your diet and doing more exercise. Volumes of research show that exercise can increase overall energy[11] levels, which will help with motivation.

B   Apart from adjusting your mental attitude, you might also find a few other useful hints in some of the countless self-help books cramming bookshops' shelves. There are plenty on motivation and they're full of advice: everything from taking some extra training to burning energising essential oils on your desk.

C   Cooper believes that this may even apply to more moderate levels of success. 'Say you take someone motivated to be successful at university – that would probably stem from teachers making them feel that they weren't very good at an early age. Basically, they need to prove that they can do it.'

D   And research backs up this view of gender differences. A recent study of 36 British Telecom employees found that the women were far more likely to want to be seen as 'experts' who did their job well, while the men were more likely to be 'climbers', motivated principally by a desire to scale the career ladder and achieve the most senior management level possible.

E   So, that's the theory[12] of where your motivational style comes from. But what can you actually do about improving your motivation levels? When it comes down to success at specific tasks or objectives, all kinds of factors can come into play. For example, how you think about a problem can seriously affect your motivation to resolve it satisfactorily.

F   Of course, many people are fairly motivated to succeed at school and work. But there's a big difference between the person who simply wants to move steadily forward in their career and the mega-achievers like Richard Branson or Bill Gates* who push themselves towards ever greater success.

G   'These two styles have proved very illuminating,' says Biddle. 'We generally find that you must have the second "task" or "mastery" motivation to play your best – it seems to be essential. Top sports people will probably have both. They don't just want to win, they want to win well, and they get motivated by improvement.'

> **Richard Branson** = *a successful British businessman*
> **Bill Gates** = *founder of Microsoft*

'I understand that if it's a success they plan to close down the whole chain.'

7 Look back at the text on pp.104–105. Find the numbered words and put them in the following sentences in the correct form.

EXAMPLE: *promotion*[1] *They decided to **promote** him because of his amazing results.*

2 Sometimes it's very difficult to .... students to study enough.

3 I'm afraid he's been having some .... problems. He may need to see a specialist.

4 You can't .... on Peter, he never does what he says he will do.

5 She made an .... attempt to break the world record. She was two seconds short of the existing time.

6 There's nothing I can do. I'm afraid I am utterly .... in this situation.

7 This is the fourth time I have .... my driving test. I may give up trying.

8 There have been some new .... in the current Middle East crisis.

9 He's made a lot of .... at school. The teachers are very pleased with him.

10 She's .... to leave school even though her parents want her to stay.

11 He's a very .... little boy. He never stops running about.

12 .... speaking you are right. But what happens in practice is rather different.

Watch Out! *few*

Which sentences have a negative meaning?
Which have a positive meaning?

1 a) *Quite a few* people achieve some degree of success.
  b) *Only a few* people achieve some degree of success.

2 a) *Few* of his friends came to watch him run.
  b) *A few* of his friends came to watch him run.

D **8** Check your dictionary to find other important forms of the words in Exercise 7 e.g. *motivate* [v] / *motivated* [adj] / *motivation* [n]. Add the words and the different parts of speech to your vocabulary notebook.

mo·ti·vate /ˈməʊtˌveɪt‖ˈmoʊ-/ *v* [T] **1** to make someone want to achieve something and make them willing to work hard in order to do it: *A good teacher has to be able to motivate her students.*

mo·ti·va·ted /ˈməʊtˌveɪtˌd‖ˈmoʊ-/ *adj* **1** very keen to do something or to achieve something, especially because you find it interesting or exciting: *They're a really good bunch of students – highly motivated and very intelligent.*

mo·ti·va·tion /ˌməʊtˌˈveɪʃən‖ˌmoʊ-/ *n* **1** [U] eagerness and willingness to do something without needing to be told or forced to do it: *Jack is an intelligent pupil, but he lacks motivation.*

(from the *Longman Dictionary of Contemporary English*)

9 Make two resolutions about things in your life that you would like to do or change. Write them on a piece of paper. Tell other people your resolutions and collect suggestions for ways to ensure that you are going to keep your resolutions.

EXAMPLE:

Resolution: *I'm going to learn some new English words every day.*

Advice: 1 *Give yourself a specific number to learn each day e.g. five, so you know your target.*

2 *Get a partner to do it with you. Then test each other.*

3 *Try and choose words which are connected to a theme e.g. weather, sport etc. It will make them easier to remember.*

Vocabulary: expressions with *make/get/ keep/gain/resolve*

1 Put the words in the boxes in the appropriate columns to form expressions with each of the verbs.

1

make	get	keep
a difference	*into trouble*	*a resolution*

a resolution	a promotion
someone feel something	your word
even with someone	an impression
on at someone	a difference

2

gain	resolve
control	*a problem*

to leave	control	experience
a problem	your doubts	an advantage

2 Complete each of the following sentences with the expressions above in the correct form.

EXAMPLE: *Have you* **resolved your doubts** *about whether to marry Mike yet?*

1 You .... a very good .... on my mother. She thinks you're great!

2 She .... a lot of useful .... through working for her uncle and now she'd like to start up her own business.

3 They .... the .... of where to send their son to school by letting him choose.

4 His teacher told him he would .... serious .... if he continued to hang around with that group of boys.

5 She .... terribly guilty when she said how upset she was that I hadn't been in touch.

6 She was so unhappy in her job that she .... by the end of the year.

7 I think we can .... a definite .... over the competition if we launch our new model in January.

8 You can never believe Jim when he promises to do something. He just seems unable to ....

9 I can't believe that Fiona humiliated me like that. I'll .... with her if it's the last thing I do.

10 I wish my boss wouldn't .... me all the time to finish the report. It doesn't have to be done until the end of the month.

11 He's managed to .... to stop smoking for six weeks now.

12 My sister has just .... Now, she's head of her department.

13 If he .... of any more newspapers, he will have a virtual monopoly of the media.

14 Passing her exams has .... amazing .... to her levels of self-confidence!

3 Discuss these questions with other students.

1 Have you ever made any 'New Year's resolutions'? If so, what were they? Did you manage to keep them?

2 If your best friend made you promise to keep a secret, under what circumstances might you not keep your word?

3 Describe a situation where someone made
 a) a very good first impression on you.
 b) a very bad first impression on you.

4 Have you had a problem recently which you have now resolved? What was it? What did you decide?

5 Did you ever get into trouble when you were younger? What kinds of things did you do?

6 If you are feeling down, what kinds of things can you do to make yourself feel happier?

7 Are there any areas of work where you would like to gain experience? What are they?

Grammar plus: emphasis

 1 Listen to this conversation and answer this question: How did Amanda embarrass Sam?

2 Listen to the conversation again and write down the missing parts from the conversation below.

1 She's really nice and so on but .... is her wicked sense of humour.
2 Anyway, ... Sam that it was a 'Roman toga' party.
3 So, of course, ... at the party in this elaborate costume.

3 Look at these pairs of sentences.

1 What is the difference in effect of using the structure beginning with *What ...* in each case?
   a) They need to prove that they can do it.
     What they need to prove *is* that they can do it.
   b) She won the race.
     What she did was to win the race.
   c) He stayed up all night revising but then he fell asleep in the exam.
     What happened was that he stayed up all night revising but then he fell asleep in the exam.
2 Identify which of the sentences above emphasises:
   • a whole sentence
   • the verb
   • the thing
3 Now add each of the sentences from the listening text to the categories in 2 above.

4 Emphasise the bracketed parts of these sentences in one of the ways shown in Exercise 3.

EXAMPLE: *I want to know (how you were treated as a child).*
      *What **I want to know is how you were treated as a child**.*

1 She (learnt all the irregular verbs off by heart).
   What she ...
2 (People who are always late) annoy me most.
   What ...
3 (He failed all his exams at school and that made him determined to be successful in business.)
   What ...
4 (She went on a management course) at the end of last year.
   What she ...
5 I'd really like to have (a new computer).
   What ...
6 (She decided finally to ask her boss for promotion but the company went bust and she lost her job.)
   What ...
7 I (started going swimming) first thing in the morning.
   What I ...
8 (She went and told her boss about how she felt.)
   What ...

 5 Listen to some possible answers to Exercise 4 on the recording and mark the main words which are stressed. Try saying the sentences with the same stress.

EXAMPLE: *What <u>I</u> want to know is <u>how</u> you were <u>treated</u> as a <u>child</u>.*

6 Choose one of these topics to speak about.

• What I particularly need to do to improve my English is to ... because ...
• I had a slightly strange experience a little while ago. What happened was ...
• What I value most about my best friend is ... because ...
• What really annoys me is people who ... because ...
• My friend *(name of friend)* really surprised me the other day. What she did was to ...

1 Make notes and prepare to speak for at least a minute. Start with the sentence you chose. Listen to the example on the recording.
2 Work in groups. Take it in turns to speak.

► Grammar reference p.192

108

7   A good friend of yours has applied for a job in a local tourist office. She/he will be helping and advising tourists who visit the town. You have been asked to write a character reference (in about 250 words) for your friend.

- Explain how you know your friend and how long you have known her/him.
- Describe the characteristics that make your friend suitable for the position. (Don't exaggerate otherwise your reference will not be taken seriously.)
- Mention any relevant weaknesses but try and avoid making them sound serious.
- Finish by recommending your friend for the job.
- Remember to write in a formal style. This reference will go to their potential employer. (Include two or three 'emphasising structures' as appropriate.)
- Check through your reference to make sure that everything is relevant to the job that your friend is applying for.

Speaking

▶ P5, Pt2 (comparing and contrasting)

1   Look at the photographs below showing different people trying to do something for the first time. Have you ever tried to do any of them? How easy or difficult was it in the beginning? Why?

2   In Part 2 of Paper 5 of the CAE exam you may be asked to 'compare and contrast' different pictures. Here are some words/phrases that will help you to do this:

appearance	contrast	qualifier
looks	on the other hand	considerably
comes across as	however	slightly
appears	whereas	far

EXAMPLE: *In Picture A there are two women who are probably in their late teens. I think one of them is trying rollerblading for the first time but she **comes across as** being fairly relaxed and confident. **In contrast**, the small boy in Picture B is starting to learn to swim and he looks **considerably** more nervous about the whole business!*

Now listen to someone comparing and contrasting Pictures A and C and note down any extra words/phrases to go in each of the categories in the table above.

3   Now do the following task trying to use some of the various words or phrases above. (Either refer to Pictures A, B and C below or Pictures A, B and C on p.217.)

Compare and contrast two pictures showing people attempting to do different things for the first time. Say how you think the people are feeling in each case and what skills or abilities they would need to be successful.

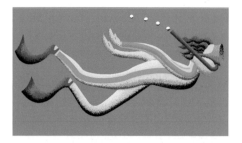

Vocabulary: leisure activities

1 Look at the words below.

- a wetsuit/an oar/a snorkel/flippers/ a mask
- a tripod/a lens/an album/an easel/ a dark room
- a choir/a rehearsal/a conductor/to sight-read/a script
- a bridle/a whip/a crash helmet/ reins/a saddle
- a chapter/lyrics/a blurb/an author/ a paperback

1 Which is the odd word out in each of the groups above?

2 Which leisure activity do the other words belong to? Explain what they mean in each case.

3 Test another student on the words above.

EXAMPLE:

Student A: *You often find it on the back of a book. It briefly describes the contents.*

Student B: *The blurb!*

2

D 1 Choose one leisure activity which you do and enjoy. Collect as many key words as you can which are connected to it. (Use your dictionary, ask other students or ask the teacher.)

2 Prepare to speak to other students about it for two to three minutes. Talk about the following points:
- how you came to take it up
- how often you do it
- what you need to be good at it
- why you enjoy it and any particularly good/interesting experiences

English in Use

▶ P3, Pt3 (error correction, spelling and punctuation)

1 Discuss with other students.

Should parents automatically leave most of their wealth to their children when they die? Why/why not?

2 Read the text below quickly. What reasons are given for not leaving children a large inheritance?

3 Discuss with other students whether you agree with the attitude of Paul Sykes.

4 In each of the lines marked with SP. there is a spelling mistake and in each of the lines marked with a P. there is a punctuation mistake. Find the mistakes and correct them.

5 Check that you
- can pronounce all the letters of the alphabet correctly.
- know the names for all the different punctuation marks you have changed or added.

Then, compare your corrections with other students.

TYCOONS PULL PLUG ON RICH KIDS

A growing number of entrepreneurs. Including Paul Sykes,   P.
the self-made millionaire, are choosing to disinherit there children rather   SP.
than 'burden' them with vast amounts of inherited welth.   SP.

Sykes, the british technology and property tycoon worth £250m,   P.
has decided not to leave his children a penny even thought there is   SP.
no family rift. Instead, he and other like minded millionaires intend   P.
to distribute their fortunes to good causes before they dye.   SP.

Financial analysts say that even succesful entrepreneurs who fall   SP.
short of milionaire status are favouring charities rather than their   SP.
offspring for their legacies the trend is being led by self-made   P.
businessmen who beleive their children should make their own   SP.
way in life.

There are many more important things to do with your money than   P.
leave it to your kids,' said Sykes. 'I don't believe in goverment   SP.
intervention in peoples lives and I don't think that parental   P.
intervention works in a monetary sense either' Sykes believes he   P.
has amply provided for his four children by giving them love and
support.

Sykes believes that his children should stand or fall on their own.
'I have never found a link, between money and happiness, but I   P.
have definitaly found a link between success and happiness.'   SP.

Grammar check: tenses

1 Read the following text and put the verbs in brackets into the correct tense: *Present Simple, Present Continuous, Past Simple, Past Continuous, Present Perfect* or *Past Perfect*. (Occasionally, there may be more than one alternative.)

NEVER SAY DIE
– *the art of survival*

What kind of person will survive an emergency? The simple answer is anyone – including you, if you 1. (**be**) determined enough. Here are just a few stories of people who 2. (**live**) to tell the tale in the most incredible circumstances.

■ An elderly man 3. (**break**) his leg while he 4. (**walk**) in the Lake District. Three weeks later he was found alive and well. The survival kit he 5. (**take**) with him was nothing more than what you would take on a day's hike.

■ A Mexican 6. (**survive**) eight days in desert temperatures of 39°C with only two gallons of water. He 7. (**travel**) 35 miles on horseback when his horse 8. (**die**) and then 9. (**walk**) 100 miles until he 10. (**reach**) help. When he was finally found he 11. (**lose**) 25% of his body weight and his hair 12. (**go**) completely grey.

■ Maurice and Maureen Bailey's yacht was hit by a whale in the Pacific. When they were rescued by Korean fishermen, they 13. (**drift**) 1,500 miles over 118 days.

You 14. (**probably think**): 'These 15. (**be**) clearly all amazing people. I could never survive what they have.' But the truth is, there isn't an easy profile of the born survivor. However, in recent years psychologists 16. (**conduct**) various surveys of emergencies which give us a few clues and it seems the most unlikely people can be the ones to pull through.

2 Discuss with other students. Are these statements true or false? Where appropriate refer to the examples in the text above to check your ideas.

1 We use the Present Continuous to talk about temporary actions and situations that are in progress 'around now'.
2 We generally use the Past Simple to talk about the past unless there is special reason to use another tense.
3 We only use the Past Continuous to refer to things that go on for a long time.
4 We use the Past Continuous to say that something was in progress around a particular past time or event.
5 We use the Past Perfect to describe something that happened a long time ago.
6 We use the Past Perfect to make it clear that something happened before something else in the past.
7 We use the Present Perfect to say that a finished action or event is related to the present in some way.
8 We generally do not use the Present Perfect with expressions that refer to a completely finished period of time, like *yesterday, last week, three years ago, in 1970*.

▶ *Exam Maximiser*

3 Choose one of the stories above. Prepare to expand it and tell it to other students in much more detail. You should speak for at least one minute.

Writing: report (1)

1 Read the report below. It is an example answer to this question:

A government department is conducting research into why students in your country are not finishing school with a sufficiently high level of spoken English. You have been asked to contribute a report entitled 'Motivating students to achieve a high level of English'. Your report should make specific reference to:

- reasons why students fail to reach a good level of spoken English
- possible ideas to improve the situation

2 Which of the points in the report do you think apply to your country?

MOTIVATING STUDENTS TO ACHIEVE A HIGH LEVEL OF ENGLISH.

This report is intended to explain why so many students finish secondary school with a low level of English. A number of students and teachers were interviewed and their suggestions for changes to the teaching methods are summarised.

There seem to be a variety of reasons why our school students fail to reach a good level of spoken English. The main problem seems to be the fact that teachers appear to place so much significance on grammar. Students appear to know a lot about grammar but can't actually speak with much confidence. What students complain about most is that lessons are boring with too many grammar exercises and gapfills.

What steps can be taken to improve the situation? What teachers need to do is to place more emphasis on developing the listening and speaking ability of students. They need to introduce greater variety into their teaching and use more games, role-plays, drama and so on. They should use as much authentic material as possible: newspaper articles, songs, extracts from films etc. (This will also help to increase student motivation.)

There are serious problems with the way that English is taught in our schools at the moment, leading to low motivation on the part of students. We believe that it is the way English teachers are trained that needs to be changed, with more emphasis on preparing students to use English in practical situations rather than approaching it as another academic subject.

3 Consider the following areas. Which one of them is a problem area in the report?

- paragraphing
- accurate grammar and vocabulary
- good range of grammatical structures and vocabulary
- linking words/phrases
- spelling/punctuation
- handwriting

4 Now add an appropriate short heading to each section of the report.

5 Decide if the following statements connected with writing reports are True or False.

1 Reports usually have a simple, clear, direct overall heading.
2 They usually have an introduction (describing the context and reason for the report) and a conclusion (often with recommendations).
3 Informal and dramatic language is often used.
4 They are often written as one, long, continuous piece of text.
5 Good use of linking words/expressions (e.g. *firstly, in addition* etc.) makes your report easier to read.

6 Decide whether one or both of the linking words/phrases in each of the sentences below are possible.

1 Unfortunately, our annual budget has been severely reduced and *in addition to this/ consequently* we cannot take on any more teachers for the next school year.
2 And, *most importantly/above all*, we should remember the dedication of Michael Harris, without whom none of this would have been possible.
3 It is as headmaster, *first and foremost/ furthermore*, my pleasure to begin by welcoming all new parents and children to the school.
4 We *clearly/therefore* need to change our teaching approach if students still can't speak any French after seven years of study!
5 The good news is that the numbers of students passing their English exam has increased since last year. *As a result of this/ moreover* there were 20% more 'A' grades.

7 Put the linking words/phrases in *italics* in Exercise 6 in the correct columns below. Then add any other linking words/phrases you know.

addition	consequence	significance
As well as this	*So*	*The main priority is ...*

8 Now attempt to improve the report on p.112 by adding linking words/phrases where appropriate. Try and add at least four.

9 Write about one of the topics below. (The first is the original question.)

- Motivating students to achieve a high level of English
- Motivating students to participate in more sports activities at school
- Motivating employees to feel more committed to the company they work for

Suggested procedure

(Work with other students who are going to write the same report as you.)

1 Decide on the different sections that will go in your report.
2 Brainstorm different ideas to put in each section.
3 Select the best ideas, put them in a logical order and think of linking words/expressions to connect them.
4 Write your report in about 250 words. Use a neutral or formal style.
   a) Begin with an introduction which states the subject and purpose of your report.
   b) End with a conclusion where you summarise your report and possibly make recommendations.
   c) Give each of your paragraphs an appropriate heading.
5 Check that you feel confident that all the areas in Exercise 3 (e.g. paragraphing, handwriting etc.) are dealt with well. Make any necessary changes.

Exam focus

Paper 4 Listening: Part 4 (multiple matching)

About the exam: In Paper 4, Part 4 you will listen to a series of five short extracts of about 30 seconds each. You will hear the five extracts twice. The speakers will all be talking about a similar topic. You will either have a multiple-matching task or a multiple-choice task.

Suggested procedure

Before you listen:

1 Read all of the prompts in Task One and Task Two before you listen the first time.
2 Predict any key vocabulary you might expect to hear.

As you listen the first time:

3 Focus mainly on Task One.
4 Make a note of any key words/phrases you hear.
5 Cross off any prompts you are sure you have matched correctly. Put a question mark next to any you are not sure about.

As you listen the second time:

6 Focus mainly on Task Two.
7 Listen particularly carefully to the extracts you are not sure about.
8 Make sure you don't leave any question unanswered.

 Exam task

You will hear five short extracts in which various people are talking about different things they have attempted to do.

TASK ONE

For questions **1–5**, match the extracts as you hear them with the activities listed, **A–H**.

A climbing a mountain

B passing an exam

C getting a job

D writing a novel

E building an extension on their house

F learning to swim

G giving up smoking

H getting on better with their sister

1
2
3
4
5

TASK TWO

For questions **6–10**, match the extracts as you hear them with **A–H** below.

A talks about how difficult it is

B can't understand why other people find it difficult to do

C did it with their best friend

D wants to do it before a particular future event

E couldn't do it because of conditions outside their control

F has had lots of advice but no success yet

G was inspired by a famous person

H talks about having to make a lot of effort

6
7
8
9
10

Remember that you must complete both tasks as you listen. You will hear the recording twice.

1 Five of the expressions with *make/get/keep/ gain/resolve* below are used incorrectly. Find them and correct them.

EXAMPLE: *I wish you wouldn't make on at me to clean my room. I will do it soon.*
  > *keep on at me*

1 I wouldn't be surprised if she makes an important promotion by the end of the year.
2 I'm going to get even with him if it's the last thing I do!
3 She made a very good impression on the interview panel, I'm told.
4 If they keep into trouble, they could be expelled from school.
5 I'm afraid it won't make any difference what you do.
6 There's no chance that we will be able to resolve this problem before Christmas.
7 If you make some experience working on the shop floor, you'll be a better manager in the end.
8 If they get their new model out by Christmas they will gain quite an advantage in terms of market share.
9 He's renowned for not being able to make his word.
10 Being with him always gets me feel great. That's why I like him so much.

2 Complete each of the following sentences with one appropriate missing word.

EXAMPLE: *What I love about him is his sense of humour.*

1 What I really can't stand about my brothers .... the way they are so bossy.
2 What .... then was that she threw a full glass of water over the interviewer.
3 What we .... in the end was to ask for our money back.
4 What really upsets me is .... I see people being cruel to animals.
5 What I want to know is .... they managed to get into the building without being seen.
6 What happened after she ran out of the church .... that her mother burst into tears and started shouting at the groom.

3 Name the thing that is being defined in each case below.

EXAMPLE: *a publisher's short description of the contents of a book, usually printed on the jacket or the cover*
  > *the blurb*

1 a place with a red light or no light, used for developing photographic film
2 a piece of equipment with three legs, used for holding a camera in position
3 a book in which you put photographs, stamps etc.
4 a long pole that is wide at one end, used for rowing a boat
5 a tube that makes it possible for a swimmer to breathe air while her or his face is under water
6 a group of people who sing together, especially in a church or school
7 a person who directs the performance of an orchestra, choir etc.
8 a seat, often of leather, for a rider on a horse, donkey etc.
9 a long thin piece of leather or rope with a handle, used for making animals move faster
10 the words of a song

4 For items 1–15, complete the following article by writing down each missing word. Use only one word for each space.

Most people only know Sir Edmund Hillary (1) ... the first man to set foot on top of Mount Everest. But it is often forgotten that he (2) ... also the first to reach the South Pole (3) ... motor vehicle and to jet-boat up the Ganges. He is a towering, affable man (4) ... doesn't look anything like his 80 years and his clear blue eyes give him a formidable presence.

(5) ... he laughs at the notion, Sir Edmund (6) ... arguably become the most influential figure in the region around Mount Everest, which he scaled (7) ... Sherpa guide, Tenzing Norgay in 1953. That feat might well have (8) ... impossible without the aid of Sherpa porters, suppliers, guides and climbers. For that and (9) ... favours, Sir Edmund initiated the first of numerous projects. When he asked villagers (10) ... they most needed, the elders (11) ... him: 'Our children have eyes but they cannot see.' So in 1961, Sir Edmund built a school in the village of Khumjung (12) ... children with no knowledge of (13) ... world beyond their deep valleys. These were the first (14) ... several generations of 'Hillary children', a number of whom have gone (15) ... to become doctors, airline pilots, teachers and wealthy businessmen.

10 The trials of technology

The schoolboy SPY

Exam focus

Paper 1 Reading: Part 2 (gapped text)

About the exam: In Paper 1 Part 2 you will read a text from which six or seven paragraphs have been removed and placed in jumbled order after the text. You must decide from where in the text the paragraphs have been removed. Only one answer is correct in each case and there is one extra paragraph which does not fit in any of the gaps. You will have approximately 18 minutes to do this task.

Suggested procedure

1 Read the main part of the text through to get a general idea of the structure and the content. Pay attention to the information and ideas before and after each gap. Highlight any linking or referencing words e.g. *However, Consequently, This idea* which will help you put the paragraphs in the right order.

2 Read the missing paragraphs and see if any of them obviously fit into the spaces in the main text.

3 Go through the main part of the text again. Stop at each gap and check each missing paragraph. Look for grammar and vocabulary links. If you are not sure about a particular gap, leave it and go on to the next one.

4 Go back and make sure that you have decided on one paragraph for each gap.

5 Check your ideas by reading the complete text in sequence. Make sure that your answers make sense.

Exam task

For questions **1–7**, you must choose which of the paragraphs **A–H** on p.117 fit into the numbered gaps in the following magazine article. There is one extra paragraph which does not fit into any of the gaps.

On the evening of April 15, 1994, six American special agents sat in a concrete basement at a secret air force base patiently waiting for an attack. Their unseen and unknown enemy had for weeks been rampaging across the Pentagon
5 network of computers, cracking security codes and downloading secret files. Defence officials feared the infiltrator was a foreign agent. They were monitoring his movements in a desperate effort to trace him to his lair.

He had first been spotted by a systems manager at the
10 Griffiss air base in New York State, the premier command and control research facility in the United States. He had breached the security system and was using assumed computer identities from the air base to attack other sites, including Nasa. He was also planting 'sniffer files' to pick
15 up every password used in the system.

> **1**

Computer specialists from the Air Force Office of Special Investigations (AFOSI) were dispatched to Griffiss air base to catch the attacker. By the end of the second week of their attempt to outwit him, their windowless basement room
20 was a mess of food wrappers, sleeping bags and empty drinks cans.

> **2**

They carefully tracked him on a computer screen as he used the access code of a high-ranking Pentagon employee to sign on. This gave him the power to delete files, copy secret
25 information and even crash the system. As he sifted through battlefield simulation data, artificial intelligence files and reports on current weaponry, the agents worked frantically at their terminals, trying yet again to establish who he was and where he had come from.

> **3**

30 Pentagon generals insisted it was essential that he should be found and put out of action. It would have been relatively simple to shut him out of the Pentagon network, but he would survive to attack again – and his identity and the information he had already stolen would have remained
35 unknown. American cyber agents were ordered to continue chasing him through the electronic maze.

> **4**

The process can often be hit and miss because of the vast amount of traffic on the Internet and the hacker's path was simply too long and circuitous to follow to its end. The agents almost gave up hope. Then old-
40 fashioned police work was brought to bear. In the cyber age, where do hackers hang out? On the Internet, of course. They 'chat' with each other through their screens.

5

Moreover, he was a particularly chatty individual who
45 was eager to engage other hackers in e-mail conversation. Naive, too. Before long, the informant had established that Datastream Cowboy lived in the United Kingdom. He even gave out his home telephone number.

Jubilant, a senior AFOSI agent contacted the computer
50 crime unit in Scotland Yard for assistance. Datastream Cowboy's number was traced to a house in a cul-de-sac in Colindale, part of the anonymous north London suburbs. In cold war days it would have been a classic address for a spy's hideaway.

6

55 American agents flew to London and staked out the address with British police officers. Detectives were cautious, however, about making an immediate arrest because they wanted Datastream Cowboy to be online when they entered the house, so that he would be
60 caught in the act.

7

One of the detectives walked up silently behind the young suspect and gently removed his hands from the computer. For 16-year-old Richard Pryce, a music student, it was the shock of his life. 'They thought they
65 were going to find a super-criminal and they just found me, a teenager playing around on his computer,' says Pryce now. 'My mother had noticed people sitting outside our house for a few days beforehand, but I didn't think much of it. I never thought I would get caught and
70 it was very disturbing when I did. It had just been a game or a challenge from which I got a real buzz. It was unbelievable because the computers were so easy to hack, like painting by numbers.'

A The agents had informants who cruised the Internet and one of these made the breakthrough. He found that Datastream Cowboy hung out at Cyberspace, an Internet service provider based in Seattle.

B It was futile. Datastream Cowboy always bounced around the world before launching an attack and it was impossible even to establish in which country he was sitting.

C Posing as a courier, one of the agents knocked on the door. As it was opened by a middle-aged man, eight policemen silently appeared and swept into the house. The officers quietly searched the downstairs and first floor. Then, creeping up the stairs to a loft room, they saw a teenager hunched in his chair tapping frantically away on the keyboard of his £700 PC World computer. They had found Datastream Cowboy.

D This was a new type of warfare, a 'cyber attack' at the heart of the most powerful military machine on earth. But the American military had been preparing for 'cyber war' and it had a new breed of agent ready to fight back against the infiltrator.

E Having identified his location, subsequent telephone line checks revealed that the hacker was first dialling into Bogotá, the Colombian capital, and then using a free phone line from there to hack his way into the sensitive military sites.

F But how? They used a process called 'fingering' in which they tried to detect every computer that Datastream Cowboy had used as stepping stones before attacking them. A computer gives its own address in the first few bytes of any communication and the agents tried to trace Datastream Cowboy's path backwards.

G The Internet automatically brought hackers to the very gates of the Pentagon's most secret files – and it could not be policed, as it had been deliberately set up without controls to ensure ease of access for nuclear survivors.

H Sitting among the debris, the American cyber agents saw a silent alarm throb on one of the many terminals packed into the 30ft by 30ft room. Datastream Cowboy, as he called himself, was online again.

Vocabulary: computers

1 Find these words/phrases in the Exam focus text, *The Schoolboy Spy*, on pp.116–117 and explain what they mean:

- a network (of computers) (l. 5)
- to download a file (l. 6)
- a (computer) screen (l. 22)
- to delete a file (l. 24)
- to crash a system (l. 25)
- a (computer) terminal (l. 28)
- a (computer) hacker (l. 38)
- to be online (l. 58)
- an Internet service provider (Paragraph A)
- a keyboard (Paragraph C)

2 Discuss with other students.

1 Do you use a computer? What do you use it for?
2 How do you feel about computers? Do you love them, hate them or have no strong feelings about them?
3 Do you think computers will ever have independent intelligence and be able to act and think for themselves?
4 What can the Internet be used for? Do you think it is a positive thing?

Grammar plus: *it* as preparatory subject / object

1 In the following cases, sentences are often begun with 'preparatory *it*'. Match each of the uses to one pair of example sentences at the top of the right-hand column.

1 when the subject of a clause is an infinitive expression
2 when the subject of a clause is another clause
3 when you want to emphasise what comes first in the sentence

a) It was Jane who showed me how to set up my new computer, not Simon.
   It was last night that Sarah called me to tell me, not last weekend.
b) It's surprising how many people still seem to be afraid of computers.
   It appears that he hasn't heard the latest news.
c) It's important to know how to use this software.
   It's unusual to see Derek so excited by his work.

2 The sentences below would sound more natural if they began with *it*. Transform each one keeping approximately the same meaning.

EXAMPLE:
a) *Even to establish in which country he was sitting was impossible.*
   It was impossible even to establish in which country he was sitting.
b) *That he should be found was essential.*
   It was essential that he should be found.

1 How easy it is to hack into government computers is unbelievable.
   It ...
2 To try and find out where he was based was futile.
   It ...
3 That an outside person knows the password to our system seems likely.
   It ...
4 For us to find out who it was is absolutely vital.
   It ...
5 When you give me back that book doesn't really matter.
   It ...
6 That the Prime Minister will resign was announced yesterday.
   It ...

3 *It* can also be used as a 'preparatory object' in this pattern.

subject +	verb +	it +	complement +	infinitive/clause
I	find	it	hard	to believe how much technology has advanced.
They	made	it	clear	that they didn't like him.

The following sentences are incorrect. Insert *it* in the appropriate place in each one.

1 His headache made difficult for him to work.
2 They thought strange that he hadn't called.
3 I found surprising to be asked to be on the committee.
4 He made impossible for me to continue working there.
5 She considered a mistake to sign the contract.

4 Look at the use of *it* in the following sentences. Which sentences are correct? Which are not correct? For the incorrect sentences, explain what is wrong and correct them.

1 I cannot bear it to see people being cruel to animals.
2 She loves it when you sing to her.
3 I find it thought-provoking hearing you talk like this.
4 She made it obvious that she never wanted to see me again.
5 I'll leave it to you to decide which film we're going to see tonight.
6 I knew it that they didn't really want to come with me.
7 They owe it to us to tell us the truth.
8 I take it you won't be coming to Mike's party at the weekend.
9 He put it to me that I should really withdraw from the election.

5 Work with another student. Take it in turns to make sentences beginning with the words below. Ask questions to get more information.

EXAMPLE: A: *It is vital that young people have the opportunity to learn to use computers at school.*
B: *Why do you feel that?*
A: *Because computers are essential in every area of work.*

- It's vital that …
- It's surprising how few/many …
- It's exciting when …
- It's definitely worth …
- It's often said that …
- I find it quite difficult to …
- I find it very interesting to …
- I find it embarrassing to …

▶ Grammar reference pp.193–194

Listening: computers

▶ P4, Pt1 (sentence completion)

1 What do you know about the man in the photo? Why is he famous? What do you think of him?

2 The game you can see illustrated is called 'noughts and crosses' in British English and 'tick-tack-toe' in American English. How do you play it?

3 Listen to this talk. Which of the following things are mentioned?

- how he had the chance to start using computers
- what he first used a computer for
- a theory about why children like computers
- predictions about what computers will do in the future
- his sense of awe at the future

4 Listen again and fill in the missing information.

1 The problem he had with the computer he wrote his first program on was that it was very
....
2 It was .... who were responsible for his first chance to use a computer.
3 They would find out who won a game by looking at the paper from a ....
4 To play a game of tick-tack-toe on computer could take nearly all of ....
5 One of the reasons why he and other children liked using the computer was that they could
....
6 Something you get from computers that you rarely get from other things is ....
7 Gates and a friend used BASIC to make the computer play games ....
8 His friend taught the computer how to play various games and it told them the strategies which
....
9 Gates thinks that children typically try and make their toys do ....

Speaking: language of approximation

1 Look at the picture above and with a partner try and describe it as fully as possible.

2 Listen to some people attempting the same task. At times they don't know the exact name for something so they use phrases to help them express what they want to say approximately. Make a note of phrases like this that you hear.

EXAMPLE: ***As far as I can see, it looks like some kind of*** *tube or machine or something.*

3 Now take it in turns to describe Picture A and Picture B (on p.216). Describe what you can see and explain what you think is happening in the pictures. If you are not sure what certain things are, use approximating phrases to express what you think.

4 Now look at the pictures on the right. Compare and contrast them. Say which of the two offices you would prefer to work in and why.

A

B

English in Use

▶ P3, Pt2 (open cloze)

1 Discuss the following questions with another student.

1 How many hours do you think it takes surfing the Internet to qualify as an 'addict'?
2 Why do you think some people become Internet addicts?

2 Read the article below. How do your answers to the above questions compare with those given in the text?

CAUGHT IN THE NET

IT CAN CONSUME UP TO 80 HOURS A WEEK, wreck relationships and damage health, and it is the world's fastest growing addiction. Internet abuse **(1)** ... created millions of on-line addicts **(2)** ... suffer withdrawal symptoms **(3)** ... they switch off their computer and panic attacks if they have no e-mail.

In the first book **(4)** ... offer health tips to the estimated 8.1 million addicts, Dr Kimberley Young of **(5)** ... University of Pittsburgh spells out **(6)** ... to kick the habit and get back into the real world. It is difficult **(7)** ... tell when entertainment becomes addiction. **(8)** ... who spends more than 40 hours a week online is probably suspect, and other clues **(9)** ... lying about the amount of time and money **(10)** ... spent online, neglect of other work and a withdrawal **(11)** ... social contacts.

The big attraction **(12)** ... the Internet is that it allows people to escape into a fantasy world at any time of the day or night. '**(13)** ... ever sees you, so you **(14)** ... be whoever you choose. It's a form of escape **(15)** ... allows people to forget their problems for a time,' Young says.

3 Go through the text again and decide which gaps you can complete quickly and confidently with one word only and which you are not sure about. Write the answers for the ones you are sure about and put a question mark for those that you aren't sure about.

4 Compare your ideas with another student.

1 Tell each other the answers you are sure about and why.
2 Then together look at the remaining gaps and try and work out the missing part of speech by looking at the surrounding context.
3 Try and suggest some probable answers. Select one of them.
4 Read the text again to make sure your ideas make sense.

5 Look at the following types of words. From your work on the above text and previous cloze texts, say which one is least likely to be tested in this part of the exam.

prepositions (*in, on, at* etc.)
articles (*a, an, the*)
pronouns (*it, that* etc.)
linking words (*although, so* etc.)
determiners (*some, much* etc.)
nouns (*lamp, earth* etc.)
auxiliary verbs (*do, will, am* etc.)

Listening: cyber dating

1 Listen to the conversation and briefly summarise the attitude of Andrew, Ben and Cathy to the subject of 'making friends over the Internet'.

2 Listen again. Which of the following attitudes do you think are expressed during the conversation? How are they expressed? Give examples.

1	disbelief	5	defensiveness
2	irritation	6	dismissiveness
3	scepticism	7	excitement
4	concern	8	joy

3 In what ways do you think getting to know someone via text online is different from meeting them for the first time in a face-to-face situation e.g. at a party?

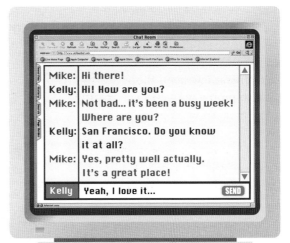

Grammar check: making comparisons

1 There are nine mistakes connected with making comparisons in the two dialogues below. Find them and correct them.

Ann: So, is Alison going to get her new computer then?

Bill: Yes, well she's says it's far much faster and has lot more memory than the old one. Personally I can't see why she needs a new one. We've only just got the old one after all.

Ann: Well, technology is changing fast and presumably she'll be able to get her work done a bit more efficiently and download things from the Internet more quicklier.

Bill: True.

Ann: Do you know what I think?

Bill: No, but I'm sure you're going to tell me.

Ann: (laughing) Seriously ... I think the most interesting and possibly the less positive thing about all these changes is the way they're isolating people.

Bill: What do you mean?

Ann: Well, people don't have to work together any more in a social context. They can all work on their own from home as long as they have their personal computer.

....

Clare: So how's the computer course going?

David: Well, I must say, it's probably most difficult thing I've ever done.

Clare: Really? But are you coping?

David: I think so but it's a bit of a struggle at home. I really need my own study. We're thinking of moving to a slightly biger flat. We've actually seen one possibility but it's not as near the tube our present one, and there are far few good shops nearby. It's also on the noisyest main road in the area, so we're probably not going to go for it!

2 Look at the following pairs of pictures and make as many comparisons as you can.

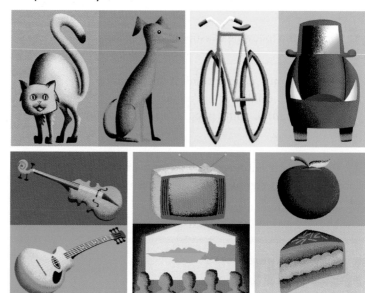

EXAMPLE: *Cats are more independent than dogs. They also need much less looking after ...*

3 Work with another student. In turn compare and contrast:

1 what you were like five years ago and now.
2 two places that you have been to on holiday.
3 your experience of learning two different subjects at school.

➤ *Exam Maximiser* **M**

Speaking: Just a minute

1 Look at these topics. Match the comments below to each topic as appropriate.

EXAMPLE: *C1*

A the use of computers for learning English
B mobile phones
C robots
D the Internet

1 It's amazing how much they can be used for. Soon they'll even be helping with major operations I hear.
2 They're very useful for people travelling alone in cars, in case they break down on the motorway.
3 It's not the same as having other people to speak to and try out new words and expressions with.
4 You almost get too much information. It's finding your way around it all which I think is the big problem.

2 Look at the topics in Exercise 1. Imagine you have to speak for one minute about each one. What would you say? Make notes.

3 Work in groups of four or five. One person in each group is the 'chair', the others are the players. Read the rules below.

Just A Minute rules

1 You must speak continuously about the subject.
2 You must not hesitate.
3 You must not deviate from the subject.
4 You must not repeat words except those of the original subject.
5 You can challenge the speaker by saying 'Hesitation', 'Repetition' or 'Deviation'.
6 The 'chair' decides whether a challenge is successful or unsuccessful. If a challenge is successful, the challenger takes over and continues to speak on the topic for however much time remains. If a challenge is unsuccessful the player continues talking on the same topic for the time remaining.
7 The winner is the player speaking after one minute.

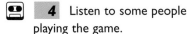 **4** Listen to some people playing the game.

5 Work in groups of four or five and play the game. Decide who is going to begin and who will be responsible for checking the time remaining.

English in Use

▶ P3, Pt6 (gapped text)

For questions **1–6** below, read the following text and then choose from the list **A–J** the best phrase to fill each of the spaces. Each correct phrase may only be used once. **Some of the suggested answers do not fit at all.** The exercise begins with an example (**0**).

ROBOTS – DREAM OR NIGHTMARE?

Members of the staff of the Franklin Institute in Philadelphia, USA were puzzled. The museum had acquired (**0**) .*J*. , but no one knew how old it was, who had made it, or exactly what it was meant to do. Once its mechanism was restored, however, the figure wrote out a short poem in French – and eerily signed it with the words, 'written by Maillardet's automaton'.

This robot, and others made by Henri Maillardet in the early 19th century, (**1**) ... designed to mimic the actions of living creatures. As long ago as the second century BC, Hero of Alexandria wrote of a theatre manned by mechanical performers, and Leonardo da Vinci is said to have built a mechanical lion to greet the King of France on his visit to Milan in 1507.

Not until the 20th century did such inventions (**2**) ... . The word first appeared in 1921, in a Czech play about rebellious humanoid machines, and is derived from the Czech word for 'forced labour'. It is mainly as helpmates, though, (**3**) ... from fiction into the real world. In particular, they are used to perform many tasks too dangerous, difficult or boring for humans.

For example, robots have explored the wreck of the Titanic, and a robot even (**4**) ... . But the main use of robots has been in industry. In Japan, which employs twice as many robots as the rest of the world put together, one company has built a factory in which robots (**5**) ... .

But the dream (or nightmare?) of the future is of robots which can build other robots – a prospect that would open up such exciting possibilities as the exploration of deep space by machines (**6**) ... .

A work nightshifts all on their own
B which could renew themselves unendingly
C has been known to make the occasional mistake
D that robots have found their way
E were by no means the first mechanical devices
F helps doctors to perform brain surgery
G may never learn to show human emotions
H come to be known as 'robots'
I has to perform a million calculations a second

J what seemed to be a mechanical doll

Exam focus

Paper 2 Writing: Part 1

About the exam: Part 1 of the Paper 2 Writing is compulsory. You will have to read about 400 words of input material i.e. text and notes. It is essential that you read all this material carefully, selecting what is significant and ignoring what is irrelevant to the task.

The task will involve writing about 250 words but this may be broken into a number of smaller parts. You may be asked to write formal letters, informal letters, reports, articles, notes or any combination of these.

Suggested procedure

1 Read the instructions very carefully and underline key words/phrases.
2 Plan your answer. Remember to organise your writing in clear and separate paragraphs.
3 Use linking words where appropriate.
4 Avoid copying long phrases from the input texts.
5 When you have written your answer, check you:
   • have written approximately the right number of words.
   • have used an appropriate style e.g. formal or informal.
   • will create the desired effect on the reader.
   • have fully answered the question.

Exam task

TASK

You are a student rep. at the college where you are studying. The director of the college has recently posted a notice outside the multi-media centre warning of its possible closure.

You subsequently organised a survey of students regarding their use of the multi-media centre. The results of the questionnaire you sent out are summarised below. You have also received a note from a friend, Pablo, who is studying at another college, about how their multi-media centre is used.

Write a letter to the director summarising the results of your survey and presenting suggestions/arguments to keep the multi-media centre. (200 words)

Also write a note to your friend Pablo to let him know what action you are taking. (50 words)

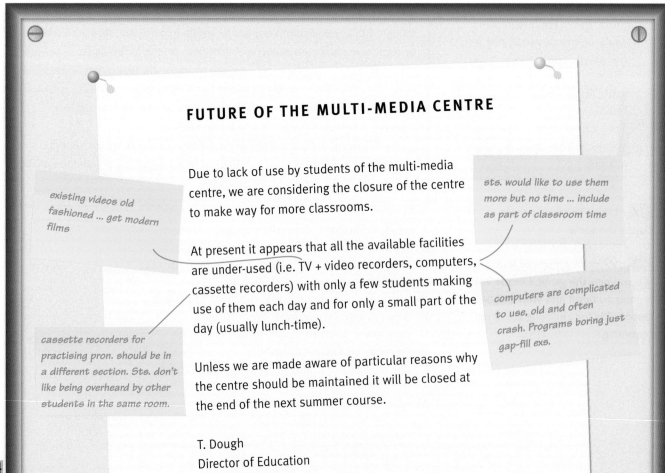

FUTURE OF THE MULTI-MEDIA CENTRE

Due to lack of use by students of the multi-media centre, we are considering the closure of the centre to make way for more classrooms.

At present it appears that all the available facilities are under-used (i.e. TV + video recorders, computers, cassette recorders) with only a few students making use of them each day and for only a small part of the day (usually lunch-time).

Unless we are made aware of particular reasons why the centre should be maintained it will be closed at the end of the next summer course.

T. Dough
Director of Education

existing videos old fashioned ... get modern films

sts. would like to use them more but no time ... include as part of classroom time

computers are complicated to use, old and often crash. Programs boring just gap-fill exs.

cassette recorders for practising pron. should be in a different section. Sts. don't like being overheard by other students in the same room.

CLARENCE SCHOOL OF LANGUAGES

Hi Brigit!

I got your note. It's good to hear that you want to do something to save your multi-media centre. Actually, it's one of the most popular things in the school here. Everyone loves it. Probably because the school makes a real effort to help people use it. Every class uses it for at least one hour a week in class time and you get shown how to use everything by the teacher. There's also a 'Student Guide To the Multi-Media Centre' which is very useful. In fact, lots of people have said that the centre is one of the main reasons why they chose to come to this particular college.

Hope that's of some use.

Let me know how it goes!

Pablo.

MULTI-MEDIA CENTRE QUESTIONNAIRE SUMMARY

Number of student responses: 40

How often do you use the multi-media centre?   80% = 0–1 hour per week

Why do you not use the centre more often?
Don't know how to operate equipment / It's not open at convenient times / Boring videos and computer programs / No one available to help or to ask questions

If the centre was improved would you want to keep it? If so, why?
75% = Yes
Students can practise the things they find difficult / They can work at own speed / They can practise pronunciation on the cassette recorders / Lots of students like working with computers

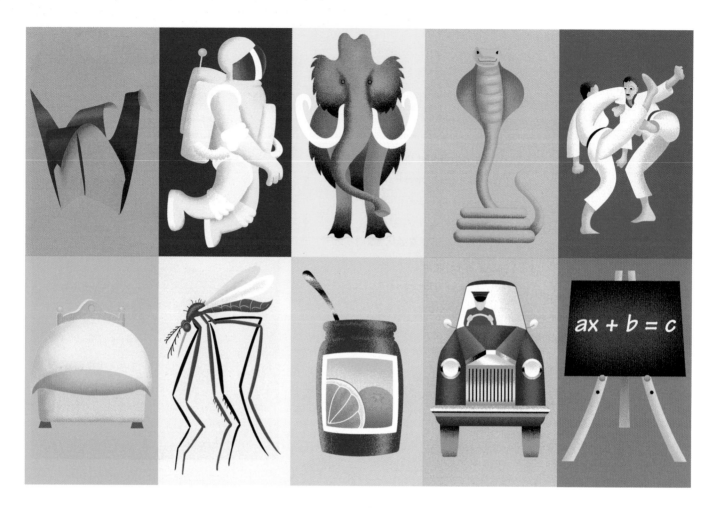

Vocabulary: words from other languages

1 The word *multi* as in *multi-media* comes from the Latin word *multus* meaning much or many. Below are some words that English has borrowed from different languages.

1 Look at the words in the box and the table below. Match the words to the illustrations. Eight of the words do not have illustrations. Which words are they?
2 Try and guess which language each word in the box comes from and put it in one of the language columns below.
3 Now use a dictionary to check the origin and meaning of any words you were not sure of.

 4 Say how you think the words are pronounced in English. Then listen to the recording to check your answers.
5 Work with another student. Check they know and can pronounce the words below like this:

EXAMPLE: A *You throw this at weddings.*
          B *Confetti.*

2 Discuss with other students.

1 Do you know any words in your language that English has 'borrowed'?
2 Are there any English words or versions of English words which have now become 'part' of your language? How do you feel about this? Is it a problem?

| cosmonaut | marmalade | chauffeur | psychology | origami | algebra | kindergarten | piano | siesta |

Greek	Spanish	Japanese	Italian	French	German	Portuguese	Arabic	Russian
drama	mosquito	karate	confetti	duvet	hamburger	cobra	mattress	mammoth
.....	.....	.....	.....	.....	.....	.....	.....	.....

Paper 3 English in Use: Part 1 (multiple-choice cloze)

1 For questions **1–15** read the text below and then decide which word (**A**, **B**, **C** or **D**) best fits each space. The exercise begins with an example (**0**).

HELP ALWAYS AT HAND:
A MOBILE IS A GIRL'S BEST FRIEND

If it fits inside a pocket, keeps you (**0**) _A_ as well as in touch with your office, your mother and your children, it is (**1**) ... worth having. This is the (**2**) ... of the (**3**) ... ranks of female mobile-phone users who are beginning to (**4**) ... the consumer market.

Although Britain has been (**5**) ... to be one of the most expensive places in the world to (**6**) ... a mobile phone, both professional women and (**7**) ... mothers are undeterred. At first, the mobile phone was a rich man's plaything, or a businessman's (**8**) ... symbol. Now women own almost as many telephones as men do – but for very different reasons.

The main (**9**) ... for most women customers is that it (**10**) ... a form of communications back-up, wherever they are, in case of (**11**) ... . James Tanner of Tancroft Communications says: 'The (**12**) ... of people buying phones from us this year were women – often young women – or men who were buying for their mothers, wives and girlfriends. And it always seems to be a question of (**13**) ... of mind.

'Size is also (**14**) ... for women. They want something that will fit in a handbag,' said Mr Tanner. 'The tiny phones coming in are having a very big (**15**) ... . This year's models are only half the size of your hand.'

0	**A** safe	**B** secure	**C** guarded	**D** protected
1	**A** totally	**B** certainly	**C** absolutely	**D** completely
2	**A** vision	**B** vista	**C** view	**D** panorama
3	**A** swelling	**B** increasing	**C** boosting	**D** maximising
4	**A** master	**B** dominate	**C** overbear	**D** command
5	**A** demonstrated	**B** shown	**C** established	**D** seen
6	**A** function	**B** drive	**C** work	**D** run
7	**A** complete	**B** total	**C** full-time	**D** absolute
8	**A** prestige	**B** fame	**C** power	**D** status
9	**A** attraction	**B** enticement	**C** charm	**D** lure
10	**A** supplies	**B** furnishes	**C** provides	**D** gives
11	**A** urgency	**B** emergency	**C** predicament	**D** contingency
12	**A** most	**B** preponderance	**C** majority	**D** bulk
13	**A** tranquillity	**B** calmness	**C** serenity	**D** peace
14	**A** crucial	**B** necessary	**C** urgent	**D** essential
15	**A** impact	**B** impression	**C** perception	**D** image

2 Use two words to complete each of the advanced future verb forms in these sentences.

EXAMPLE: _We'd better hurry. The film **is due** to start in five minutes._

1 I'm on the .... ringing the police about all the noise those people are making.

2 All those taking part in the parade .... meet outside the main building at four o'clock.

3 You've been away so you won't .... about what happened in the meeting.

4 By the end of the year the number of people using mobile phones will .... by 2%.

5 It won't be long before we'll all .... the Internet to buy our groceries instead of going to the supermarket.

6 Will you .... immediately after the conference or could you spare a few minutes to talk to reporters?

7 They .... about .... launch their new software package and everyone is very excited.

3 Choose between the alternatives to complete these sentences.

1 He's in his early fifties but he still takes a _childlike/childish_ delight in many aspects of life.

2 She very seldom _loses/looses_ her temper.

3 The actress Greta Garbo was always saying that she wanted to be _alone/lonely_.

4 She had been working really _hard/hardly_ and needed a holiday.

5 Would you mind if I changed the _canal/channel_?

6 The painting in the Louvre may be a _priceless/worthless_ fake.

7 It's important to get there early _especially/specially_ if you want a good view of the parade.

Paper 3 English in Use: Part 4 (word formation)

4 For questions **1–15** read the two texts. Use the words in the boxes to the right of the texts to form **one** word that fits in the same numbered space in the text. Write the word in the space. The exercise begins with an example (**0**).

TRAINING FOR A MARATHON		
A (**0**) _successful_ marathon training programme starts slowly, (**1**) ... gradually and then tapers off before the big race to (**2**) ... maximum energy. A typical schedule for a beginner lasts six weeks, which is enough time to build up the endurance and (**3**) ... needed to run twenty-six miles while avoiding (**4**) ... . Before you begin training you should be capable of (**5**) ... running for 45 minutes. The most important element in the programme is long runs, as these allow you to develop the physical and mental (**6**) ... that will enable you to run for several hours without (**7**) ... . To be fresh for the race, make your final run two or three weeks before the marathon.	0	SUCCESS
	1	INTENSE
	2	SURE
	3	STRONG
	4	INJURE
	5	COMFORT
	6	TOUGH
	7	INTERRUPT

BORN TO BICKER		
It seems so petty and (**8**) ... ! While we expect sibling (**9**) ... among our children we're often embarrassed to find similar emotions ourselves. Yet we do sometimes have (**10**) ... animosities that can cause some of the most (**11**) ... problems of adult life. (**12**) ... is inherent in all aspects of life. If nations compete, it shouldn't be surprising that siblings do too – for their parents' affection and then for the (**13**) ... of bosses, peers and friends. As we grow older we usually find that there is enough love and (**14**) ... to go round. Some siblings may be more (**15**) ... while others have more urgent needs for love and attention and this can produce conflict.	8	CHILD
	9	RIVAL
	10	PAIN
	11	RESOLVE
	12	COMPETE
	13	ADMIRE
	14	RECOGNISE
	15	ASSERT

5 Use the prompts to write sentences with preparatory *it*.

EXAMPLE: *Mary/study/aeronautical engineering/university*
It was aeronautical engineering that Mary was studying at university.

1 difficult/know/what/do
2 essential/I/get in touch/David
3 Jane/lent/me/mobile phone
4 Tuesday/Bill/leave/Australia
5 terrible/few people/use public transport
6 seem/she/not know/meeting/cancelled
7 his parents/make/clear/they/ not like/new girlfriend
8 important/obtain/student visa
9 I/find/hard/understand/why/I/ not get job

6 Match the prefixes to the words or stems.

a) auto-		1	intellectuals
b) im-		2	come
c) ir-		3	conception
d) over-		4	biography
e) mono-		5	logical
f) un-		6	mature
g) il-		7	logue
h) mis-		8	loyal
i) psuedo-		9	believable
j) dis-		10	relevant

7 Form sentences by changing the order of these words.

EXAMPLE: *people who ignore pedestrian crossings annoys me most is what*
What annoys me most is people who ignore pedestrian crossings.

1 left his passport at home happened he what was
2 what stay at home is like to do and watch a video I'd
3 is her sense of humour what most about Clara I like
4 to the airport was to hitchhike what she did
5 the way he's always gossiping is what on my nerves really gets
6 what to find out about using my mobile phone outside Spain need to do I is

Paper 3 English in Use: Part 5 (register transfer)

8 For questions 1–13, read the following e-mail message. Use the information in it to complete the numbered gaps in the notice. **Use no more than two words for each gap.**

E-MAIL MESSAGE

To: Irene Harman: Director of Studies

From: Tina McMahon: Computing Services

Subject: Computer Centre

Hi Irene,

Can you include the following in the notice to teachers? There's an official opening next Monday. From Tuesday someone from computing services will be there every day and we'll be offering introductory courses on word processing, e-mail and the Internet. I hope you'll get your students to come along. Teachers are most welcome too. In fact, we're not going to let people use the equipment until they've shown us they know how or have taken one of the courses. There are a few more rules we've had to make. Can you emphasise that these are to stop people wrecking the machines?

Here goes:

(1) No eating, drinking or smoking while using the equipment.
(2) No using the internet while others are waiting to use word processing software.

If they break these rules more than once I'm afraid we'll have to stop them coming into the centre.

Tina

NOTICE

Computer Centre

The Centre opening will (**0**) *be held* on Monday 9th March. From Tuesday 10th March the Centre will (**1**) ... by members of the Computing Services Department. Teachers are asked (**2**) ... students to attend the courses on word-processing, e-mail and the internet and are urged (**3**) ... so themselves. No one will be (**4**) ... use the equipment unless they (**5**) ... their competence to staff or (**6**) ... a course. In order to (**7**) ... to the equipment two (**8**) ... rules have (**9**) ... by centre staff. They are (**10**) ... :

(1) Eating, drinking and smoking while using the equipment (**11**) ... .
(2) Word processing users are (**12**) ... priority over Internet users.

Please note: repeated breach of these rules will (**13**) ... denial of the right to use the centre.

9 Complete these sentences using one or two words in each gap.

1 He .... a very positive impression on the interview panel.
2 No one has been able to resolve the .... of what to do with nuclear waste.
3 He made me .... so stupid when he showed them all the old photographs.
4 By the fourth lap Criville had already .... a considerable advantage over the other riders.
5 After her marriage broke up she couldn't .... her doubts about her ability to sustain a relationship.
6 Having a decent breakfast really .... a difference to the way I feel half way through the morning.
7 You can trust John. He always .... his word.
8 He .... the promotion he'd been wanting for years.
9 After two months of not allowing herself to so much as smile she finally .... some control over the class.
10 He got into some sort of .... with the authorities and they refused to renew his residence permit.
11 She gained invaluable .... working with her father in the summer holidays.
12 We resolved .... on better together.

Getting away from it all

Speaking: agreeing to disagree

1 The British Tourist Authority wants to produce its own set of postcards to promote tourism in Britain. Look at the different possibilities. Say what you like and don't like about each one and decide which three you think would be most popular with tourists and why.

2 Listen to other people attempting the above task. Which three did they choose in the end? What were the main reasons for their choices?

3 Listen again and make a note of three phrases you hear used to disagree very politely.

4 Discuss the following questions and practise the phrases you noted above where appropriate.

1 What kinds of reactions do people have to tourists in your country? Why is this?
2 What should tourists try and do to reduce the possibilities of having a negative effect on the places they visit?
3 How do you think living and working in another country might be different from just going on holiday there?
4 Do you think the amount and types of holidays that people are taking these days are changing? If so, why?
5 If you could go anywhere in the world for a two-week holiday, where would you go and why?

5 Work in groups of four or five. You are going to roleplay a meeting of members of the local tourist board. You have been asked to come up with three or four practical ideas to help significantly increase levels of tourism in your area.

Student A refer to p.217
Student B refer to p.216
Student C refer to p.219
Student D refer to p.220
(optional Student E refer to p.221)

Changing of the Guards at Buckingham Palace

Scenes from around Britain

Playing the Bagpipes

S C O T L A N D

Wales

Nottinghill Carnival

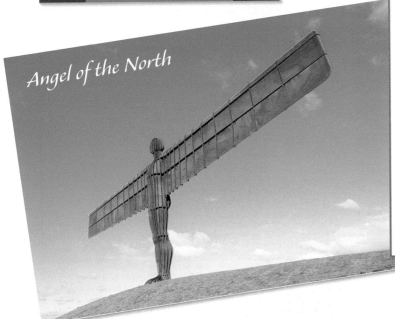

Angel of the North

Listening

▶ P4, Pt2 (sentence completion)

1 In Part 2 of Paper 4 you will hear a monologue of approximately two minutes, which you will hear only once. You will have to complete either sentences or notes with missing information (a maximum of three words).

2 Discuss with other students.

1 Do you enjoy travelling by plane? Why/why not?
2 Are there any places in the plane that you prefer to sit or not sit?
3 Have you had any bad experiences when travelling by plane?

3 You are going to listen to someone's views about the best places to sit on a Boeing 747. Complete the sentences in the box following this procedure.

Suggested procedure

1 You will have 30–45 seconds to look at the questions before the monologue begins. Read all the sentences and try and predict what the missing words might be.
2 Listen and make a note of the missing words. You will hear the words you need in the text but you may have to make changes to the words you hear in the text so that they fit grammatically with the rest of the sentence.

WHERE TO SIT ON A BOEING 747

Seat 30C is good if you're feeling ill as it's near to the (1)..................................... . (British Airways flights receive support in (2)..................................... from MedAir.) Sit in seats 30 AB and C or 31HJ and K if you need to disembark from the plane (3)..................................... . (Alternatively try and sit (4)..................................... of the plane in case you are allowed to use both exits.) If you sit in seats 46-52DEFG, you'll have to wait until last to get your (5)..................................... . And if you want to enjoy the (6)..................................... make sure you sit in seats 55ABCHJK or 45ABCHJK. For those travellers who want some (7)..................................... , make sure you avoid seats 30C, 31C & H, 32C & H. Everyone wants to sit in seats 54ABC and HJK as these have more (8)..................................... than other seats.

Exam focus

Paper 1 Reading: Part 4 (multiple matching)

About the exam: Part 4 of Paper 1 Reading is a multiple-matching task. You are usually required to read a text of 700–1,200 words. This is often made up of a group of short texts or sections of text.

You will be required to match the questions with the relevant information from the text. There may be more than one correct answer for some questions.

You should spend no more than 18 minutes on this task.

Suggested procedure

1. Read the instructions carefully.
2. Read all of the prompts, highlighting key words/phrases.
3. Read the whole text to get an idea of the content of each section.
4. Make a note of any answers you are confident about.
5. Go back to the prompts you are not sure about. Take each one in turn. Decide which sections they might refer to. Scan those sections carefully for 'parallel expressions'.
6. Check you have answered all the questions.

Exam task

Answer these questions by referring to the article on p.133 about different railway journeys you can take in different parts of the world. Choose your answers from the list of train journeys. (When more than one answer is required, these may be given in any order. Some choices may be required more than once.)

On which train journey(s)		
should you admire the actual construction of the railway?	**1** ... **2** ...	
can you be treated like royalty?	**3** ...	**A** The Bullet Train
is speed a characteristic?	**4** ...	**B** The Trans-Siberian Express
can you see very old historical sites?	**5** ... **6** ...	**C** Venice Simplon–Orient–Express
does it pay to be a foreigner?	**7** ...	**D** Across the roof of Norway
is there a literary connection?	**8** ...	
might you glimpse a rarely seen animal?	**9** ...	**E** Rocky Mountain Divide
can you tour round a whole country?	**10** ... **11** ...	**F** Crossing Canada
will you get very good value for money?	**12** ...	**G** Peruvian Andes
do you not have to choose which way to face?	**13** ...	**H** The whole of India
do you go through large areas where there used to be wildlife?	**14** ...	
can you pass through three or more countries?	**15** ... **16** ...	

The best
RAILWAY JOURNEYS
in the world

A *The Bullet Train*

You can whiz past the snow-capped Mount Fuji, travelling from Tokyo to Osaka on one of the fastest trains in the world. The Shinkanses bullet train is covered by the Japan Rail Pass, which is only available to foreign visitors – you must buy it before you go. The state-of-the-art railways and stations are extraordinary and an experience in themselves and the network is fast and efficient, making it much the best way to travel around the country.

Many companies offering tours in Japan use the bullet trains in their itineraries. Explore Worldwide (01252 344161) follows the ancient Nakasendo Highway through the mountainous centre of Japan. But after trekking and staying in traditional inns, you are transported into the modern world by bullet train back to Osaka.

B *The Trans-Siberian Express*

Covering about 11,000 kilometres in seven days, if you go for the non-stop option, the Trans-Siberian Express has to be the classic epic rail journey. It leaves from Moscow and crosses Siberia to either Beijing via Mongolia or Manchuria or the port of Vladivostok – quite literally the end of the road. It is still cheaper than flying and surprisingly comfortable. Even better is to take advantage of stopovers and see Baikal, the deepest lake in the world, or the remote town of Novosibirsk.

The Imaginative Traveller (0181 742 8612) advertises its Trans-Siberian train trips as costing 'from less than 4p per kilometre'. The company also offers extensions to Hong Kong, travelling south from Beijing through China and a 'silk route' journey by rail, taking in the ancient cities of Tashkent and Bukhara in Uzbekistan.

C *Venice Simplon–Orient-Express*

Travel in style, as in the famous Agatha Christie novel *Murder on the Orient Express*. The service has figured in people's imagination since 1883, when prominent people like princes, spies and film stars started travelling in this sumptuous train across Europe. As well as the classic London–Paris–Venice journey you can also travel to Florence, Rome, Prague. New destinations for 1998 are Monte Carlo and, en route to Istanbul, you can now stop at the central European capitals Budapest and Bucharest.

You can also travel in Southeast Asia from Singapore to Bangkok, in an Orient Express railway carriage with an eastern feel. From December, Australia will also have its own Orient Express, the Great South Pacific Express from Brisbane to Cairns and Sydney.

D *Across the roof of Norway*

Spacious trains and seats that revolve to face the direction of travel are a few of the features of the Bergen line, a service which operates in Norway. It travels into the Hardangervidda plateau, a remote mountainous region of glaciers, peaks and wild moorland, before reaching the fjords that make Norway's coastline uniquely spectacular. It's not only the landscape that will impress you; the engineering of the railways is also amazing.

Inntravel (01653 628811) runs seven-day journeys in both summer and winter, travelling from Oslo to Bergen with a three-night midway break in Geilo, a picturesque mountain village.

E *Rocky Mountain Divide*

When people think about travelling in the US, they usually think of the classic road trip – cruising along Route 66. But the best views and most comfortable ride across the Rockies is by train. Travel from one great city to another across the Rockies and the vast, empty Great Plains where buffalo once roamed. The journey from Seattle to Chicago brings home the sheer scale of the Midwest. Amtrak's service is skeletal but scenic and you can make reservations through agents in the UK. There are also several 'historic railroads', such as the Durango & Silverton Narrow Gauge Railroad in Colorado, which takes passengers across parts of the Rockies and the western US. LeisureRail (01733 335599) offer AmTrak services across the US, and also represents Rocky Mountaineer Railtours, which cross the Canadian Rockies.

F *Crossing Canada*

Canada is vast, so it could be a daunting experience to cross the country by rail. But the Via Rail network provides efficient and comfortable travel through some of the most beautiful and remote parts of Canada. Cross from Halifax, Nova Scotia through Quebec and the capital Ottawa and north of the Great Lakes before heading on to the Rockies and Vancouver on the Pacific coast. Other, smaller networks, such as the E&N Railiner on Vancouver Island and the Rocky Mountaineer, serve specific regions, so it is feasible to travel around Canada entirely by rail. The Rocky Mountaineer is a two-day 965-kilometre journey running during the summer between Calgary, Banff or Jasper to Vancouver.

North American Highways (01902 851138) offer a wide range of tours, tailor-made itineraries and help with independent travel. Leisure Rail (01733 335599) also handles VIA Rail bookings and offers special packages on several of the Rocky Mountain routes. The company will also put together a tailor-made itinerary for all those wanting to cross Canada by train.

G *Peruvian Andes*

This is one of the world's highest railways and links the amazing sights of the ruins of Machu Picchu with Lake Titicaca, the birthplace of the Incas and the bustling mountain town of Cuzco. The massive stoneworks and idols of the Incas are made relatively accessible by this rail route along the Peruvian Central Valley alongside hand-tilled fields. Between Puno on the shores of Lake Titicaca and Cuzco, the train passes the source of the Amazon.

Journey Latin America (020 8747 8315) the leading UK specialist in South and Central America, has seven trips available that include the rail journey. One involves spending the night at the Inca ruins of Machu Picchu.

H *The whole of India*

India's rail network is the second largest in the world, carrying 14 million people every day. It is still the best and cheapest way to see the country – but it doesn't have to be cheap and crowded. A growing number of specialist companies are hosting luxurious private tours, particularly in the palace province of Rajasthan, where you can travel in the sumptuous style of an Indian prince. Take in sights such as the Taj Mahal at Agra, the 'pink city' of Jaipur and ancient Jodhpur. Abercrombie and Kent's (020 7730 9600) acclaimed Journeys of Discovery include an escorted Highlights of India using road, rail and air. The company also offers other Indian tours by train and private car. Cox and Kings (020 7873 5025) offers a Palace on Wheels package, which it claims is India's most luxurious train, fitted out in classic Rajput style. The week-long journey also includes a visit to the impressive Ranthambore National Park, rated as one of the places you have most chance of seeing the elusive and endangered tiger.

Grammar plus: relative clauses (advanced features)

1 Look at the two examples of relative clauses below. Why is a) known as a 'defining' relative clause and b) as a 'non-defining' relative clause? What is the difference in meaning between them?

a) The tour which lasted 21 days went to all the places I wanted to visit.
b) The tour, which lasted 21 days, went to all the places I wanted to visit.

2 Here is one example of a relative clause from the text on p.133. How many others can you find? (Look in paragraphs C, D, E and H.) Are they defining or non-defining relative clauses?

EXAMPLE: *The Shinkanses bullet train is covered by the Japan Rail Pass, which is only available to foreign visitors.*

3 Decide if the statements on the left below are true of defining or non-defining relative clauses.

	defining relative clause	non-defining relative clause
that can be used in place of *who* or *which*		
the relative pronoun can be left out		
commas are generally used before (and after) the relative clause		

4 Correct the mistakes in each of these sentences.

1 It's the kind of scenery, that you only see once in a lifetime.
2 The cost of the trip was much lower than we had imagined, what came as a very pleasant surprise.
3 We met a young man, who was terribly helpful, when we got lost.
4 The company which train this is don't seem to want to spend money on improving the state of the interior.
5 The guy led the tour was very experienced and very helpful.
6 This is the hotel which we used to stay.
7 We were unable to discover who the documents had been sent.
8 I took some great photos which everybody wanted copies of them when we got back.

5 Join each of these pairs of sentences to make one sentence, using a relative clause.

1 The train was at least 35 minutes late. It came to a halt again.
2 They didn't understand why he was so angry. It was very upsetting.
3 She was a teacher in my school. We all had immense respect for her.
4 By Friday we had seen an amazing variety of wildlife. Friday was the last day of the tour.
5 This is the gentleman. I was telling you about his son.
6 A young woman gave me this packet. She asked me to hand it in to the police.
7 Stephanie asked me if I was resigning. I only had one thing to say.
8 That's the restaurant! Jim finally proposed to me there!

> ## Watch Out!   *what*
>
> *What* can act as a noun + relative pronoun together and means 'the thing(s) which'. Which of these sentences is possible?
>
> 1 We listened carefully to what the travel agent was saying.
> 2 We listened carefully to everything what the travel agent was saying.

► Grammar reference pp.195–196

Listening: on the slow train

1 Discuss with other students.

1 What are the pros and cons of travelling by train?
2 If you could go on any train, through any part of the world, where would you go and why?

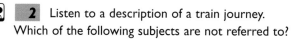 **2** Listen to a description of a train journey. Which of the following subjects are not referred to?

- an important local official
- different types of accommodation on the train
- the general state of the train
- the refreshments available on the train
- the surrounding scenery
- the cost of the travel
- unplanned stoppages

3 Listen again and make a note of the significance of the following:

EXAMPLE: 1 *4p.m. >* **the time they go to the station**

1 4p.m.
2 29
3 a box of dates
4 5p.m.
5 4,000
6 899
7 wooden struts
8 a personal stereo
9 a vacuum pipe

4 Discuss with other students.

How would you feel about going on a journey like this?

Vocabulary: expressive description

1 Here are some phrases which are expressed slightly differently in the extract you listened to in Listening Exercise 2. Listen again and replace the underlined parts with the actual expressions the speaker uses.

EXAMPLE: 1 *crowds are already milling around*

1 ... groups of people are already walking around
2 ... shakes hands with us all in a friendly way
3 ... the whistle makes a loud noise
4 ... the large, heavy train begins to move
5 ... a large number of people running towards the train
6 ... a pale half moon lights up a landscape of silver sand
7 ... finished cigarettes being thrown out of the windows

2 Discuss with other students the difference between the expressions above and the expressions in the extract. What impact do the ones in the extract have on the listener?

3 Imagine that you have been asked to write an article for a travel magazine about a memorable travel experience that you have had.

1 Describe the experience to another student.
2 Now write a brief description of one part of it in no more than 100 words. Be prepared to read your description to other students. Try to make the description as vivid as possible to keep your readers interested.
3 Listen to other students' descriptions. Make a note of any particularly expressive words/phrases they use.

Writing: brochure

1 Look at these extracts from different kinds of brochures. Brochures generally aim to a) inform b) attract their readers. How do the examples try and achieve their purpose? Identify any particular words or phrases which you think are effective.

2 Work with one or two other students and plan your answer to the task below.

TASK

You have been asked to prepare part of a brochure for your local tourist authority. Your section should inform visitors about all that the local area has to offer. In particular, make reference to special features of the area, the alternative types of accommodation available and the variety of activities that can be enjoyed.

Write the text for your part of the brochure in 250 words.

1 Discuss the typical kinds of people who will read this kind of brochure.
2 Decide how many paragraphs you will have, the subject of each paragraph and any ideas as to the possible content of each paragraph.
3 Decide on possible headings for your paragraphs.

3 Write a rough draft of your text. Keep in mind the typical people who will read it. Show it to other students. Can they suggest any improvements?

4 Now write a final version of your text. Check for mistakes and include any new vocabulary/expressions that you have found.

5 Finally, with other students, discuss what pictures or illustrations you might use to make the design of your brochure as attractive as possible to potential visitors.

DURHAM UNIVERSITY

'I got off at Durham ... and fell in love with it instantly in a serious way. Why, it's wonderful – a perfect little city ... If you have never been to Durham, go there at once. Take my car. It's wonderful.'

BILL BRYSON *Notes from a Small Island*, 1995

High fliers
96% of our students gain their degrees.
This is 7% above the national average. 93% of our students gain first or second class degrees.

The College system
We are a Collegiate University. Our Colleges are unique.

We're accommodating
Two thirds of our undergraduates are in University accommodation.

Bright future
Durham graduates have an excellent employment record. Recent surveys show us doing consistently well in employment league tables.

From IT to Italy
Our flexible degree structure offers you a wide range of degree options. You also have the opportunity to develop your Information Technology, foreign language and numerical skills, and in many subjects the chance to spend a year abroad.

Extra curricular
At Durham we promote a broad view of education. You will have the opportunity to join over 50 University sports clubs and over 100 University societies, as well as countless College-based groups.

Take care
Departmental staff, College tutors, our health, careers and welfare services, our Students' Union and chaplaincy support networks are there to ensure you can make the most of your University experience.

Easy reach
You will be in easy reach of most UK and European centres. Durham is just 264 miles from London (less than 3 hours by train), 125 miles from Edinburgh (less than 2 hours by train) and 187 miles from Birmingham (just 3 hours by train). We are on the main North-South rail network, two miles from the A1(M) and 30 minutes drive from Newcastle International Airport. Find out more ...

Disneyland
Paris

This year make your dream come true at Disneyland, Paris.

ONCE UPON A TIME is now! A year inspired by the most magical dream of all: yours. Be prepared for spectacular Disney parades, shows, events, entertainment and good old-fashioned fun all year round. It's going to be a marvel-a-minute around every corner. Big or small, you'll thrill, amaze and smile your way into a whirlwind of impressions. So come dream with your eyes wide open. It's Disney magic!

Discover the wonderful world of Disney festivities that Disneyland Paris has in store especially for you. Start with a magical tour, visiting the continents of the world in the giant, new **Disney's ImagiNations Parade.** Then, in Adventureland, zoom and whoosh your way on a new adventure: **Indiana Jones and the Temple of Peril: Backwards**! Here you'll discover the hero inside on a high-speed chase up, over and under the ruins of an ancient temple before thrilling your way into a spiralling 360-degree loop. All this and more ... **100% backwards!**

Next stop: Deep in the heart of the jungle, you are in the middle of a legendary tale: **The Tarzan Encounter**, a spectacular new show at the Chaparral Theater in Frontierland. After this you will be thrilled by **The Main Street Electrical Parade**, a magical symphony of colours and lights. And after the Parade glows by, you'll see stars in your eyes with the shimmering, glimmering **Tinker Bell's Fantasy in the Sky Fireworks Show.**

Disneyland Paris, it's a year inspired by the most magical of dreams: Yours.

Take advantage of our very attractive special offers:

 'Four nights for the price of three' and

'Three nights for the price of two' on certain dates in April, May and September.

Grammar check: linking words

1   Read the following letter to a newspaper. Which of the following linking words/expressions could go in each gap?

> however   because   although   therefore
> on the one hand   firstly   in spite of   to begin with
> in the first place   secondly   despite   because of
> finally   on the other hand   as a result   so

Dear Sir/Madam,

There has been much debate recently concerning the issue of tourism in our town. **(1)** .... , I would like to say that, in my opinion, there is an immediate need for a tourist information office where tourists can go to find out about accommodation, places to visit etc. It has been said that this would be expensive and not worth the cost. **(2)** .... , at present, many tourists are unaware of the range of accommodation available and the variety of places of interest and facilities on offer and, **(3)** .... this, they are leaving with a correspondingly low opinion of the town.

Some have argued that we shouldn't be encouraging tourists to come at all. Whilst **(4)** .... , I can understand the fear that we will lose some of the traditional character of the town, **(5)** .... , given the current high level of unemployment I think it is clear that the local economy needs some kind of boost.

(6) .... the various points that have been made about keeping the numbers of tourists low, I still believe that tourism needs to play a key role in our economy in the years to come. If we ignore this fact, we run the risk of suffering from a slow but inevitable decline, something which I am sure that none of us would want.

Yours,

2   Put the different linking words/expressions from the box in Exercise 1 in the appropriate columns below. (Which of the linking words/expressions don't fit in any column?)

listing ideas	showing consequence	making contrasts
firstly	*therefore*	*however*

3   Add one more linking word/expression to each column.

4   Note down any of the linking words that were new to you and write an example sentence for each of these in your vocabulary notebook.

Reading

1 What different reasons might someone have for deciding to walk across an entire continent? What kind of person do you imagine they might be?

2 Divide into two groups. Group A will read the following article. Group B will read the article on p.221. Read your article and make notes of the answers to the following questions.

1 Which of the following adjectives do you feel describe Ffyona based on what you have read in your article. What evidence is there to support this?

> thoughtful awkward determined mean sincere self-centred conventional self-righteous

2 Summarise what you learn about Ffyona's upbringing and her relationship with her parents.
3 What reasons does she give for wanting to walk?
4 What is Ffyona's attitude to her sponsors?
5 What did Ffyona confess recently?
6 What are her plans for the future?

3 Work with a student who read a different article. Compare your answers to the different questions in Exercise 2. From hearing the answers of your partner, has your impression of Ffyona Campbell changed at all?

SUPERWOMAN

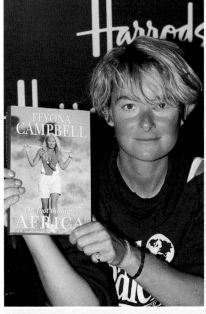

WHAT would make a young woman, not yet out of her teens, begin walking, and walking, and walking, and walking until she had become the first woman to walk around the world? 'Frankly° I just thought,' Ffyona Campbell says, 'that I'd go for a long walk
5 and figure out what I was going to do with my life.'

And so she did. She set out on her trek of self-discovery in John O'Groats at the northern tip of Scotland in 1983, when she was just 16. Over the next 11 years she walked across North America, Australia, Africa and Europe.
10 Along the way, she went through 100 pairs of running shoes, in part because she walks so fast – five miles an hour (most people walk three). She also nearly wore herself to a frazzle as well. In Australia, for example, she doubled her normal walk load to an average of 50 miles a day. 'My feet were covered in blisters,' she says. 'I was pulling
15 a litre of pus out a week.'

In Africa she suffered near-constant diarrhoea and bouts of malaria and typhoid. In Zambia, where an irate villager held a knife to her throat, she was mistaken for a spy. In Morocco she had to be guided through a minefield.
20 One of the most formidable obstacles Campbell had to cope with was her own thorny personality. She made an impressive list of enemies – from corporate sponsors to the drivers who carried her food and supplies. In the United States she angered the Campbell Soup Company, which felt she wasn't doing enough to raise money
25 for charity. She even ran afoul of journalists who went along from time to time. As one commented: 'Actually[1], it's true she's horrible. Unless you're talking about her, she goes into a shell.'

138

MELLOWS OUT

Her father, Colin, was a Royal Marine captain whose changing assignments took the family through two dozen homes and fifteen
30 schools by the time Ffyona was 16. They moved so often that Campbell described the occupation of their mother, Angela, as 'she moves house <u>basically</u>'.[2]

Campbell says she got her blind determination from her father, who <u>obviously</u>[3] had a penchant for driving Ffyona and her sister
35 Shuna, now 29, to the limits of their endurance. 'The motto in our family was, "One last-ditch effort",' she says. 'When you'd been on a particularly nasty camping trip, in muddy fields and with ice in the tent, and you hadn't complained, you earned your green beret.'

The walk was <u>apparently</u>[4] the only way she felt she could make
40 good the gaps in her upbringing. 'I had to do something to test myself. I had to be in an extreme situation to find out who I was and who I wanted to be.' But now the trek is at an end she feels 'comfortable with who I am' and is not planning any new physical challenges.

45 After a holiday in Greece with her 29-year-old sister Shuna and trips to Europe and South Africa to promote her book, *On Foot Through Africa*, she wants to build on the camaradarie that she has enjoyed on the British stage of her journey after years of travelling alone. And, unashamedly, she says she finally wants to get married
50 and settle down. 'I know I am a long way off that point. But <u>personally</u>[5] I feel that motherhood is the most important thing that anyone can do. A family may be some way away but, and you will have heard me say this before, I am determined to do it.'

Vocabulary: adverbials expressing attitude

1 Look at the numbered and underlined adverbials in the text 'Superwoman mellows out'. Discuss with another student the meaning of each one and how they are used to convey the attitude of the speaker or writer.

EXAMPLE: *'Frankly, I just thought,' she says, 'that I'd go for a long walk and figure out what I was going to do with my life.'*
> used to show you are speaking directly and honestly.

D **2** Check your ideas in a dictionary.

3 Decide which of the alternatives in each case below is the most likely.

1   The young man was breathing heavily and was *actually/personally/obviously* unwell.
2   Well, *basically/apparently/personally* the teacher told me I had to work every day of my holiday.
3   I've known Beatriz for years. *Actually/Basically/Personally* she's my closest friend.
4   *Frankly/Personally/Apparently* we had hoped that you would have stayed with the firm to the end of the financial year.
5   I couldn't go unfortunately but *actually/apparently/frankly*, by all accounts, Jo's party went really well.
6   *Obviously/Apparently/Personally*, I think it was a mistake to take on another secretary.
7   *Obviously/Frankly/Basically* no one is suggesting for a minute that you had anything to do with the disappearance of Mr. Penfold's wallet.
8   It's easy to claim the insurance. You just *basically/frankly/obviously* have to fill in a short form.

Exam focus

Paper 3 English in Use: Part 5 (register transfer)

About the exam: In Paper 3 English in Use, Part 5 you are required to read two texts and transfer information from one to the other. The second text will have gaps in and be written in a different register from the first e.g. more formal/informal. You must complete the gaps with no more than two words and NOT use words from the first text. You must also ensure that your answers are grammatically accurate as well as the appropriate register.

Suggested procedure

1 Read both texts to get the general idea of what they are about.
2 Read the second text again, sentence by sentence, and make sure you understand the meaning of each sentence which includes a gap.
3 Refer to the equivalent part of the first text to check the exact meaning of the missing part.
4 Underline or highlight the relevant words/phrase in the first text, if necessary.
5 Decide on the part of speech of the missing word(s).
6 Complete the gap, paying careful attention to the form and spelling of the words you insert.
7 Do not use words which appear in the first text.

Exam task

For questions **1–13**, read the following statement of objectives by a modern holiday company. Use the information to complete the numbered gaps in the informal letter to a friend below. **Use no more than two words for each gap.** The words you need do not occur in the statement of objectives.

STATEMENT OF OBJECTIVES

Tourism is the world's fastest growing industry and brings many benefits to the host country and to you, the traveller. However, we realise that not all the effects of travel are positive. In an effort to encourage sustainable tourism with manageable growth and minimal environmental impact, we have various aims with regards to the environment which include

▶ promoting understanding and respect for all local cultures, environmental issues and wildlife by providing our clients with background information and Responsible Travellers' Guidelines to help ensure minimal impact on the area visited.

▶ ensuring our tour leaders promote and involve our clients in environmentally responsible practices in all respects, particularly regarding waste disposal on treks and safaris.

▶ using locally owned hotels and various local modes of transport where practical and encouraging clients to utilise local products and facilities so that the local economy is stimulated at source.

▶ involving clients in the assessment of our environmental performance, encouraging their suggestions and undertaking to react positively to any environmental criticism.

LETTER TO A FRIEND

Dear Jenny

Sorry I haven't written for ages but I'm only just back from my summer holidays when I went on one of those small group adventure tours. Well, actually it was absolutely fantastic! One great thing about it was their whole (0) ...attitude... to the environment. You see their aim is to make the effect of the tours on the local environment (1) ... as possible.

For a start, we were given lots to (2) ... to help us learn about the people, places and (3) ... that we would be seeing. As well as that, we all had to be really (4) ... about getting rid of all our (5) ... whenever we set up (6) ... .

Generally we didn't stay in big, (7) ... hotels but smaller local ones which were fine and had lots of character. They also tried to make sure that we always (8) ... equipment etc. made in the (9) ... . All in all, it was good to feel that we were doing something towards (10) ... the economy of the area.

At the end, they were really (11) ... to know what we (12) ... of the tour and environmental issues and to get any (13) ... that we might have for improving things.

1 Read the description of someone's experience of whitewater rafting below.

I had never been whitewater rafting before. There were 8 of us sitting in a rubber boat with paddles. The leader sat in the back. I was nervous. I hadn't really wanted to do this but a friend had persuaded me. The river looked very rough. Apparently, there had been a lot of rain in the previous week.

After getting some basic instruction we set off. Almost immediately we were being thrown about by the water. It was difficult to hear the instructions the leader was shouting. We were trying hard to avoid the large rocks all around us. Then we came to a large drop. A lot of water came into the boat. Then I felt myself falling backwards into the river. ...

1 It is written in quite a simple and basic way. Rewrite it so that it is more dramatic and has a greater range of structures and vocabulary.
2 Now write the following paragraph, describing what happened next.

2 In **most** lines of the following text, there is **one** unnecessary word. It is either grammatically incorrect or it does not fit in with the sense of the text. For each numbered line **1–16**, find this word. Some lines are correct. Indicate these lines with a tick (✓). The exercise begins with two examples (**0**) and (**00**).

SURVIVAL IN THE SKY

0	Armando Socarras Ramirez <u>who</u> flew from Cuba to Spain on June 4,
00 ✓	1969. However, unlike the other 143 passengers on the nine-
1	hour flight, which the Cuban student travelled under rather than
2	inside the Iberia Airlines DC-8. When airport mechanics opened
3	the compartment during the aeroplane's routine post-flight
4	service in Madrid, one very cold stowaway dropped him onto the
5	tarmac. By some miracle, Socarras who was still alive. He was
6	rushed to hospital where to be treated for exposure and shock.
7	Socarras, was dressed only in a shirt and trousers, had endured
8	a temperature of −40°C, pressures a quarter of those at the sea
9	level, and a lack of oxygen that had rendered him unconscious
10	for almost the entire journey. Any one of these that should
11	have killed him. Baffled scientists who could explain Socarras's
12	survival only as a remarkable example of human hibernation.
13	When the body's temperature decreases, so does its own
14	demand for oxygen. Socarras's temperature had, what it seems,
15	dropped by just the right amount. This did not freeze him, but
16	it reduced his need for oxygen and was enabled him to live.

3 Some of these sentences are correct. In others an incorrect (or unlikely) adverbial has been used. Find the incorrect adverbials and replace them with possible alternatives.

1 He may look quite young but he's actually in his forties.
2 I didn't know before but, basically, Claire is now living in Moscow.
3 From the way she was behaving she personally didn't want to go to the party.
4 Frankly, I have always had my doubts about hiring people without proper interviews.
5 Although it's not very exciting I think she is basically very happy with her life.

Mind over matter

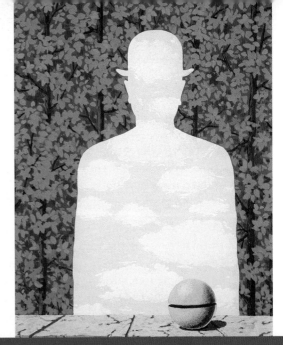

Reading

▶ P1, Pt2 (gapped text)

1 Look at the pictures.
Do you like them? Why/why not? How do they make you feel?
Do you think the artist is trying to make a particular point?

2 Look at the title of the article. Predict what you think the article will be about.

3 Now read the article (in not more than 17 minutes) and insert the missing paragraphs from p.143 in the correct place. (There is one extra paragraph which does not fit in any of the gaps.) Make sure you can justify your answers by referring to words/phrases within the text.

4 Read the complete text again and discuss these questions with other students.

1 How do you imagine it would feel to be Dr P.?
2 Apart from the 'mistakes' mentioned in the text, what other problems do you imagine he might have in day-to-day life?

The man who mistook his wife for a hat

Dr P. was a musician of distinction, well-known for many years as a singer, and then, at a local School of Music as a teacher. It was here, in relation to his students, that certain strange problems were first observed. Sometimes a student would present himself, and
5 Dr P. would not recognise him; or, specifically, would not recognise his face. The moment the student spoke, he would be recognised by his voice. Such incidents multiplied, causing embarrassment, perplexity, fear – and sometimes, comedy. For not only did Dr P. increasingly fail to see faces, but he also saw faces when there were no faces to see:
10 genially, when in the street, he might pat the heads of water-hydrants and parking-meters, taking these to be the heads of children.

(1 ———)

Well aware that it could affect his eyes, Dr P. consulted an opthalmologist, who took a careful history, and examined his eyes closely. 'There's nothing the matter with your eyes,' the doctor
15 concluded. 'But there is trouble with the visual parts of your brain. You don't need my help, you must see a neurologist.' And so, as a result of the referral, Dr P. came to me.

(2 ———)

And yet there was something a bit odd. He faced me as he spoke, was oriented towards me, and there was something the matter – it was
20 difficult to formulate. He faced me with his *ears*, I came to think, but not with his eyes.

(3 ———)

'What seems to be the matter?' I asked him at length.
'Nothing that I know of,' he replied with a smile, 'but people seem to think there's something wrong with my eyes.'
25 'But you don't recognise any visual problems?'
'No, not directly, but I occasionally make mistakes.'

(4 ———)

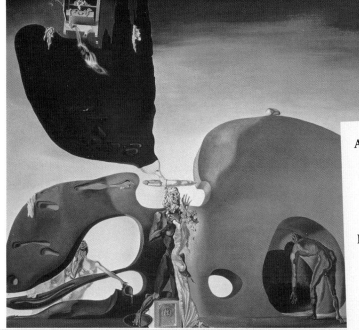

A These, instead of looking at me, 'taking me in', in the normal way, made sudden strange fixations – on my nose, on my right ear, down to my chin – as if noting these individual features, but not seeing my whole face, 'me' as a whole.

B I showed him the cover, an unbroken expanse of Sahara dunes.
'What do you see here?' I asked.
'I see a river,' he said. 'And a little guest-house with its terrace on the water.' He was looking into mid-air and confabulating non-existent features, as if the absence of features in the actual picture had driven him to imagine the river and the terrace.

C 'My eyes,' he explained, and put a hand to his foot. '*This* is my shoe, no?'
'No, it is not. That is your foot. *There* is your shoe.'
'Ah! I thought that was my foot.'
Was he joking? Was he mad? Was he blind? If this was one of his 'strange mistakes', it was the strangest mistake I had ever come across.

D 'Smell it,' I suggested, and he again looked somewhat puzzled, as if I had asked him to smell a higher symmetry. But he complied courteously, and took it to his nose. Now, suddenly, he came to life.

E I had taken off his left shoe and scratched the sole of his foot with a key – an essential test of a reflex – and then, excusing myself to screw my opthalmoscope together, left him to put on the shoe himself. To my surprise, a minute later, he had not done this.

F At first these odd mistakes were laughed off as jokes, not least by Dr P. himself. Had he not always had a quirky sense of humour? The notion of there being 'something the matter' did not emerge until some three years later, when diabetes developed.

G I left the room briefly, to talk to his wife. When I came back Dr P. was sitting placidly by the window, attentive, listening rather than looking out. 'Traffic,' he said, 'street sounds, distant trains – they make a sort of symphony, do they not?'

H It was obvious within a few seconds of meeting him that there was no trace of dementia in the ordinary sense. He was a man of great cultivation and charm, who talked well and fluently, with imagination and humour. I couldn't think why he had been referred to our clinic.

What a lovely man, I thought to myself. How can there be anything seriously the matter? Would he permit me to examine him?
30 'Yes, of course, Dr Sacks.'
I stilled my disquiet, his perhaps too, in the soothing routine of a neurological exam – muscle strength, co-ordination, reflexes, tone ... It was while examining his reflexes – a trifle abnormal on the left side – that the first
35 bizarre experience occurred.

(5 ———)

'Can I help?' I asked.
'Help what? Help whom?'
'Help you put on your shoe.'
'Ach,' he said, 'I had forgotten the shoe,' adding, *sotto voce*,
40 'The shoe? The shoe?' He seemed baffled.
'Your shoe,' I repeated. 'Perhaps you'd put it on.'
He continued to look downwards, though not at the shoe, with an intense but misplaced concentration. Finally his gaze settled on his foot: 'That is my shoe, yes?'
45 Did I mis-hear? Did he mis-see?

(6 ———)

I helped him on with his shoe (his foot), to avoid further complication. Dr P. himself seemed untroubled, indifferent, maybe amused. I resumed my examination. His visual acuity was good: he had no difficulty seeing a pin on the
50 floor.
He saw all right, but what did he see? I opened out a copy of the *National Geographic Magazine*, and asked him to describe some pictures in it.

(7 ———)

I must have looked aghast, but he seemed to think he had
55 done rather well. There was a hint of a smile on his face. He also appeared to have decided that the examination was over, and started to look round for his hat. He reached out his hand, and took hold of his wife's head, tried to lift it off, to put it on. He had apparently mistaken his wife for a hat!
60 His wife looked as if she was used to such things.

Vocabulary: expressions with *take*

1 Join a sentence from section A with a sentence from section B.

A

1. He frequently **took** parking meters **to be** the heads of children.
2. It took a while for him to **take it** all **in**.
3. You've really **taken to** James, haven't you?
4. You can't **take anyone else on**.
5. You always **take things in your stride**.
6. You **take people** just **the way that you find them**.
7. You mustn't **take advantage of him**.
8. You've **taken** your wife **for granted** for too long.
9. You completely **took my breath away**.
10. You mustn't **take** the responsibility for looking after your mother all **upon yourself**.
11. Running the department single-handedly while Jim's been sick has **taken a lot out of you**.
12. You should **take** this issue of promotion **up with** your boss.

B

a) You never seem to get flustered or upset.
b) Your brother should do his bit too.
c) He's a very trusting sort of person and a little naive.
d) Well, he is very good-looking.
e) It was a very complicated lecture.
f) Now she's ill you can see just how much work she does.
g) You really should have a holiday.
h) We can't afford to pay the staff we've got.
i) He would pat them in a benevolent manner.
j) He should have put you in charge of your department when Tina resigned.
k) You don't make assumptions or pre-judge them.
l) I can't believe you paid that much for your house.

2 Now say what you think the expressions in bold in column A mean.

EXAMPLE: 1 > *mistakenly think*

3 Complete the following sentences. Use a word from Exercise 1 to fill each gap.

1. Peter took it .... himself to sell the car while I was away.
2. As we cannot seem to reach an agreement, I'm afraid I must take this matter .... with my lawyer.
3. It's surprising how much looking after the kids for just a few hours takes .... of you.
4. I took .... Sarah as soon as I met her. Something just clicked.
5. When you visit some of the poorer parts of the world it makes you realise just how much we take for ....
6. It rather took my .... away when she told me we were going to have triplets.
7. My parents think she takes .... of me but it's not true. She does as much for me as I do for her.
8. You've got to take things more in your .... Just try and relax. Don't get so worked up about everything.
9. We need to take .... some more staff for the summer. Bookings are way up on last year.
10. We took her to .... truly fond of Michael but she didn't really care for him at all.
11. I really like Julie. She's very accepting of other people. She always just takes them the .... that she finds them.
12. He spoke so quickly and it was so complicated. I had trouble taking it all ....

4 Work in pairs. Tell a story or describe a situation to illustrate one of the expressions from Exercise 1. The student listening should respond at the end with the appropriate expression.

EXAMPLE: Student A: *I've been spending quite a bit of time with Simon just recently. You know he's really good fun and very intelligent. He's also one of the most interesting people I've met in ages. He's travelled all over South America, you know.*

Student B: *You've really **taken to** him, haven't you?*

Student A: *I guess I have. I think he's great!*

Listening: song

 1 Listen to this song. Decide if it is about:

- a visitor from outer space
- someone with a serious case of amnesia
- an old person thinking about the past

2 Before you listen again, read the words to the song below and attempt to complete the gaps with an appropriate word in each case. If you're not sure, make a guess.

3 Listen again and check your answers.

4 Imagine that one day you found yourself wandering in an unknown street. You couldn't remember who you were or anything about yourself. What would you do?

Grammar plus: emphasis with inversion

1 What is the difference in the impact on the reader of each of the sentences in a) and b) below?

a) Not only did Dr P. increasingly fail to see faces, but he also saw faces when there were no faces to see.
b) Dr P. increasingly failed to see faces and he also saw faces when there were no faces to see.

a) Seldom have I come across such a strange 'mistake'.
b) I have seldom come across such a strange 'mistake'.

2 What is the difference in the way the two sentences in each pair are formed grammatically?

3 Read the following sentences. Match each sentence with one of the people in the box and then guess what the situation might be.

> witness newsreader politician accountant parent
> university lecturer

1 'No sooner had I turned the corner, than I saw these three men in balaclavas.'
2 'Rarely has this country been in such need of strong leadership.'
3 'Under no circumstances can we be late with the figures for next year.'
4 'At no time in recent history have we seen such rapid technological change.'

 4 Say each of the above sentences with appropriate emphasis and sentence stress. Then listen to the recording.

I don't REMEMBER

I got no means to show identification
I got no (1) .... (to) show you what I am
You'll have to take me just the (2) .... that you find me
What's gone is (3) .... and I do not give a damn
Empty (4) .... , empty head
I got empty heart and empty (5) ....
     I don't remember
     I don't remember

I don't remember, I don't recall
I got no memory of anything at all
I don't remember, I don't recall
I got no memory of anything at all
     – anything at all

Strange is your language and I have no
     (6) ....
Why don't you (7) .... your intentions clear?
With eyes to the sun and your mouth to the soda
Saying "Tell me the truth, you got nothing to
     (8) .... "
Stop (9) .... at me like a bird of prey
I'm all mixed up. I got (10) .... to say.
     I don't remember
     I don't remember

I don't remember, I don't recall
I got no memory of anything at all
I don't remember, I don't recall
I got no memory of anything
     – anything at all

I don't remember, I don't recall
I got no memory of anything at all
I don't remember, I don't recall
I got no memory of anything absolutely anything at all
     I don't remember

5 Make the following sentences grammatically correct. You may need to add words. (They all refer to past time.)

EXAMPLE: *Never/I (be)/so insulted!* > ***Never have I been so insulted!***

1 Not only/he (miss) the meeting/but (fail) to finish/ report on time.
2 Rarely/I (meet)/such/interesting individual.
3 At no time/I ever (believe)/Ms Stevens (take)/ money.
4 Hardly/I (leave) the room/I (hear)/someone calling my name.
5 Only after (sign)/the agreement/she realise/what a terrible mistake she (make).
6 No sooner/judge (enter) the courtroom/defendant (start) shouting.
7 Scarcely/we (get) on the plane/the flight attendants (ask) us/go back to the departure lounge.
8 Under no circumstances/we (allow)/enter the building without an identity pass.

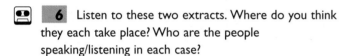 **6** Listen to these two extracts. Where do you think they each take place? Who are the people speaking/listening in each case?

7 Listen again. What differences do you notice between the two extracts?

8 Listen to the second extract again. Make a note of four sentences you hear which include inversion structures.

9 Now write your own short political speech. Include at least three sentences using inversion for emphasis.

Watch Out! ◄

What difference do you notice in the way these two sentences are formed?

1 No sooner had he left the room than they started talking about him.
2 Hardly had he left the room when they started talking about him.

► Grammar reference p.193

► *Exam Maximiser* M

Exam focus

Paper 5 Speaking: Parts 1–4

About the exam: The Speaking paper takes about 15 minutes for a pair of candidates. There are two examiners but only one of them speaks with the candidates. There are four parts to the test:

Part 1: Candidates have to respond to questions from the other candidate and the examiner. These questions usually ask for the candidate to give personal information about, for example, where they come from, their family, their free time etc.

Part 2: Candidates speak for one minute (without interruption). Each candidate comments on a different set of pictures or photographs. Candidates are also asked to speak briefly after their partner has spoken.

Part 3: Candidates work together and discuss a problem-solving task for about three minutes.

Part 4: Candidates respond to questions from the examiner related to the issues raised in Part 3. The questions become more abstract as the discussion develops.

Suggested procedure

- Listen carefully to the instructions that the examiner gives you for each part of the test.
- Be positive in your attitude. Speak clearly and fully when responding to questions and prompts.
- If there is something you don't understand, ask the examiner.
- Use a good range of language when responding to the various tasks.
- When discussing with your partner, be cooperative and give them to time to participate as well.
- Don't worry if the examiner stops you before you have finished speaking.

Exam task

Work with another student. Decide who is Candidate A and who is Candidate B. Listen and respond to the examiner's questions and instructions on the recording. Candidate B's photos are on p.218.

Part 2
Candidate A's photos

Part 3

INFORMATION TECHNOLOGY

www.com

TRANSPORT

WORK

CLIMATE

FAMILY LIFE

Grammar check: questions

1 Read the article below and answer this question.
Did the writer conquer her fear of flying?

a flying phobic

The day dawned wet and miserable, an accurate reflection of my state of mind. My task was to conquer my fear of
5 flying which had prevented me from going on a plane for four years. The solution, I hoped, was to attend a course for first-time passengers or people
10 whose fear was stopping them flying.

During the first morning we were introduced to the cabin crew, who would have the daunting task of coping with potentially hysterical passengers. Then
15 came a session with a psychiatrist, who taught us breathing and relaxation exercises. He made us close our eyes to experience the flight in our imagination. The closing of eyes was our ticket
20 to further relaxation, and we were soon asleep. After waking up, we were driven in coaches to the airport, where several people experienced
25 minor panic attacks.

The rest of us chatted nervously and, seemingly without worry, boarded the British Airways shuttle. As the plane moved towards the runway, my mind
30 was thrown back into reality. The trance which had led me from the hotel to the aircraft subsided, and I realised they had won; I was on a moving plane.

2 Read the article again and make appropriate questions for the answers below:

EXAMPLE: 1 *What was the day like?*

1 Wet and miserable.
2 It prevented her from flying for four years.
3 Attend a course for people afraid of flying.
4 Cope with potentially hysterical passengers.
5 To the airport.
6 Because she was on a moving plane.

3 Decide if each of these questions is correct or not. If not, correct the mistake.

1 Couldn't you have tried to stop him leaving?
2 Who did give you permission to leave school early?
3 Did you use to have many friends at school?
4 About what is that book you're reading?
5 Aren't you going to have a holiday this year?
6 Did he tell you whether he would be coming or not?
7 Will you please tell me where did you go last night?

4 Write four questions to ask another student.

The first question must be exactly six words.
The second question must be exactly seven words.
The third question must be exactly eight words.
The fourth question must be exactly nine words.

► *Exam Maximiser* M

Listening

▶ P4, Pt2
(note taking)

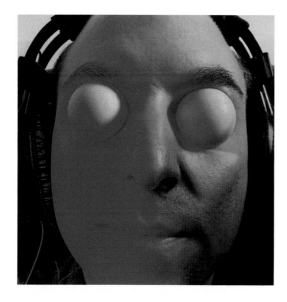

1 You will hear a radio journalist describing some of the work of the Koestler Parapsychology Unit at Edinburgh University. As you listen, complete the information sheet for questions 1–10.

KOESTLER PARAPSYCHOLOGY UNIT.

Founded in: (1) ....

Name of key test: 'ganzfeld'

Necessary equipment: (2) .... ,
red light, (3) ....

Prior to commencement of experiment:

a) parts of (4) .... placed on
   subject's eyes

b) headphones placed over subject's ears

On commencement of experiment:

a) computer chooses picture from
   (5) ....

b) 'sender' tries to project this telepathically

c) computer chooses (6) ....
   more pictures and shows them all

d) person in sealed room tries to
   (7) .... what was transmitted
   by sender.

Number of years Morris has been at institute:
(8) ....

Number of 'ganzfeld' tests performed in recent
research:
(9) ....

Odds against 48% success rate:
Under 1 in (10) ....

2 Listen to the information again. Make notes so that you will be able to explain to someone else:

1 how a 'ganzfeld' test works and
2 why the results are significant.

Vocabulary: sound and light

1 Divide the following words into a group of

1 types of sound
2 types of light

> hiss flash flicker crash hum
> screech sparkle bang roar beam
> thud twinkle glow

2 Match one of the words above to each of these sounds.

3 Match one of the words above to each of the illustrations below.

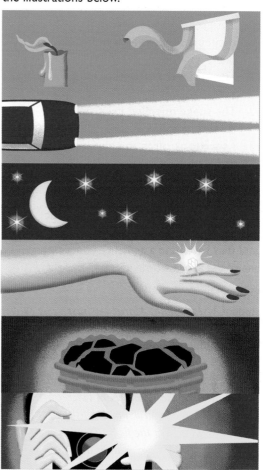

4 Now think of one other situation for each of the sounds and types of light above.

5 Complete each of the sentences with one of the words in Exercise I in the correct form.

1 The torch gave out a strong .... of light so they could see where everyone was.
2 There was a .... of lightning and then all the lights went out.
3 His eyes .... for a second and then he lay still.
4 The audience .... with laughter when she told her first joke.
5 His cigarette .... in the dark.
6 The tree fell through the bedroom window with a terrible ....
7 The barn owl gave one last piercing .... and flew away.
8 I love the sound of the insects .... in the sunshine.
9 The snowball hit the window with a dull ....
10 Her eyes .... with excitement when he told her the plan.
11 The gun went off with a loud ....
12 The snake uncoiled itself slowly making a loud .... noise.
13 As we took off in the plane, the lights of the town .... below us.

6 Work in groups. Create a dramatic story. Each person continues the story until they have used a sentence containing one of the above words of sound or light.

EXAMPLE:

Student 1: *Last night Maria was just going up to bed when she heard a loud* **crash** *from the living room.*

Student 2: *She ran back downstairs, and into the living room where she found a large bowl of fruit in pieces on the floor. Then she saw a* **beam** *of light outside in the garden.*

Writing: article

1 In Paper 2, Part 2 you might be asked to write an 'article'. Articles can be on a range of different topics and for different audiences but there are some core features which are true of any good article. Work with another student. Think about any articles you have read recently and suggest possible characteristics of a good magazine article.

2 Read the following general interest magazine article and discuss a possible title which will attract the reader and make them want to read the article.

'It's a Friday afternoon and you're sitting in a small, dark room at Edinburgh University. All you can see is a haze of pink light. All you can hear is a gentle hissing. And somewhere, someone is sending you a
5 *psychic message ...'*

This is just part of an everyday routine experiment for Professor Robert Morris who probably has one of the most fascinating jobs in the world. He is director of the Koestler Parapsychology Unit – Britain's very own X-Files laboratory –
10 and Britain's leading investigator of the paranormal. For the past 10 years what they have been attempting to do is to conduct a series of paranormal experiments, in search of scientific evidence to finally prove or disprove whether some human beings possess Extra-Sensory Perception (ESP).
15   Morris and his team have devised a range of rigorous tests for ESP ability since they began back in the late 1980s and they've produced some startling results. For example, the proportion of people able to select one picture from several that has been telepathically 'beamed' to them was 48% –
20 almost twice the rate expected. The odds against doing this by fluke alone are less than one in 39 million.
  But under no circumstances do orthodox scientists appear prepared to take parapsychology seriously just yet. Why is that? Because, in fact, most scientists believe that any
25 explanation – fluke, error, even fraud – is more plausible than the reality of ESP. 'In situations like this,' says Professor Lewis Wolpert of London University, 'I think we must follow the philosopher David Hume, who said that extraordinary claims require extraordinary evidence.'
30   Morris and his colleagues fully accept this, and their strategy for convincing sceptics was neatly summed up by the writer Sir Arthur Conan Doyle: 'When you have eliminated the impossible, whatever remains, however improbable, must be the truth.'

TASKS

1   Stress is an increasing problem for students in this college. Have you got any ideas that will help students combat stress, particularly in the lead-up to exams? Your college magazine needs an article on this topic and is offering a free day in a local health club for the best article.

2   You have been asked to write an article for an international magazine about the problem of homelessness in your country. Describe some of the reasons as to why you think homelessness might occur and any action that you think should and could be taken.

3   Your college magazine is including a special section on the contribution of older people (over 60) to society. You have been asked to contribute a short article profiling an extraordinary older person that you know. Write the article describing the special characteristics and/or achievements of this person.

---

3   Here are some suggestions for what might make an article interesting to the reader. How many of these are included in the text on p.150?

1   attention-grabbing title
2   intriguing/thought-provoking opening paragraph
3   direct questions to reader
4   addressing readership as 'you'
5   special grammatical structures to give extra emphasis
6   surprising or remarkable information/facts
7   range of interesting vocabulary
8   concrete examples, not just general statements
9   direct speech quotations from relevant people
10   concluding final paragraph

4   You are going to write one of the following articles in approximately 250 words. Choose one of the tasks in the box and work with another student who has made the same choice. (The article you write in the exam will not require any specialist knowledge.)

5   Plan and write your article. Follow the suggested procedure below.

Suggested procedure

1   First, decide how you are going to organise your article. How many paragraphs will you have? What will be the general subject of each one?

2   Look at the various points in Exercise 3. Make notes of how you might include each one in your article. (They may not all be appropriate!)

3   Write your article.
   • Exchange your article with your partner. Make notes of suggested improvements to their article.
   • Discuss your suggestions with your partner.
   • Read the model article on p.210 Writing reference. Check that you are following the Dos and Don'ts suggested. Can you incorporate any of the suggested 'Useful Language' in your article?
   • Write your final article. Make sure your handwriting is clear and easy to read.

Speaking: memory

1 Look at the objects in the first picture on p.219 for 30 seconds. Then shut your book and see how many you can remember. Compare your result with other students.

2 Now read this short text about a strategy for remembering things. Discuss with other students any strategies you use to improve your short-term memory. How did you try and remember the items in the picture?

> In the days before autocue, Greek and Roman politicians used 'memory theatre' to order their speeches. They mentally placed objects they wished to remember close to familiar places in their homes, in a street, or indeed in a theatre. It is said they could remember thousands of items this way. And the method persisted. If you respond to those ads that appear regularly in the papers offering memory improvement courses this is how they will tell you to do it.

3 Look at the lower pictures on p.219. Do they spark off any memories from your childhood? Try and link each picture to something from your past. Describe the connection to another student in as much detail as you can.

4 Prepare to talk about another childhood memory. Speak for one minute without interruption. Think about a time when you:

- were very embarrassed.
- did something you were told off about.
- were very happy.

English in Use

▶ P3, Pt4 (word formation)

1 What different uses are there for hypnotism? How would you feel about being hypnotised?

2 Read the text below to see if the writer seems positive or negative about 'self-hypnosis'.

OUT FOR THE COUNT		
'You are what you think you are,' says self-hypnotist Jonathan Atkinson. So there are 20 of us lying on our backs trying to communicate with our (**1**) ... minds. We start by describing our problems. I've got the usual (**2**) ... : tiredness, insomnia, (**3**)	1	CONSCIOUS
	2	COMPLAIN
	3	ANXIOUS
Six years ago, Jonathan was a typical 40 cigarettes-a-day executive under too much (**4**) ... . Then he learnt self-hypnosis. What is particularly (**5**) ... is that he can stop the bleeding when he cuts himself shaving, and have his teeth filled without needing an (**6**)	4	STRESSFUL
	5	IMPRESS
	6	INJECT
Gradually what started off as weird becomes (**7**) ... . While in hypnosis, Jonathan tells us that whenever we count to ten, with the (**8**) ... of going into self-hypnosis, we'll be able to do it. Amazingly, it seems to work.	7	UNDERSTAND
	8	INTEND

D **3** Read the text again.

1 Look at each gap and decide on the appropriate part of speech.
2 Write down what you think is the correct form of the word in capitals.
3 Check your idea in a dictionary.
4 Record in your notebook the important forms of each word that you didn't know before.

▶ *Exam Maximiser* 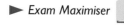 M

1 For questions 1–15, read the text below and then decide which word best fits each space.

YOUR AMAZING MEMORY

The age-old (1) ... that a drowning man's whole life passes before him in a (2) ... before he dies is perfectly true. Or so Canadian neurosurgeon Wilder Penfield, who (3) ... research into the (4) ... in the 1950s, concluded. And it happens not only when a person drowns, but when he or she believes death is imminent, say those who have been saved at the last (5) ... .

A curious (6) ... of the experience is that in those (7) ... moments of consciousness one's life is replayed *backwards*; forgotten people, places and events crowd into the mind's eye with (8) ... clarity. Penfield believed that this occurs because the brain normally (9) ... all memories, but only a special trigger can (10) ... them, such as death, or the belief that death is imminent.

Another theory is that the temporal lobes, where memories are stored, are especially (11) ... to interruptions in the supply of oxygen to the brain, and these in (12) ... wreak havoc with the brain's electrical signalling system. People suffocating, drowning or being hanged, for instance, (13) ... conscious long enough to (14) ... the bizarre effect of this oxygen starvation. This projects every (15) ... memory into the consciousness.

	A	B	C	D
1	conviction	belief	impression	judgement
2	ray	flicker	sparkle	flash
3	prepared	pioneered	developed	launched
4	phenomenon	happening	event	episode
5	time	period	point	moment
6	mark	feature	trait	quality
7	final	end	conclusion	eventual
8	absolute	entire	full	downright
9	hoards	deposits	reserves	stores
10	remind	remember	recall	reminisce
11	vulnerable	unprotected	damaged	powerless
12	order	place	turn	side
13	endure	remain	wait	continue
14	behold	spectate	witness	scan
15	vacant	convenient	employable	available

2 Rewrite these sentences beginning with the words given. Do not change the meaning of the sentence.

1 Simon broke a bone in his foot and also dislocated his shoulder.
Not only ....
2 He walked through the front door and immediately the phone rang.
No sooner ....
3 I shouted at Jerry for not waking me up but then I remembered it was the weekend.
Only after ....
4 It's the first time I have been so attracted to someone.
Never before ....
5 We moved into our new house and almost straightaway the central heating stopped working.
Hardly ....

3 Replace each of the underlined phrases below with an appropriate expression with *take*. Look at p.144 if necessary.

1 If we don't <u>hire</u> more people to work over the holiday period, we're not going to cope.
2 <u>I was really shocked</u> to hear that she had been fired. It seemed impossible.
3 We really <u>liked</u> Gail from the beginning. She's just our kind of person.
4 Having to look after my mother after her stroke has <u>been pretty exhausting</u>.
5 You should <u>raise</u> this matter with the council. Something has to be done.

An interesting business

Listening: market place economics

▶ P4, Pt1 (sentence completion)

1 How would you define *poverty*? What images does this word conjure up in your mind's eye?

2 Listen to Muhammad Yunus speaking in an interview on a radio programme. What is he trying to do? How is he trying to achieve this goal?

3 Listen again. For questions 1–8 fill in the missing information.

Despite his excitement about the economic theories he was teaching, Muhammad began to have
(1) ....

When Muhammad first saw Sufia she was making
(2) ....

The price of the bamboo to Sufia was approximately
(3) .... pence.

Sufia sells the stools in order to (4) ....

Each working day Sufia makes a
(5) .... of about one penny.

Muhammad found that the number of people in Jobra in a similar position to Sufia was (6) ....

To get a loan Muhammad's clients have to show proof of how
(7) ....

Every month Muhammad's bank receives from its clients nearly (8) ....

4 Discuss with other students.

1 What do you think of what Muhammad Yunus is doing? Why do you think that almost all of the money he lends is repaid promptly?

2 One problem that many countries have is the debts they owe international banks and the interest they must keep paying on their loans. What arguments are there for and against such banks cancelling these debts?

Grammar check: passives

1 Read the following text and then summarise the main points to another student.

2 Read the text again. There are six mistakes connected with passives (two in each paragraph). Find them and correct them.

THE SEARCH FOR A CORPORATE IDENTITY.

Today, many companies are being marketing products or services which are similar. Think of Burger King and McDonalds, Reebok and Nike, Coca Cola and Pepsi. So, in order to encourage customer loyalty, companies seek to establish a clear image or identity for their products, one which will instantly recognised and remains consistent.

The logotype (a word which generally shortened to 'logo') is one way this is achieved. A logo is an emblem or other device that is identifies an organisation or its products. Logos sum up the company image using a kind of visual shorthand.

Visual identity is not a new concept. Throughout history and in different societies, colours and symbols have used to represent particular groups or interests. In medieval Britain the system of heraldry – the patterns on a knight's shield and battle regalia – was developed partly because the heavy armour and helmets made it difficult to distinguish one knight from another. Each knight chose his own pattern and colours and these were then passing on to his descendants.

3 Look at the box below which outlines three uses of the passive.

> *The passive is used:*
> 1 to talk about actions, events and processes when the action, event or process is seen as more important than the agent.
> *A large number of political biographies have been written in recent years.*
>
> 2 to put new information later in the sentence.
> *This photograph was actually taken by my grandfather.*
>
> 3 to put longer expressions at the end of the sentence.
> *I was upset by the way she continually tried to ignore me the other night.*

4 Now match each of the sentences below with one of the uses of the passive outlined in the box above.

1 This kind of pottery was first made by native American Indians.
2 Santa Cruz was founded in 1495.
3 They were horrified by Simon's appalling behaviour in the middle of the party.

5 Transform each of these sentences into the passive form. Name the verb tense where possible.

EXAMPLE: *I take my dog for a walk every morning. – My dog **is taken for** a walk every morning. (Present Simple passive)*

1 They are giving her an award for bravery.
   She ....
2 Journalists asked him lots of questions.
   He ....
3 They were showing her the new museum of modern art at 9 a.m. this morning.
   She ....
4 Mr Jacobs has asked me to tell you a little about how the company began.
   I ....
5 I hear they are going to make him chairman of the board.
   I hear he ....
6 Bad weather must have delayed the plane.
   The plane ....

► *Exam Maximiser* M

Speaking: expressing uncertainty

British Telecom

1 Above are some logos used by different companies. Say if you think each one is effective or not. If you are not completely sure what you think, use one of the phrases below for expressing uncertainty:

- *I don't think I can put my finger exactly on what I don't like about this one but ...*
- *I'm not entirely sure what I think about this one but ...*
- *It's hard to say why I think this is quite effective but perhaps it's because ...*

2 Look at these four alternative ideas for a logo for a new language school called Language Link. Discuss with another student which two you think are the most effective and why.

Reading

▶ P1, Pt3 (multiple choice)

1 Discuss with other students.

1 What is the link between the two photographs?
2 What is unusual about the radio in the photograph?

2 Read the text quickly to find out the answers to the above questions.

The Wind-Up Merchant

He was not at all what I'd expected. Short and barrel-chested, he has a belly that has taken much time and effort to achieve. Frequent and <u>explosive</u>[1] laughter rumbles from its depths. There's a hole in
5 the toe of his dusty black desert boots and in the sleeve of his well-worn blue jumper. The luxuriant moustache that warms his upper lip is white with a hint of golden yellow. This, ladies and gentlemen, is the <u>description</u>[2] of a genius, Trevor
10 Baylis, the inventor of the wind-up radio.

Perhaps Trevor was always destined to be a star. At the age of 15 he swam for his country. In 1970 he became 'Ramses II' and <u>performed</u>[3] an underwater escapology act in a Berlin circus –
15 they'd blindfold him, tie him up, stick him in a coffin, nail the lid down and drop him into a pool about 10 feet <u>deep</u>[4].

Trevor points to his TV. 'I was watching this thing on telly, a programme about AIDS in Africa.
20 The image that stopped me dead was some youngsters, kiddies with hollow eyes, lying on rush mats, <u>covered</u>[5] in flies, dying of this filthy disease. Then there was a burial party, putting people down a hole – quite graphic stuff.
25 'But the important thing was the message coming over, that the only way they could possibly stop this terrible disease was through education. And there was the problem,' says Trevor. 'People weren't receiving the information. Radio is the
30 most effective way of bringing information to the 600 million people in Africa, but most don't have

electricity. And batteries are horrendously <u>expensive</u>[6].
'I was sitting there watching this when suddenly
35 I had this strange picture of all those old colonialists in the films with their monocles and fly swats, listening to their wind-up gramophones. And I thought, if you can get all that noise by dragging a nail round a piece of old Bakelite using
40 a spring, maybe we could use a spring to drive a dynamo that could drive a radio ...'

It took Trevor five minutes to shift from his chair in front of the telly to his workshop to start on his idea. He made the first prototype from a
45 cannibalised radio and a few bits of plastic and <u>metal</u>[7] from his scrapyard of a workroom. Two or three months later, he made it work for 15 minutes. 'Then came the worst part. Every British company I went to turned me down. I was so
50 <u>humiliated</u>[8], angry and frustrated.
'But then the BBC World Service put me in touch with the TV science programme, Tomorrow's World. When the show came out, the phone didn't stop ringing. It was just lovely, people
55 phoning up saying. "Well done Trev," and kiddies ringing up saying, "Can I be an inventor?" That was absolutely magic. Those people kept me going.'

There is a certain sweet <u>logic</u>[9] to what came
60 next. His appearance on television, that bastion of high-technology, was the catalyst that turned Trevor's wind-up radio from a dream into a reality. 'A fellow called Christopher Staines faxed me and said he could help me,' says Trevor. Chris Staines'
65 plan was that he and partner Roy Stear should work for Trevor and share in his success. Together they set up 'BayGen', the company that now makes the wind-up radio.

At first it wasn't easy, every potential British
70 manufacturer they contacted turned them down on cost or risk grounds and in the end they had to go to South Africa to get funding. In 1996, Trevor was flown to South Africa to visit their factory for

the first time. The factory in Cape
75 Town is staffed by <u>disabled</u>[10]
workers and turns out around
60,000 Freestyle radios a month.
All the staff – many of them in
wheelchairs – were lined up to
80 greet him. 'As I walked through
the door, I was stunned by all the
activity: the smiling faces of all
these physically damaged people.
It was too overwhelming. I cried
85 my eyes out.'
  Trevor has met the Queen, to
pick up his OBE, and Nelson
Mandela. He is feted as a <u>hero</u>[11]
and he's already a millionaire on
90 paper. And he hasn't finished yet.
He has recently launched the
wind-up torch, and there are
other new designs on the way: the
solar-powered wind-up radio,
95 which gives a choice of power
sources – both free, both green;
and even the wind-up lap-top
computer.
  Then he grabs what looks like a
100 child's electronic toy – a book that
'speaks' when you touch its
pictures with the attached pen.
'I'm going to do something about
adult <u>literacy</u>[12] and numeracy.
105 This book could be on land mines
or insects. Touch the picture of
the land mine with the pen and it
would tell you what you should
and shouldn't do. You could do
110 <u>translations</u>[13] into any language,
using the radio for power and
sound. So you take literacy and
numeracy into the wilderness or
the jungle without the need for
115 electricity.'

3 Read the article again and then choose the correct alternative in
each case below.

1 From the journalist's description, Trevor

  A makes an effort to keep in shape.

  B seems quite reserved.

  C doesn't take much care of his appearance.

  D is quite fashion-conscious.

2 Trevor was originally moved to design his radio because of

  A the lack of good education in Africa.

  B the price of radios in Africa.

  C the link between information and health in Africa.

  D his first hand experience with disease in Africa.

3 Trevor had the idea for his radio after

  A using his imagination.

  B seeing an old movie about the British in Sudan.

  C experimenting with a nail, some Bakelite and a dynamo.

  D visiting the Sudan.

4 A consequence of being on television was that Trevor

  A was constantly stopped in the street.

  B had his self-confidence restored.

  C wanted more people to become inventors.

  D was introduced to Chris Staines.

5 Trevor's main reaction to visiting the factory in South Africa was to

  A feel very distressed.

  B be amazed that the workers could produce so many radios.

  C feel embarrassed at their gratitude.

  D be moved by the positive attitude of the workers.

6 Now Trevor clearly seems

  A quite surprised by his success.

  B full of new ideas.

  C interested in making money for charities.

  D most concerned about the problem of landmines.

7 The journalist's attitude to Trevor is

  A neutral.

  B mixed.

  C admiring.

  D cynical.

157

4 Discuss with other students.

1 What is your general reaction to Trevor Baylis? Would you be interested in meeting him and talking to him? Why/why not?

2 Given the obvious problems with famine, disease etc. in certain parts of the world such as Africa – what kinds of assistance, if any, should wealthier nations provide?

5 Look back at the text on pp.156–157. Find the numbered words which are underlined and put them in the following sentences in the correct form.

EXAMPLE: 1 **explosive** > *There was a terrible* **explosion** *when the bomb went off.*

2 She doesn't give her opinion. It's a purely .... account.

3 It was a remarkable .... The applause went on for ages.

4 I was very surprised at the .... of the hole.

5 The recent visit of the Queen to Australia received a lot of media ....

6 They wanted to decorate their home in the latest style and no .... was spared.

7 I heard this strange .... sound coming from the bathroom.

8 Then she threw the glass of wine over her boss and his .... was complete.

9 He knew .... what the next step should be.

10 This building is suitable for use by people with various ....

11 Her actions in saving the little boy from drowning were truly ....

12 I don't believe we are producing great .... at the level of Shakespeare and Dickens these days.

13 Do you know any .... who are fluent in Polish and Portuguese?

D **6** Write a paragraph describing someone you know well, giving a vivid sense of what they are like in a similar way to the first paragraph of the article on p.156. Where possible, use a dictionary like the *Longman Language Activator* to help you research appropriately evocative language. Look at p.220 to see how the *Activator* might help you find interesting ways of describing a thin person.

Grammar plus: participle clauses

1 Participles e.g. *rushing* can combine with other words to become 'participle clauses' e.g. *rushing out of the front door*. They are often used to give more information about the idea expressed in a sentence. They are found more in written English.

Look at the pairs of sentences below. There is little difference in the essential meaning but participle clauses are often used in more literary writing to create a stronger visual picture for the reader.

Compare the pairs of sentences and comment on the difference in the way they are formed.

1 The image that struck me was some youngsters lying on rush mats.
The image that struck me was some youngsters who were lying on rush mats.

2 Anyone wanting to help should sign the form that is being passed around.
Anyone who wants to help should sign the form that is being passed around.

3 I found him sitting at a desk piled high with files.
I found him sitting at a desk which was piled high with files.

4 Who is that man talking to your father?
Who is that man who is talking to your father?

2 Express the meaning of the following sentences using participle clauses.

1 We all noticed his sister, who was standing next to the exit.

2 The students who finish first should get on with their homework.

3 Not all the people who were asked to come actually turned up.

4 The piece of wood which was keeping the window open has disappeared.

5 There's the Indian tiger which is sleeping as always.

6 You should apply for the job which pays the most.

3 Participle clauses can be used to replace words like *because*, *so that*, and *after*. Look at these examples. What words/phrases could replace the underlined words?

EXAMPLE: *a) because > as*

a) reason:
   We all took umbrellas <u>because</u> we had noticed that it was raining.
   We all took umbrellas, having noticed that it was raining.

b) result or consequence:
   She had been told that she could fail her final exams, <u>so</u> she started studying all hours of the day and night.
   Told that she could fail her final exams, she started studying all hours of the day and night.

c) time:
   <u>Once</u> she had finished the report, she decided it was time to go home.
   Having finished the report, she decided it was time to go home.

4 Express the meaning of the following sentences using participle clauses and removing the linking words/expressions.

EXAMPLE: *We have two young children and as a result we don't go out very much. >* ***Having*** *two young children, we don't go out very much.*

1 Since we were so late, we decided to catch a taxi.
2 Sarah received a large salary rise earlier this year so she is thinking of getting a new car.
3 I'm going to start going swimming again, now I have more time.
4 He shouted to his PA that he'd be back soon as he rushed out of the office.
5 I was enjoying a long Sunday morning lie-in and consequently I was not pleased to hear a loud banging on the front door.
6 As their children have all left home, they are thinking of moving somewhere smaller.
7 He expected some thanks after he showed them what the problem was.
8 Shouldn't you get someone to help you since you are under so much pressure at the moment?

▶ Grammar reference p.195

▶ *Exam Maximiser* M

5 Rewrite the text below. Make it more interesting to read by using a wider range of vocabulary and including some participle clauses.

EXAMPLE: *Jeremy and Sue's holiday was turning into a nightmare ...*

Jeremy and Sue's holiday wasn't going very well. They had arrived at the youth hostel the day before. After they had booked in they were told that they should leave all their valuable items at reception. They were looking forward to exploring the town the next day so they decided to go to bed early that night. In the morning they woke up early because there was a lot of noise coming from the reception area. They went to see what was happening. There were a lot of angry people. Someone told them that there had been a burglary in the night. All the valuables in the reception safe had been taken. Jeremy and Sue had lost their passports, cameras and all their travellers' cheques. They were very unhappy and didn't know what to do.

Exam focus

Paper 3 English in Use: Part 2 (open cloze)

About the exam: Paper 3 English In Use, Part 2 is an open cloze of approximately 200 words containing 15 gaps. One word is required to fill each gap. The emphasis is on grammatical words.

Suggested procedure

1   Read the complete text to get the general idea of it.
2   Go through the text again and make a note of the answers you are confident about.
3   For the remaining gaps look carefully at the surrounding context. Decide on the part of speech of the missing word. Remember, the missing words are usually small 'grammatical' words e.g. prepositions, auxiliaries and articles.
4   Read the complete text again to make sure that all your answers make sense in context.

Exam task

For questions **1–15**, complete the following article by writing down each missing word. Use only one word for each space.
The exercise begins with an example (**0**).

GET A JOB THE ON-LINE WAY.

(**0**) *Of* the estimated 6.5 million people in the UK using the Internet, a fifth are using it (**1**) ... look for work. Applying for a job in (**2**) ... manner is quick, convenient and a tacit claim (**3**) ... you are on the technological ball.

The positive side to internet job hunting for the applicant is the ability to find out (**4**) ... an organisation. You can prepare thoroughly (**5**) ... both application and interview from the comfort of your PC. The main downside is that, (**6**) ... printed applications, Internet forms have almost limitless amounts (**7**) ... space for applicants to enter their details. 'There's always (**8**) ... danger they will ramble on. It is important to remain focused on (**9**) ... key points an employer will (**10**) ... looking for,' says Karen Skewies, an on-line recruitment specialist. A growing number of companies use software packages to scan applications, (**11**) ... including the right key words is essential. 'These programs look for specific skills, qualifications or relevant experience. They (**12**) ... so by searching for particular words or phrases,' she explains.

This must be balanced (**13**) ... the need to communicate your personality and attitude. Other computer tracking systems identify particular traits, (**14**) ... as responsibility or reliability. Where possible, (**15**) ... original in your language and avoid clichés.

Vocabulary: language of business

 1   Listen to the recording and put the words below in the order in which they are described. Write a number by each word.

EXAMPLE: *h) shareholder > Number 1*

a) turnover
b) get the sack
c) to take maternity leave
d) be laid off
e) to take early retirement
f) to go bankrupt
g) to work flexitime
h) shareholder

2   Now complete these sentences with a word or phrase from Exercise 1 in the correct form.

1   I'm looking forward to going back to work after my .... My husband works from home so he's going to look after the baby.
2   The recent economic recession has meant that many small companies have ....
3   He's only 55 but he's been offered this good deal by his company and he'll get a good pension so he's seriously thinking of ....
4   Two thousand workers have been .... by the country's largest supermarket chain. Falling profits have been blamed.
5   .... are angry that several high level executives have awarded themselves massive pay increases despite the company's poor performance this year.
6   My brother .... yesterday for swearing at one of the company's most important clients.
7   I love .... because it means I can work longer hours for a few days and then have a morning off.
8   We have increased our annual .... to £14 million but profits are still lower than we anticipated.

D **3** Check the correct word stress of each word below in a dictionary (such as the *Longman Dictionary of Contemporary English*). Then make a sentence to illustrate their meaning. Write down other forms of the words that you know.

EXAMPLE: *an employee – He's been an employee of this company for nearly 30 years. – employer, employment, unemployment*

an employee	a subsidiary
a competitor	a promotion
monopoly	efficient
production	economical
personnel	investment
to manufacture	viable

4 Discuss with other students.

1 What businesses or companies are in the news at the moment? Why are they in the news?
2 Name one or two very successful businesses or companies. Why are they so successful?

Speaking: starting your own business

1 Work with two or three other students. You are going to start your own business. Here are some suggestions of what the business will be. Choose one of these or something else.

2 Discuss these questions with your business partners and prepare to convince your local bank manager to give you a loan.

- What will your business do/sell?
- Who will its target market be?
- Where will you locate your business?
- What kind of premises do you need?
- How many people will you employ at the beginning?
- What will be the name of your business? (Design a possible logo if appropriate.)
- How and where will you advertise?

3 Roleplay a meeting with your local bank manager.

Loan Applicants: You must convince your bank manager of the viability of your proposed business venture. Persuade her/him that your business will succeed and you will be able to pay the loan back in due course.
Bank Manager: You have recently been criticised for lending money to businesses that fail and therefore can't repay their loans. Check very carefully that this proposed venture is likely to succeed.

4 Do one of the following writing tasks in approximately 250 words with reference to the company you created above.

1 Write a letter to your local bank manager. Describe
  - the plans for your new business
  - the need for a substantial loan
  - how you will be able to pay it back.
  Conclude by requesting a meeting to discuss this further.

2 Imagine your business has been going for a year. Write an information leaflet for visitors to your company.
  - Give a brief history of the company.
  - Describe its main activities.
  - Mention any other points that you think are important.

English in Use

▶ P3, Pt1 (multiple-choice cloze)

1 Discuss with another student.

What are the pros and cons of being an office worker?

2 Read the article below and compare your ideas with the results of a survey.

3 For questions 1–15, read the text again and then decide which word below best fits each space.

	A	B	C	D
1	weight	force	heaviness	pressure
2	published	printed	publicised	proclaimed
3	outlooks	odds	prospects	views
4	important	impressive	heavy	significant
5	quality	calibre	excellence	worth
6	rank	status	degree	grade
7	pliable	elastic	amenable	flexible
8	safety	security	sanctuary	protection
9	failure	defeat	deficiency	lack
10	indisposed	unwell	injured	sick
11	pestered	inflamed	irritated	ruffled
12	behind the times	expired	out-of-date	invalid
13	fertility	capacity	value	productivity
14	compensation	damages	reimbursement	atonement
15	idiosyncratic	unique	personal	individual

OFFICE STRESS

Stressful atmospheres, (1) ... of deadlines and long hours dominate office life, according to a survey (2) ... recently.

The majority of those questioned said a good salary and career (3) ... were their main reason for working. But (4) ... numbers did not believe their employers offered either. In general the survey found that most felt that (5) ... of life was more important than (6) ... and company perks. Most would prefer employers to offer (7) ... hours, challenging tasks and job (8) ... rather than perks such as company cars and private health care. Many employers' (9) ... to understand this meant more than a third worried about their work on holiday, and 40 per cent took days off (10) ... when not ill.

Workers were also (11) ... by the conditions they had to work in. A fifth struggled with (12) ... technology, badly lit offices and chairs which caused backache. Half said their (13) ... would increase if their environment improved.

On the plus side, the biggest (14) ... was the friendship offered by colleagues, and it appears that the office also affords the chance to flirt with colleagues, make (15) ... calls to friends abroad, steal stationery and play computer games.

Writing: job application

1 Read the advertisement on the right. Would you be interested in a job like this? Why/why not?

'I've called this meeting to decide if there's any point in holding a meeting'

cooper

EXCITING SALES POSITIONS

English language publisher wants keen, committed individuals as local representatives.

You must have a clear interest in the English language and the teaching of English as a foreign language. A significant part of your responsibilities will involve visiting teachers in schools in your local area and telling them about our excellent range of teaching materials.

You will be working in a largely English-speaking environment with opportunities for sales training in the UK.

No previous experience necessary. All training provided. A good level of English is required.

Company car, competitive salary package, definite career opportunities.

All applications in writing to Ms. B. Dickinson (Personnel Manager), BritBooks, Scotland House, Harlow, Essex CM33 5HU, England.

2 Now read this letter of application. In each case choose the more appropriate preposition.

Rua Miguel Bombarda 2-1°,
2561 Torres Vedras
Portugal
5.10.00

Ms. B. Dickinson (Personnel Manager),
Scotland House,
Harlow,
Essex CM33 5HU,
England.

Dear Ms. Dickinson,

I am writing (1) *in/with/of* reply to your advertisement in the Sunday Times (3/10/2000) (2) *to/for/by* local sales representatives.

As you can see (3) *at/from/into* my enclosed CV, I finished my degree in Economics last year and since then I have been working in my father's company and consequently have some experience (4) *of/by/from* sales. I have also been trying to improve my English through evening classes and have reached an advanced level.

I am very interested (5) *in/by/from* starting a possible career in sales and I feel very enthusiastic (6) *about/with/from* the possibility (7) *in/of/at* working (8) *at/about/with* teachers and English language teaching materials. I have actually studied from some of the books you have published and know their high quality.

I should mention that I am available (9) *with/for/to* attend an interview (10) *at/of/by* any time which might be convenient.

Please don't hesitate (11) *in/to/with* contact me at the above address if you need any further information.

I look forward (12) *in/to/by* hearing from you.

Yours sincerely,

Elia Ribeiro

Elia Ribeiro

3 Read the letter again. Find, and make a note of, any phrases or expressions which might be useful in <u>any</u> job application letter.

4 Now attempt to write <u>your own</u> application for the job advertised on p.162 without referring to the letter.

5 Read this advertisement for a summer job. Highlight key words and phrases.

Summer opportunity

Come to Kent, the 'garden' of England. We have places for flexible, hard-working individuals to spend the summer with us on our farm. You will be expected to join in with all the various activities on the farm including fruit picking, working with animals, looking after the children etc.

We have been inviting foreign students to stay with us for a number of years now and many come back year after year. We want you to have a great summer and the chance to improve your English in a warm, friendly, family environment.

All accommodation and food is provided plus a small weekly allowance.

Write, giving full information about yourself to:

Jim and Mary Bryant, Park Gate Farm, Lyminge, Kent CT3 6FH, England.

6 Write a letter applying for the job advertised in Exercise 5. Make notes of what you might write in your letter:

1 State your reason for writing.
2 Give relevant information about yourself; highlight anything which will show your suitability for the job.
3 Say why you are interested in this job.
4 Explain how and when you can be contacted.
5 Close your letter appropriately.

7 Show another student your notes and see if they have any suggestions for changes or additions.

8 Write your letter. Check your use of prepositions and try and use a range of appropriate expressions for a letter of application.

Vocabulary: phrasal verbs with *up/down*

1 Look at these groups of sentences containing phrasal verbs with *up* or *down*. Match each one to a general meaning of *up* or *down* that is common to all the phrasal verbs in each group.

EXAMPLE: *1d)*

General meanings
a) to indicate a decrease in size or intensity
b) to indicate that something is being improved or prepared
c) to indicate thoroughness or completeness and usually of ending or change
d) to indicate that someone is moving closer to someone else
e) to indicate an increase in quantity or intensity

1 It took me ages to *catch up with* them.
  She walks so fast, it's difficult to *keep up with* her.
  He *ran up to* the old man and started shouting at him.
2 This clock needs *winding up*.
  I'll be back in a minute. I just need to go and *freshen up*.
  We should *tidy up* the living room before my parents arrive.

3 The party started to *liven up* when Jack arrived.
  If you don't *speed up* we'll never get there.
  Could you *speak up* a bit? I can't hear very well.
4 We've *narrowed* it *down* to three possible culprits.
  I really must *cut down on* the amount of chocolate I eat.
  Will you please *calm down*! Now, what is the matter?
5 It sounds like the children have finally *settled down*.
  I'm afraid we're going to have to *close down* our branches in the south west.
  I finally managed to *track down* that missing report.

2 Read the following sentences and decide if the missing particle in each case is *up* or *down*.

1 Jim sidled .... to Mary and whispered in her ear.
2 Apparently it's now economically viable to melt .... old glass.
3 The fire blazed .... and all we could do was to stand back and watch.
4 You'll have to wait a minute while the soup cools ....
5 Don't creep .... on me like that. You scared the life out of me!
6 He touched .... the car a bit and finally managed to sell it.
7 I'm afraid the debts are mounting .... Something must be done.
8 They agreed to water .... the final document so that everyone was prepared to sign.
9 We're going to fix .... the flat and then move in at Christmas.
10 We're going to hunt this man .... until we find him.

3 Work with another student and test each other on the phrasal verbs in Exercises 1 and 2 like this.

EXAMPLE:
Student A: *It means to repair or improve something.*
Student B: *to fix up*

Student B: *It means to make something more interesting or exciting.*
Student A: *to liven up*

1 Rewrite the following sentences without changing the meaning but using one of the phrasal verbs in the box.

> keep up with   narrow down   creep up on   fix up
> freshen up   settle down   mount up   water down
> liven up

EXAMPLE: *I couldn't go as fast as Jim. His car's a lot more powerful.*
*I couldn't **keep up with** Jim. His car's a lot more powerful.*

1 I'd like to wash and make myself look neat and tidy before we eat.
2 This place needs to be made more exciting. There's nothing to do in the evenings.
3 We've reduced the number of possible candidates for the job to five.
4 They got comfortable and ready to watch the film.
5 The number of reports I have to write before the end of the month is increasing all the time.
6 I was sure that some kind of animal was coming towards me slowly and silently.
7 We are going to plaster and redecorate the spare bedroom so that it's ready for my parents to come and stay.
8 He was furious because he was sure the orange juice had been diluted.

2 Complete each sentence with the correct form of the word in brackets.

1 He's terribly .... He always wants to win. [COMPETITION]
2 This way of working is terribly .... We must change it. [EFFICIENCY]
3 Some of our most important .... industries are in decline. [MANUFACTURE]
4 Tell me what you think about the commercial .... of the proposed project. [VIABLE]
5 I believe that Keynes is the greatest .... to have ever lived. [ECONOMICS]
6 We have had a very .... day today. We got an awful lot done. [PRODUCTION]
7 I hate the way he always .... the conversation. [MONOPOLY]

3 In most lines of the following text, there is either a spelling or punctuation mistake. For each numbered line **1–16**, write the correctly spelled word(s) or show the correct punctuation. Tick those lines which are correct. (Spend no more than 15 minutes on this task.) The exercise begins with three examples.

THE FUTURE OF WORK

	technology
0	Information <u>tecnology</u> has transformed the organisation of work,
00 ✓	but instead of liberating workers from humdrum tasks it
000	can put people out of work and intensify <u>pressure⁄ on</u>
1	those still employed. The idea of a job for life has gone
2	on the scrap heap. In a recent survey, more than a third of
3	middle-class workers feared that they would lose there jobs
4	in the next 12, months and nearly 75% believed that a
5	university-degree would no longer be a springboard to a good
6	career. Increasingly, we are told to be receptive to the possibilitys
7	of part-time working and of retraining in different skills).
8	Information technology may even be making the
9	workplace itself redundant. Offices are extremly expensive,
10	a drain not only on Company profits but also on the time
11	and energy of the employees who spend large parts of the day
12	commuting to and from them. Already more, than two million
13	british employees are 'teleworkers'. Some work from home
14	full-time, keeping in touch with headquaters by e-mail and
15	the phone. Many employees welcome the break with tradition,
16	claiming that teleworking has improved their lives' enormously.

It's only natural

Listening

 1 Look at the pictures of cats above. Brainstorm with other students any words and phrases you associate with cats.

EXAMPLE: *independent ... curious ...*

2 Listen to (and read) this poem. Which of the following is the attitude of the poet to cats?

1 He dislikes them.
2 He is in awe of them.
3 He pities them.
4 He is confused by them.

The Tom-cat

*At midnight in the alley
A Tom-cat comes to wail,
And he chants the hate of a million years
As he swings his snaky tail.*

*Malevolent, bony, brindled,
Tiger and devil and bard,
His eyes are coals from the middle of Hell
And his heart is black and hard.*

*He twists and crouches and capers
And bares his curved sharp claws,
And he sings to the stars of the jungle nights,
Ere cities were, or laws.*

*Beast from a world primeval,
He and his leaping clan,
when the blotched red moon leers over the roofs
Give voice to their scorn of man.*

*He will lie on a rug tomorrow
and lick his silky fur,
And veil the brute in his yellow eyes
And play he's tame, and purr.*

*But at midnight in the alley
he will crouch again and wail,
And beat the time for his demon's song
With a swing of his demon's tail.*

3 Listen to the poem again. Mark the words which receive particular stress. Then read the poem to another student following the same stress pattern.

Exam focus

Paper 3 English in Use: Part 4 (word formation)

About the exam: Part 4 of Paper 3 is designed to test awareness of word formation. The task requires candidates to form an appropriate word, using the given prompt words, to fill each of the gaps in the two short texts. You should spend no more than 15 minutes on this part of the exam.

Suggested procedure

1 Read the whole text through first to get a general idea of the subject.
2 Read the text sentence by sentence, looking at the specific context of each missing word.
3 Decide on the part of speech of the missing word and whether it should have a positive or negative meaning. (Some items may require the addition of a prefix as well as a change to the end of the word.)
4 Write the correct form of each word paying careful attention to accurate spelling.

Exam task

For questions **1–15**, read the two texts below. Use the words in the boxes to the right of the two texts to form **one** word that fits in the same numbered space in the text. The exercise begins with an example (**0**).

ANIMALS	
Most cat or dog owners would swear their pet was virtually human. It's pleased to see you and shows its (**0**) *disapproval* when you go. It may not be particularly (**1**) ... or a genius at mathematics but it sees grass as green and inhabits a rich world of smells (**2**) ... to us. Until recently such notions of a pet's inner life, with (**3**) ... to our own in some ways would have been met with a (**4**) ... sneer in many respected (**5**) ... circles. Nowadays in fact, claiming (**6**) ... for your pets is commonplace. The problem now is providing an adequate (**7**) ... of what this actually means. Is it about having sensations like hunger and pain, or is it more about the ability to be aware that you are experiencing something?	0 APPROVE 1 TALK 2 IMAGINE 3 SIMILAR 4 KNOW 5 SCIENCE 6 CONSCIOUS 7 DEFINE

VOLCANOES	
Midnight on the tiny island of Reunion in the Indian Ocean, and a dazzling (**8**) ... of light and colour is in full swing. For the past three months, Piton de la Fournaise has been showing considerable signs of (**9**) ... , including shooting molten rock into the sky. The flames are (**10**) ... even from space. Volcanoes are notoriously (**11**) ... . But with over 100 eruptions recorded in the past 300 years, this one virtually guarantees a (**12**) ... show. Volcanologists arrived some time ago. Here was an (**13**) ... chance to study the physical (**14**) ... of the earth's centre, as the magma reaches the top and emerges as lava. Many now look on in awe at the ferocious (**15**) ... of the volcano.	8 EXHIBIT 9 ACTIVE 10 VISION 11 PREDICT 12 SENSATION 13 RIVAL 14 COMPOSE 15 STRONG

Reading

▶ P1, Pt3 (multiple choice)

1 Discuss with other students.

1 What different animals do you know which are in serious danger of extinction?
2 What are the reasons for this?

2 Read the following newspaper article and then answer questions 1–6. Give only one answer to each question. (Don't take more than 17–18 minutes to do this question.)

The Tale Of A Tiger

We may soon be living in a world without these fierce and playful big cats. These intimate photos of Sita and her family show us what we could be missing.

She is, in some respects, an unlikely goddess. She is 16 years old. Deer die regularly under the assault of her jaws and claws. From another point of view,
5 her beauty, grace, charisma – and rarity – mark her out as divine. Sita the tigress, named after the Hindu deity of purity and virtue, lives in Bandhavgarh National Park in one of 23 areas set aside
10 as tiger sanctuaries across India. Since 1986 she has produced six litters, totalling 18 cubs. Sadly, half of them have died. One of her daughters drowned in a flood; one son was savaged by an adult male tiger. The others have been lost to poachers.
15 This tragic family history is emblematic of the plight of all tigers. At the beginning of the 20th century there were something like 100,000 roaming Asia and Eastern Europe. Now, it seems incredible but estimated populations are dangerously low; a few thousand at
20 most in the whole of India, just hundreds in other countries such as Malaysia and Russia and as few as 20 or 30 in southern China, where the animal is thought to have got its stripes more than a million years ago. Three entire subspecies – the Caspian, Bali and Javan tigers –
25 were long ago driven into extinction.
Humans, it seems, are largely to blame. Wars, deforestation, farms encroaching on tiger territory, and the hunting of deer and other classic tiger prey, have all done their bit to eliminate these massive cats. More
30 sinister is the demand for body parts for use in traditional Chinese medicine. Poaching to sell the tiger bodies is an attractive career option for some: a single tiger skeleton can earn several times a legitimate annual salary in some places.
35 Not all tigers are killed for their bones. With the escalation of India's population for example, the buffer

zones that used to ring the reserves have been eroded, often by farmers needing land to graze their cattle. Tigers have preyed on the livestock,

40 and as a result, have been seen – not unreasonably – as pests. Farmers are supposed to receive government compensation for lost cattle, but this can be slow to arrive and might cover only a percentage of the animals' value. The World Wide

45 Fund for Nature (WWF) sees both sides: ways must be found to protect people and livestock from tigers, as well as vice versa.

These are not pussycats after all. An adult tigress like Sita gets through an average of 13lb of

50 meat a day, and will kill more for her cubs. 'I saw Sita kill a couple of times,' says Michael Nichols, the photographer who took these photos. 'They only ever kill what they need to eat. I was speaking to a journalist recently who said, "From

55 my observations, the tiger is cruel." I mean, come on, it's a *predator*.'

Many of the photographs were taken with a telephoto lens with the aid of another member of the animal kingdom. 'Sita is not at all comfortable

60 with humans on foot,' says Nichols, 'but if you want to watch her properly, the best thing is to get up on an elephant. She seems to think humans on an elephant are part of the animal.' Other shots were taken using camera traps – devices triggered

65 by animals breaking an infrared beam. 'We put seven cameras around the park and let the tigers take their own pictures.' The results are delightfully intimate: a rare glimpse of how these animals behave in the absence of intrusive humanity. 'I

70 want to get more photos of Sita's cubs though. I'd like to have a proper record of their development.'

The last Nichols heard was that Sita was well, but she was struggling to feed herself and her growing cubs. As he says, 'She might have a year

75 or so left before her life reaches the end of its natural span. That's a kind of survival.'

1   The journalist thinks Sita

   A   is just an ordinary animal.

   B   is an evil force.

   C   has an unusual mix of characteristics.

   D   should be worshipped.

2   The fall in the tiger population globally over the last hundred years has been

   A   unbelievable.

   B   steady.

   C   predictable.

   D   lower than expected.

3   The compensation for the farmers for lost cattle

   A   is often not paid.

   B   is complicated to work out.

   C   depends on where the animal is killed.

   D   is sometimes inadequate.

4   Nichols' general attitude towards the view that the tiger is 'cruel' is one of

   A   shock.

   B   sympathy.

   C   sadness.

   D   exasperation.

5   Some of the photos were taken

   A   by training the tigers to operate the cameras.

   B   while the tigers were unaware of the cameras.

   C   in spite of the tigers' dislike of the cameras.

   D   by tricking the tigers.

6   Nichols feels that in the circumstances Sita has had

   A   a reasonable life.

   B   a very fortunate life.

   C   a miserable life.

   D   a dangerous life.

3   How do you feel about Sita's story? What, if anything, do you think should be done about the plight of these tigers?

Grammar plus: reported speech (advanced features)

1 Look at the reported speech sentences below and then find the direct speech versions in the article on pp.168–169.

> 1 It has been suggested that the tiger is 'cruel'.
> 2 He told us Sita wasn't comfortable with humans on foot.
> 3 He recommended that we should get up on an elephant to watch Sita properly.
> 4 He explained that they put seven cameras around the park.
> 5 He says that he wants to get more photos of Sita's cubs.
> 6 He believed that she might have a year or so left.

2 Compare the reported and direct speech pairs that you have found. Then match them to the appropriate rule below which they exemplify.

1 If the reporting verb is in a past tense, certain modals (e.g. *would*, *should*, *could*, *might*, *ought*) will not always change their form.
2 It is not absolutely necessary to report past tenses with a shift into the past perfect if the sequence of events is clear.
3 After present, future and present perfect reporting verbs, tenses don't usually change.
4 The conjunction *that* is often dropped (after common reporting verbs) in informal speech. (However, it is not usually dropped after nouns.)
5 Certain reporting verbs can be followed by *should* (or more formally, the subjunctive) e.g. *advise*, *agree*, *recommend* etc.
6 Certain reporting verbs can be used in the passive, introduced by *it* e.g. *announce*, *believe*, *suggest* etc. (This is when the speaker does not want to take personal responsibility for a statement or may be reporting the views of a group of people.)

▶ Grammar reference p.196

3 Four of the following sentences contain a mistake connected with one of the rules from Exercise 2. Find the mistakes and correct them.

1 We agreed that we all spend the night at Jim's house.
2 It believed that the poachers responsible for the recent killings all live locally.
3 The kids said they loved the trip to the safari park.
4 He disagreed with my view it was wrong to put animals in zoos.
5 She said that if she had had more time she could have helped me fix the car.
6 They recommended that we should go home immediately.
7 It has announced that the government will raise interest rates next week.
8 They said it would be good if I could start the new job immediately.

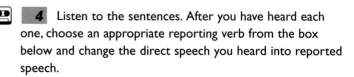 **4** Listen to the sentences. After you have heard each one, choose an appropriate reporting verb from the box below and change the direct speech you heard into reported speech.

> congratulate admit introduce warn remind invite decide advise complain

EXAMPLE: *She invited them both to spend the night at her house.*

 5 Say the following sentences to another student using direct speech. Use appropriate intonation. Then listen to possible answers.

1 He conceded that he had been wrong to get angry.
2 He boasted that he had earned over £100,000 the previous year.
3 She claimed never to have met him before.
4 She retorted that she knew how to keep a secret.
5 His father urged him to think about what he was doing.
6 He stressed that this would be her last chance.
7 He muttered something about needing to change things completely.
8 He whispered her name over and over again.

 6 Listen to these two sides of the same story. Then write a brief summary of what was said using reported speech. Finally, compare your versions with that of another student. Are they essentially the same?

EXAMPLE: *The man said that he and his girlfriend had been getting on really well but the woman had a different view. She thought that ...*

Vocabulary: text-referring words

1 Look at the extract below from the text on pp.168–169. Which three verbs repeat the idea of 'dying' but in a different form?

> Sadly, half of them have died. One of her daughters drowned in a flood; one son was savaged by an adult male tiger. The others have been lost to poachers.

2 Here are some nouns which can be used to repeat (and summarise) a previous idea. Complete each of the sentences below with the most appropriate word from the box.

> trend situation view aspect issue
> problem question topic

1 Should we increase the penalties for cruelty to animals? This is a(n) .... the government must consider urgently.
2 Global warming is having serious effects on weather conditions around the world. This .... looks set to worsen.
3 Everyone is talking about the forthcoming royal wedding. It is a(n) .... that has gripped the nation's interest.
4 Inflation is rising, as are taxes. In fact the general financial .... is looking pretty grim.
5 One important .... of modern society is that women will be successful in their work life as well as their home life.
6 Many newspapers are saying that the Prime Minister should resign. This .... is being echoed in recent opinion polls around the country.
7 More and more people are working from home. This .... has led to individuals feeling isolated and cut off from their colleagues.
8 They have spent weeks discussing what to do with the growing amount of nuclear waste. This .... has already caused immense controversy.

3 Read the following paragraphs. Find pairs of text-referring words/phrases which have similar meaning.

EXAMPLE: *The Chief Inspector this morning spoke to journalists about the recent allegations of corruption amongst the police. His <u>reaction</u> to the charges was to flatly deny any kind of cover up and to question the motives of those making the accusations. At the end of his <u>response</u> to the press he said there would be a full-scale investigation by the local police authority.*

1

POLLUTION

> *Pollution in our cities appears to be getting worse and worse. The government recognises that the current situation is unacceptable and has pledged that something will be done about this appalling state of affairs.*

2

MEMORANDUM

To _____

From _____

```
The student committee has come up with
an idea to deal with the problem of
new students not being able to afford
books for their courses. The key seems
to be to encourage leaving students to
pass on their books to new students.
One possible solution then might be
for the students' union to arrange to
buy books from old students and sell
them on cheaply to new students.
```

Listening

▶ P4, Pt2 (note taking)

1 Discuss with other students.

1 What are Vesuvius and Krakatoa? Which countries are they in? What else do you know about them?
2 Name different types of natural disasters that you know. Do you know any actual examples? What happened?

2 You will hear part of a talk about volcanoes. As you listen, complete the notes for questions **1–8. Listen very carefully as you will hear the recording ONCE only.**

VOLCANOES

After-effects of Krakatoa eruption:
a) drop in world's temperature
b) (1) ....
c) ash and aerosol circled the equator

Number of volcanoes that have erupted over last 10,000 years: (2) ....

Country where first eruption recorded:
(3) ....

Number of people threatened by volcanic eruption:
(4) ....

Possible reasons for volcanic eruption:
a) changes in sea level
b) positioning of (5) ....
c) underlying earthquake patterns
d) ground deformation
e) release of (6) ....

Official time allowed for evacuation around area of Vesuvius: (7) ....

Dobran's suggestions:
a) advise (8) ....
b) build 30m high barriers

3 Discuss with other students. What do you think of Dobran's suggestions? Are they sensible or alarmist?

Vocabulary: word + prepositions (2)

1 Complete each of these sentences with a preposition from the box.

| to   for (×2)   by   of (×2)   about |

1 We are due .... another major volcanic eruption.
2 Just how concerned should we be .... this?
3 We were shocked .... the attitude of the government to the danger.
4 He was highly critical .... their emergency plans.
5 They are totally indifferent .... the latest research findings.
6 Who is responsible .... financing further research into this area?
7 The lava is capable .... moving much faster than you imagine.

2 Match the halves of the sentences below.

EXAMPLE: *1 f)*

1 He was terribly ashamed
2 Many students are eligible
3 You know that you are immune
4 This course is open to anyone irrespective
5 Scientists are completely baffled
6 The one thing which was absent
7 My young niece seems to be addicted
8 I'm feeling a bit anxious
9 I'm sure there's something wrong

a) to chickenpox if you've already had it once.
b) by the latest set of test results.
c) from the discussion was any kind of reference to objective facts.
d) to the computer game I bought her for Christmas.
e) about travelling around India on my own.
f) of the way he had behaved at the party.
g) with my car. It's making a funny noise.
h) of previous education or experience.
i) for some kind of financial support.

3 Look again at the sentences in Exercises 1 and 2. In your vocabulary notebook, list which prepositions follow different adjectives.

EXAMPLE 1: *to be ashamed **of** something*

4 Complete the following sentences.

EXAMPLE: 1 *Sometimes I wonder if I'm addicted to coffee. I probably drink six cups a day!*

1 Sometimes I wonder if I'm addicted to ...
2 I occasionally feel a little anxious about ...
3 There's definitely something wrong with ...
4 I feel completely indifferent to ...
5 My father/mother/best friend is quite critical of ...
6 One thing I am very concerned about is ...
7 I don't think I am capable of ...

English in Use

▶ P3, Pt5 (register transfer)

For questions 1–13, read the following notes left by someone preparing an instruction leaflet on caring for cats. Use the information in the notes to complete the numbered gaps in the instruction leaflet which follows. **Use no more than two words for each gap.** The words you need do not occur in the notes. The exercise begins with an example (**0**).

NOTES

- Cats or kittens can be great BUT you need to look after them well.

- It's a serious business to have a cat or kitten so you do need to think about what it means e.g. cost of food and seeing the vet (vaccinations!) + making sure he will be looked after if you go away.

- To help your cat stay healthy you need to feed it properly — good cat foods are absolutely fine. Remember that dried cat food provides the right amount of all the important things your cat needs so this is what he should be eating most of the time. (Make sure your cat doesn't get fussy about what types of food he will and won't eat.) To get rid of fur balls, try giving him oily fish. And for a treat let him have an egg but REMEMBER eggs need to be cooked otherwise danger of poisoning.

INSTRUCTION LEAFLET

A cat or kitten makes a very worthwhile pet, (**0**) <u>providing</u> that he is properly (**1**) ... for. However, before you take on the (**2**) ... of owning one, it is (**3**) ... to give serious thought to what it will involve. For example, there is the cost of feeding and veterinary (**4**) ... (including the cost of vaccinations) and you will need to ensure adequate (**5**) ... for when you are away.

In terms of keeping your cat in good physical (**6**) ... , it is totally (**7**) ... to give your cat a regular diet of better-quality cat foods. In general, high-quality dried food gives the best (**8**) ... of minerals and vitamins and should therefore be the (**9**) ... of your cat's diet. (Remember not to let your cat (**10**) ... to you which brand or flavour he will eat.) Oily fish can be given as this is very good for the (**11**) ... of fur balls. Most cats also like an occasional egg but it must be (**12**) ... that this must be cooked so as to (**13**) ... the risk of salmonella poisoning.

Speaking: sounding interested

1 Listen to these three people giving their opinions about zoos.

1 Which one sounds the most involved in what they are saying?
2 Which one doesn't sound very interested?
3 What effect does this have on the listener?

2 Discuss this question with another student. How do you feel about the role of zoos in society?

- Begin the conversation by expressing your view in a bored way.
- Then change to sound mildly interested in what you are saying.
- Finally change to sound interested, engaged and involved in the conversation.

3 Work with a different student. Student A refer to the questions on p.216, Student B refer to the questions on p.220. Take it in turns to ask your partner one of the questions. Respond to the questions you are asked in a positive, interested way!

Writing: report (2)

1 Look at this task and the three plans below. Which plan do you think is best? Why?

TASK

You were contacted by an international research company looking at sporting activities in your area. You agreed to interview fifty people using the questionnaire below and to write a report describing the existing level of participation in sporting activities in your community including any factors which discourage people from taking part in sport and recommending ways of encouraging more people to take up a sport.

QUESTIONNAIRE ON PARTICIPATION IN SPORTING ACTIVITIES
Do you take part in sporting activities? If so, which ones?
What prevents you from taking part or from taking part more?

Please submit your report to Dr Betty Nurchison, Quality Assurance, River Drive, Cardiff.

Write your report.

Plan A
1 Survey questions
2 Description of people questioned
3 Problems with survey
4 Analysis of survey results

Plan B
1 Description of the problem
2 Survey results
3 Reasons for popularity of football and jogging
4 Best sports for healthy living

Plan C
1 Introduction
2 Participation in sports
3 Factors preventing fuller participation
4 Recommendations

2   Here is some advice for writing reports. There are eight Dos and one Don't. Can you find the one negative piece of advice?

1   begin by stating the purpose of your report
2   summarise information succinctly by using invented statistics
3   use lists of points where appropriate
4   use footnotes for extra information, definitions and clarification
5   divide your report into sections according to the input
6   develop the ideas in the task input
7   use clear layout with headings
8   let your report look like a discursive composition
9   use an impersonal, formal style

3   Read the model answer to the Exercise 1 task on p.208 Writing reference.

1   Which plan from Exercise 1 did it follow?
2   Check your Dos and Don'ts from Exercise 2.

4   Look at these two tasks. Decide which one you are going to answer.

TASK 1

An international organisation has asked you to write a report for a survey it is carrying out into trends in weather change around the world. They would like you to describe the main seasons in your country and typical weather conditions associated with these seasons. You should also describe any changes in weather patterns over the last 25 years that you are aware of and suggestions as to possible causes. They have asked you to indicate any consequences of these changes in weather and make any recommendations as to action that you believe should be taken.

Write your report in about 250 words.

TASK 2

Your school/college is considering 'adopting' a particular animal in danger of extinction. This would involve giving money and distributing information about the plight of the animal. You have been asked to select one particular animal that you believe is at serious risk of extinction and to write a report describing the animal and its habitat, the reasons why it could become extinct and any action that you think that could help save its future. You should conclude your report by saying why you believe this animal in particular deserves the support of your school/college.

Write your report in about 250 words.

5   Look at the useful language section on p.209 Writing reference. Make a note of three or four new phrases or sentences that you are going to try and include in your report.

6   Think carefully about who your report is for and what it is trying to achieve. Then, write your report, making sure that you:

- describe the subject and reason for your report in your introductory paragraph.
- divide your work into paragraphs. Each paragraph should have a separate purpose. (You may wish to use sub-headings.)
- use some of the expressions in the Useful Language box on p.209 Writing reference.
- write your report in a neutral or formal style.
- use linking words to connect sentences and/or paragraphs in a logical way.
- do everything that the question asks you to do.

Listening: weather

▶ P4, Pt4 (multiple matching)

You will hear five short extracts in which various people are talking about weather conditions. **Remember that you must complete both tasks as you listen. You will hear the recording twice.**

TASK ONE

For questions **1–5**, match the extracts as you hear them with the people, listed **A–H**.

A   a tour guide

B   a football player

C   a doctor

D   a holidaymaker

E   a TV weatherman

F   a gardener

G   a mountaineer

H   a politician

	1
	2
	3
	4
	5

TASK TWO

For questions **6–10**, match the extracts as you hear them with the descriptions of the speakers, listed **A–H**.

A   aware of a kind of illness

B   hoping for a good result

C   frustrated with the delay

D   surprised by how extreme the weather conditions are

E   angry with the weather forecasters

F   wanting to avoid a dangerous situation

G   planning practical precautions

H   enjoying the weather conditions

	6
	7
	8
	9
	10

Grammar check: countable/uncountable nouns

1   Look at the alternatives in the sentences below. Which is possible/likely? Which is not? Why?

1   I need some advice/advices about how to look after a kitten.

2   This bed is incredibly heavy. Is it made from an iron/iron?

3   There hasn't been much news/many news about the recent volcanic eruptions in central Africa.

4   We had a very interesting time/very interesting time when we visited Vesuvius last month.

5   We are only just beginning to learn about the true extent of space/the space.

6   We need additional information/an additional information about this before we decide what to do.

7   They want to do research/a research into the possibility of time travel through black holes.

8   Oh look. There's a hair/hair in my soup!

9   A travel/Travel is one of my main interests.

10   Would you like a coffee/coffee before we start working?

2   Work with other students. What nouns do you know which are usually uncountable? What nouns do you know which can be both countable and uncountable but with different meanings?

3   Work with other students. Identify the uncountable nouns in the following quotations. Then, discuss your opinions of the quotations.

> 1   *Advice is seldom welcome; and those who want it the most always like it the least.* (Lord Chesterfield 'Letters to his son' 1771, 22/2/1748)
>
> 2   *We have no more right to consume happiness without producing it than to consume wealth without producing it.* (George Bernard Shaw 'Candida' [1898])
>
> 3   *Love doesn't just sit there, like a stone, it has to be made, like bread; remade all the time, made new.* (Ursula K. Le Guin, 'The Lathe of Heaven' (1971) chap. 10)

▶ *Exam Maximiser*   M

1 Complete each of the following sentences with an appropriate reporting verb in the correct form. (You have been given the first letter in each case.)

1 They c.................... me warmly on my recent promotion.
2 We all u.................... him to change his mind but he paid no attention.
3 She b.................... to anyone who would listen about how well she had done in the exam.
4 He finally c.................... that I was right and that he should have gone to the police straightaway.
5 My parents w.................... me not to accept lifts from anyone I didn't know.
6 'Why didn't you r.................... me that it was Dad's birthday?'
7 He w.................... something to me but I couldn't hear what it was. There was too much noise in the room.
8 He c.................... bitterly that no one ever listened to his opinion.

2 Suggest an alternative word or phrase to replace the underlined text-referring word. It should convey the same meaning.

1 This state of affairs can't go on much longer.
2 This could be the answer that we've been looking for.
3 This is not the only side to the problem that we are concerned about.
4 This reaction by the minister is typical of his uncaring attitude.
5 This is a subject which has provoked much interest in the media.
6 This opinion is not one shared by the main trades unions.
7 This tendency for young couples to both work and employ a child minder is causing concern.
8 This matter has been the source of intense controversy.

3 For gaps 1–6, read the following text and then choose from the list A–J the best phrase given below it to fill each of the spaces.

ASTEROID ATTACK

It was just very recently that astronomers warned that a large asteroid, known as 1997 XF11, might hit Earth in the year 2028 (**0**) *J* . So, just how concerned should we be about this?

First of all we need to understand (**1**) ... . The asteroid belt, which lies between Mars and Jupiter, consists of lumps of rock and ice which scientists used to think came into being after a planet exploded. Today most scientists believe that the asteroids are fragments left over from material (**2**) ... when the other planets in the solar system were being formed. Nasa estimates that 1,000 to 4,000 asteroids larger than half a mile in diameter cross the Earth's orbit. Of these, scientists have identified 108 PHOs (Potentially Hazardous Objects) which may pose a threat to mankind.

The danger actually arises from the kinetic energy released when one of these asteroids, (**3**) ... , enters the Earth's atmosphere. In fact, it is believed that around 140 large asteroids have hit the Earth since it was formed.

For example, in 1908, a fragment of ice weighing around 100,000 tonnes exploded above the sparsely inhabited Lake Tunguska region in Siberia, releasing a fireball (**4**) ... . This resulted in an area of 1,000 square kilometres being flattened. In 1994, a meteor skimming through the Earth's atmosphere was spotted by US spy satellites and mistakenly identified as a possible nuclear missile.

According to Nasa scientists, the chances of being killed directly or indirectly by an asteroid are greater than the chances of being killed by wild animals, fireworks, terrorist bombs and airline hijackings. In fact Dr Victor Clube, an astrophysicist at Oxford University, says that civilisations have a good chance (**5**) ... . In theory, however, a potentially dangerous asteroid millions of miles away would only need a small nudge (**6**) ... . Scientists believe, for example, that a nuclear warhead detonated just off the surface of the asteroid could divert it into a different orbit.

A with 2,000 times the force of the Hiroshima bomb
B and it takes four years to circle the sun
C of being devastated every 3,000 to 4,000 years
D exactly what asteroids are
E their mass is less than that of the moon
F because of their motion in relation to the stars
G that failed to fuse together millions of years ago
H to be shunted into a safer orbit
I travelling at speeds of around 45,000 miles per hour

J and cause a global catastrophe

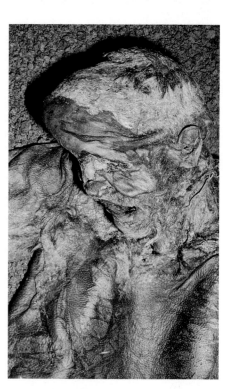

UNIT
15 It's all in the past

Reading

▶ P1, Pt2 (gapped text)

1 Discuss with other students.

What do you think is the connection between these two pictures?

2 Read the following article quickly and answer these questions.

1 What is one possible explanation of the 'bog murders'?
2 What does the writer fear may happen to the bogs?

THE LIVING DEAD

It was just a flap of skin hanging out of the peat. It was soft and wrinkled but unmistakably human skin. It had actually come to light when one of the workers
5 employed in cutting the peat (used in domestic gardens) had thrown what looked like a piece of wood on to the ground. As the muck bounced off it, the wood was revealed to be the lower part of a human leg with a foot attached.
10 Rick Turner, the county archaeologist was called and spent the next morning searching in the bog.

What Rick Turner was to unearth following the discovery of that stray human leg would
15 become known as Lindow Man, alias Pete Marsh, the almost complete remains of someone estimated to have died nearly 2,000 years ago. The find would change Turner's life. His name would be associated permanently
20 with one of the best-known archaeological finds in Britain.

(1 ———)

In the end, it was not just Turner but more than 50 scientific specialists who contributed to the British Museum's first substantial
25 report on Lindow Man. And while 'Pete Marsh' excited the press and television (more than ten million viewers watched the first of two BBC programmes on the find), he gripped academics too. He was at the centre of the type
30 of multi-disciplinary project that has come to characterise the best of modern archaeology.

(2 ———)

Hi-tech scientific analysis of the remnants of this last meal indicated it had been heated briefly to 200–250°C – too hot for an oven but
35 achievable on a griddle. He was a healthy, well-built man about 5'6" tall, aged 25, with good teeth and fingernails. His short beard and moustache had been trimmed with scissors. He was naked except for a fox fur armband
40 worn just above his right elbow.

And his mode of death was, to say the least, curious. The first thing to be noticed was a hole in the top of his head. And when his chin was gingerly lifted away from his chest, a neat
45 cut in his throat was revealed.

(3 ———)

In 1984, Lindow Man was thought to be the first bog body found in Britain. But it was well known that there were many such remains elsewhere in Europe. The new British find,
50 and the large scientific project that grew up around it, inspired archaeologists to take a fresh look at these remarkable discoveries, of which nearly 2,000 have now been catalogued. Who were all these people? How did they get
55 into the bogs, and why are they preserved so well?

(4 ———)

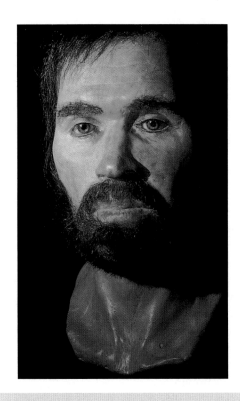

3 Read the article again and choose which of the paragraphs below fit into the numbered gaps. There is one extra paragraph which does not fit in any of the gaps.

A In addition to these, the forensic report on the body identified two further injuries, each of which on its own would probably have been fatal. The head had been hit hard enough to send splinters of skull deep into the brain and the man had also received a heavy blow in the centre of his back, breaking a rib.

B But for what possible reason might these individuals end up in the bogs in the first place? The Danish archaeologist P. V. Glob, in a popular book entitled *The Bog People* explored the notion of a bog religion. He noticed that while bog bodies ranged from several thousands of years old to almost modern, many seemed to originate from just a few centuries either side of the birth of Christ.

C It came to be realised that his clothes actually provide a unique insight into bronze-age European dress. First, he was wrapped in an undergarment of coarsely-woven wool with an embroidered hem that hung to his knees. Then, over this he wore a skin cape, threaded close around his neck.

D Today, he still feels deep affection for the man whose remains he saved then; he often talks of feeling 'protective', as if the deceased were a son, or a lost brother. It was unclear at first but it soon became obvious to Turner that he had stumbled on an extremely rare and important find.

E This, however, is just one strand of a huge debate raging in the archaeological world and, unfortunately, opportunities to resolve the issues with new finds and modern analyses are fading rapidly. Peat cutting exposed the bodies. But now industrial peat quarrying and our huge appetite for garden peat compost has all but removed the bogs.

F In order to begin one's investigation into this weird world of bog bodies, it is important to realise that while skin, hair, nails and internal organs can be exceptionally well preserved, bones are soft and pliable, and may not even survive. It is the leathery, tanned skin that keeps things together. A good bog body is literally a bag of bones and flesh.

G Many things came of this work. A concentration of certain minerals on Lindow Man's skin suggested he had been painted green or blue, and further research indicated that this might have been what Caesar was referring to in a famous passage about painted Britons. The contents of his stomach were well-preserved. And it appears that they consisted largely of a chapati-like bread made from two varieties of wheat and barley.

It used to be thought that the key to preservation was peat bog water. The natural acidity dissolves the minerals
60 in bones, leaving only the soft tissues. With no oxygen, on the other hand, corrupting bacteria cannot act. Recent research has revealed another and more important factor, the ubiquitous
65 peat-building Sphagnum moss. This plant releases a chemical called sphagnan, which both immobilises bacteria and tans the bodies.
(5 ———)
He noted as well that the Celts of
70 northern Europe were said to drown deserters, cowards etc. in swamps. To them, human sacrifice was a common punishment. Many of the best preserved bog bodies, it seems, were
75 spring sacrifices of such people to the Mother Goddess.
(6 ———)
With the loss of unique environments and ecosystems go the loss of the archaeology, and of the bogs as
80 repositories of myth and mystery. Unfortunately, an appreciation of this will increasingly have to depend on books and museums. Unless the government can move rapidly to rein
85 in the exploitation, the bogs themselves will be but part of the myth. Who then are the bog murderers?

Grammar plus: passives (advanced features)

1 Read the following news item reporting the original discovery of Lindow Man. Answer these questions.

1 What problem has Rick Turner had since the discovery?
2 Why has this discovery led to some controversy?

Announcer: <u>It is believed</u> that one of the most important finds in recent archaeological history has been made in the middle of a Cheshire bog.

The body was first discovered yesterday morning as workers were cutting and removing peat from the bog. As one piece of wood was thrown aside, it soon became apparent that this was actually the lower part of a human leg and Rick Turner, the county archaeologist, <u>was called</u>.

Apparently, Turner informed a local journalist soon after about the find and since then <u>has been besieged</u> by reporters for the national papers.

This finding has stirred up some controversy after the government's announcement last week that funding for archaeological research <u>would be significantly reduced</u> next year.

2 Look at the news item again. A number of examples of the passive have been underlined. Match each of the uses below with one of the examples in the news script.

1 We use the passive when the active form would require the use of an indefinite or vague pronoun e.g. *someone, they, people.*
2 We often use the passive with verbs such as *think, believe, know, say* to give a general opinion.
3 Using the passive means we can make a statement sound more impersonal and less connected to the speaker.
4 Using the passive means we can avoid an awkward change of subject in the middle of the sentence.

3 Decide whether it is possible to make the underlined part of the following sentences passive. If so, make the transformation.

EXAMPLE: *<u>Someone removed several valuable items</u> from the local history museum last night. > Several valuable items **were removed** ...*

1 Unfortunately, <u>management is going to make over 20% of the workforce</u> redundant.
2 <u>Someone will be along shortly</u> to answer all your questions.
3 <u>They say that</u> archaeologists are close to discovering the secret of the construction of the Pyramids.
4 <u>People have been asking</u> if there is any chance of your giving a talk about life in Roman Britain.
5 <u>Everybody believes that</u> the government has made a terrible mistake.
6 She was worrying about how she would pay the phone bill and then the next day <u>the people at the Inland Revenue sent her a large cheque</u> through the post for wrongly paid tax.
7 <u>You must clean up your room</u> before you can go out with your friends.

4 Listen to the news item in Exercise 1. Then do the following tasks.

1 Practise reading it aloud with appropriate stress/intonation for a TV news report.
2 Construct a report for the TV evening news. Use as many examples of the passive as possible/appropriate. Report on either:
   a) an exciting new archaeological or scientific discovery.
   b) another important news event e.g. a famous criminal has been captured.
3 Practise reading your report aloud. Read your report to other students. They should note down how many examples of the passive you managed to include.

EXAMPLE: *Last night, near Stonehenge, archaeologists are believed to have finally found definite proof that ...*

▶ Grammar reference p.195

Listening: a world language

▶ P4, Pt1 (sentence completion)

1 Do you think it is possible to create a 'world language'? Do you know of any attempts where this was done in the past? What happened?

2 You will hear part of a talk about 'a language for the world'. For questions **1–8**, fill in the missing information. You will hear the recording twice.

St. Hildegard's language had its own vocabulary and [_____] **1**

Wilkins's new language was completely different from any [_____] **2**

People tried [_____] **3** artificial languages at the end of the 19th century.

The main problem with Volapük was the way it depended on [_____] **4**

Zamenhof's idea of Esperanto came from his childhood where there was considerable [_____] **5**

People thought that Esperanto might improve the chances for [_____] **6**

The Japanese find Esperanto easy although its structures are completely [_____] **7**

There have been both magazines, books and [_____] **8** produced in Esperanto.

3 What different languages have you attempted to learn? Which ones were easier to learn and which were more difficult? Why?

English in Use

▶ P3, Pt3 (error correction, extra word)

1 Discuss with other students.

1 How long do you think people have been wearing jeans? Who originally wore them?
2 How fashionable are jeans nowadays? Do you wear them? If so, when?
3 Do you think there is much difference between all the different brand names?

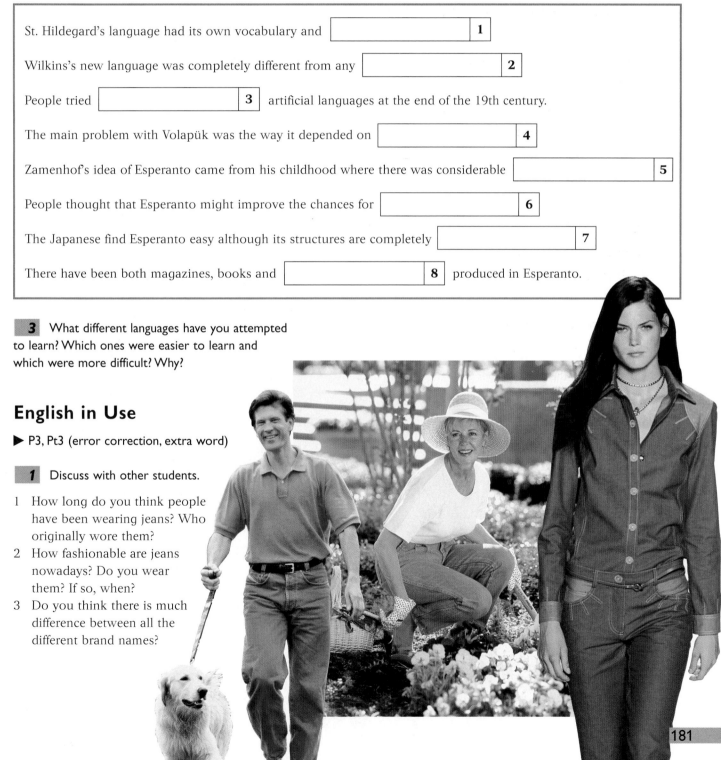

2 In **most** lines of the following text, there is **one** unnecessary word. It is either grammatically incorrect or does not fit in with the sense of the text. For each numbered line **1–16**, find this word and underline it. Some lines are correct. Indicate these lines with a tick (✓). The exercise begins with two examples (**0**) and (**00**).

BLUE GOLD

0	In 1853, a 24-year-old immigrant from Bavaria <u>was</u> named Levi
00 ✓	Strauss arrived in San Francisco, intending to make his fortune by
1	selling out supplies to the throngs of miners who arrived daily in the
2	big city to outfit themselves before heading off to the gold fields. Levi
3	came up to be a well-known and respected figure around the city and
4	immersed himself in the business, cultural and religious life of San Francisco.
5	But despite of his stature he always insisted that his employees call
6	him Levi and not Mr Strauss. In 1872, Levi received a letter from Jacob Davis,
7	a tailor from Nevada. Davis was one of those Levi's regular customers
8	and had hit himself upon the ingenious idea of strengthening jeans
9	with copper rivets. Legend has it made that Davis was fed up with
10	repairing miners' trousers over and over again because they were filled
11	their pockets with heavy rock samples. Davis and Strauss patented up a
12	method of 'fastening the corners of pockets in wearing apparel in order
13	to prevent them from tearing' in 1873. By the time of the Strauss's death
14	in 1902, Levi's jeans which had made their inventor a millionaire. But he
15	could hardly have guessed that by the 1970s, his heavy-duty work clothes
16	would have to become fashionable garb for everyone, including princesses!

---

3 Look at the 'extra words' you have identified. What types of words are they? Are there any other types of words that are often tested in this part of Paper 3?

Speaking

Discuss with other students.

1 Is it important to have a knowledge of history? If so, why?

2 What 'history' do you think children should be taught at school? (e.g. history of their country/other countries)

3 What kind of 'history' were you taught? Could it have been/ be taught more effectively or interestingly?

Grammar check: *have/get something done*

1 Complete the second sentence in each pair below. Use the structures *have something done* or *get something done*. The second sentence should have approximately the same meaning as the first sentence.

EXAMPLE: *Someone stole our mobile phone last night.*
*We had **our mobile phone stolen last night.***

1 My car is being repaired at the moment.
I'm ...
2 He ordered me to get my hair cut.
'Get ...
3 I'll make sure the police arrest you if you do that again.
I'll have ...
4 Someone eventually came and fixed my computer.
I eventually got ...
5 I refuse to allow you to use my house as a hotel.
I won't have ...
6 It will take me until 9p.m. to do my homework.
I won't get ...

2 Consider the examples in Exercise 1 and decide which one of the following rules is not true.

1 *Have/get something done* usually describes a service performed for us by someone else.
2 *Have/get something done* can also refer to 'experience', particularly to describe something unfortunate that happens to someone.
3 *Get something done* can be used to mean 'finish doing something'.
4 *Get something done* is often used in orders and with imperatives.
5 *Get something done* is used in more formal contexts than *have something done*.

3 Imagine you had unlimited money. Make a note of four or five things that you would have done for you. Then tell another student and see how similar your lists are.

EXAMPLE: *Firstly, I would have my flat cleaned from top to bottom. Then, I would have my hair cut by a top stylist.*

► *Exam Maximiser* M

Vocabulary: idiomatic language of talking/communication

1 Look at the underlined expressions and say what you think they might mean from the context.

1 His mode of death was, <u>to say the least</u>, curious.
2 I hate these kind of parties. I'm just no good at <u>making small talk</u> with people I don't know.
3 Steven Jenkins was extremely naughty today. I had to give him a real <u>talking-to</u>!
4 Will you please <u>get to the point</u>! I haven't got all day you know!
5 It's so boring when you two <u>talk shop</u>. Not everyone works in the computer business you know!
6 I'm sorry but I couldn't <u>make head or tail</u> of what he was saying. I think he enjoys using really obscure words that I've never heard of!
7 I think she's <u>got the wrong end of the stick</u>. She thinks her boss wants to get rid of her but I'm sure he's actually thinking of giving her a promotion!
8 He just talks and talks and talks. I couldn't <u>get a word in edgeways</u>.
9 I think we've been <u>talking at cross-purposes</u>. I was talking about my brother-in-law not my brother!
10 I hate the way he always <u>talks down to me</u> as if I've never done this kind of work before.

2 Work with another student. Describe a situation. Your partner should guess the expression you are illustrating.

EXAMPLE: Student A: *I was having this discussion with my brother and his friend. As usual my brother was going on and on about what he thought. And it was impossible for me to actually say anything.*

Student B: *You mean ... you couldn't **get a word in edgeways**!*

3 Discuss these questions with other students.

1 How do you feel about making small talk in social situations? Are you good or bad at it?
2 Do you know anyone who always takes ages to get to the point? How does that make you feel?
3 How do you feel about people talking shop when they aren't at work? Do you ever do it?
4 If a child has been caught shoplifting, do you think it is enough for them to be given a good talking-to?
5 Do you know anyone who regularly talks down to you? How does that make you feel?

Exam focus

Paper 4 Listening: Part 4 (multiple choice)

About the exam: In Part 4 of Paper 4 you will listen to a series of five short extracts of about 30 seconds each. You will hear the five extracts twice. The speakers will all be talking about a similar topic. You will either have a multiple-matching task or a multiple-choice task. In this section you will focus on the multiple-choice task (cf. p.114 for the Exam focus on the multiple-matching task).

Suggested procedure

1 Read the stem and the options for each question before you listen. (Remember, there will be two questions for each extract.)
2 Listen out for key words which relate to the options. Listen to the complete context in which you hear the keyword; sometimes they can mislead you.
3 Make sure you don't leave any question unanswered.

Exam task

You will hear five short extracts in which different people are talking about their memories of school and exams. For questions 1–10 choose the correct option **A**, **B** or **C**.

1 The speaker is still disturbed by memories of

A not preparing enough for an exam.
B a particularly difficult exam.
C answering the wrong question in an exam.

2 How does the speaker feel?

A angry about exams in general
B surprised by the impact of the exam
C confused about the significance of the dream

3 What happened while the speaker was supposed to be revising?

A She fell asleep.
B She would walk around the house.
C She became distracted.

4 What's the speaker's attitude to her parents?

A She's sure that they had the right approach.
B She would definitely not treat her children in the same way.
C She can see some benefits from the way they treated her.

5 Students at the school were motivated because

A they had interesting projects to work on.
B they didn't have exams.
C they could make some of their own decisions.

6 The speaker feels that his school

A prepared him well for later life.
B made him work harder than other schools.
C gave the pupils too much responsibility.

7 The speaker's approach to exams

A appears to have been largely successful.
B has caused her some serious problems.
C was completely based on luck.

8 In retrospect, the speaker

A is sure her approach was mistaken.
B has some doubts about her approach.
C is entirely positive about her approach.

9 The speaker's experience of school

A appears to have prepared him well for later life.
B was overwhelmingly positive.
C was strongly affected by his substitute family.

10 The speaker's commitment to school was because

A of an inadequate home life.
B he was a very good all-rounder.
C he wanted to be popular with the other pupils.

Vocabulary: revision

Work in groups of four or five.

1 Write down on separate pieces of paper: two nouns, two verbs, two adjectives which you have learnt recently.
2 Mix all the words together in a pile.
3 In turn, take a word from the top of the pile. Tell the group whether it is a noun, verb etc. and illustrate the word without speaking. The first person to guess the word correctly then illustrates the next word for the others to guess.

Speaking

1 Discuss with other students.

1 Your worst memory of a test or exam. Why was it so bad?
2 Your best memory of a test or exam. Why did you feel like this?
3 Any general strategies you have for preparing for tests or exams a) months before b) weeks before c) days before d) the day before.
4 Any special things you do on the day of an exam.
5 If you think it is a good or bad idea to talk about an exam immediately afterwards with other people who took the exam.
6 How you deal with disappointing results.

2 Look at these ideas for helping you revise. With another student decide which three ideas you think are the most useful.

REVISION TIPS

Typical mistakes
Go through old compositions and homework. Make a list of typical mistakes that you make so that you can try and avoid making them when it comes to the actual exam.

Fitness
It's important to get exercise. Exercise relaxes you and stimulates the brain and nervous system. Plan a routine which includes time off for a sport or exercise you enjoy.

Immersion
Make sure that you immerse yourself in English just before the exam. Read books, magazines and newspapers in English. Watch British films or TV if possible.

Visualisation
Take in a deep breath and hold for as long as is comfortable. Release the breath and feel all the tension leave your mind and body. Close your eyes and imagine there is a large coloured switch marked 'Study with ease'. Now, mentally turn on that switch, open your eyes and return to your work.

Practice exams
Do some complete CAE practice exams. Pay careful attention to doing each paper within the allocated time. If necessary, look again at the Exam focus sections in earlier units of *Advanced Gold*.

Nutrition
Blood sugar control is crucial for both revision and on exam days. Eat little and often – every two hours or so. Eat starchy carbohydrates rather than sugary foods such as chocolate bars. Wholemeal bread, bananas, raw vegetables, high-fibre crispbreads are good snacks.

Memorisation
Learn by heart some of the expressions in the useful language boxes in the Writing reference section of *Advanced Gold*. These may help you and give you confidence when you come to answer the questions in CAE Paper 2 Writing.

Posture
Sitting at a desk all day is not a good idea and it's beneficial to have breaks and change positions. Every so often, lie flat on the floor with knees bent and head supported. Relax for five to ten minutes and allow the spine to re-align.

Writing: Paper 2 overview

1 In Paper 2 (Writing) there are two parts. You have to do two tasks: a compulsory one in Part 1 and one from a choice of four in Part 2. You have two hours to do the two questions. Each question carries equal marks. The choice of text types in Part 2 you will be required to produce may include:

- a newspaper or magazine article
- a contribution to a leaflet or brochure
- a personal note or message
- a formal or informal letter
- a report
- a review
- a competition entry
- an information sheet
- a memo

2 Work with another student. Decide which of the above you generally find easier to write. Discuss why.

3 Look at the task and read the answer above right.

TASK

You have seen the following announcement of a competition in a magazine you get, and have decided to enter.

HOLIDAY OF A LIFETIME
We are offering you the chance to choose one of a range of exotic holidays, all expenses paid for two weeks, for you and a friend. All you have to do is write to us, describing the most exciting holiday you have ever had in about 250 words. Winning entries will be published in our August edition.

Send entries to: The Editor, Today Magazine, P.O. Box 743, London.

HOLIDAY OF A LIFETIME

Perhaps my most exiting holiday was when I went on my motorbike with a group of friends to the south of Sinai. We were all working in the Cairo and this was going to be a 2-week summer holiday. I was looking forward to it for months. The thought to get away from the noise and pollution in the city was very good.

We set off from Cairo on 3 bikes and drove down the west coast of Sinai. You feel very free when you are on a bike on the open road. There's nothing like it really. The scenery was amazing. It was incredibly rocky and sometimes quite lonely. About halfway down the coast we stopped to see St. Catherine's monastery. You can stay overnight. In fact, we decided to walk up the near Mt. St. Catherine so that we could see the sun rise. We sat together in silence and savoured the moment. It was very beautiful.

We continued our journey down to Sharm El Sheikh in the south. We stayed in a cheap hotel and every day we were snorkelling or scuba diving. There's an incredible range of fish and coral and the colours are out of this world! We also made friends with some Australians who had come down from Israel. I still write to them.

4 Read the task and the answer again. Decide if the answer would be classed as a band 3 (satisfactory) or band 5 (very good) on the CAE Paper 2 marking scale given below.

Band 5	Minimal errors: resourceful, controlled and natural use of language, showing good range of vocabulary and structure. Task fully completed, with good use of cohesive devices, consistently appropriate register. No relevant omissions. N.B. Not necessarily a flawless performance. Very positive effect on target reader.
Band 3	Either (a) task reasonably achieved, accuracy of language satisfactory and adequate range of vocabulary and range of structures or (b) an ambitious attempt at the task, causing a number of non-impeding errors, but a good range of vocabulary and structure demonstrated. There may be minor omissions, but content clearly organised. Would achieve the required effect on the target reader.

5 Look at these Examiner Comments on the answer. Then rewrite the answer to improve it.

Content

The task has been completed even though it is slightly underlength.

Organisation and Cohesion

Sensible opening to the entry. However, it ends rather abruptly. Appropriate use of paragraphs.

Range

Some range has been demonstrated by the candidate e.g. *out of this world, savoured*. However, the language is generally not very ambitious and there could have been more use of longer, complex sentences.

Register

Consistently and appropriately informal. The tone is lively and engages the interest of the reader.

Target Reader

Would consider shortlisting this entry for the competition.

Accuracy

There are some minor errors which do not prevent the reader understanding the writer's message e.g. *exiting, the Cairo*.

6 Now choose **one** of the following writing tasks (or the task in Exercise 3). Your answer should follow exactly the instructions given. Write approximately 250 words.

TASKS

1 You have received a request from your local town council to write a short report on the state of public transport in your area with recommendations on how to encourage the local population to use public transport more and their cars less.

    Write the **report**.

2 A magazine for students of English as a Foreign Language wants an article outlining sensible ways to prepare for English language exams which test Speaking, Listening, Reading, Writing, Grammar and Vocabulary. You should suggest general strategies to help students organise their revision timetable in the weeks before the exam and specific ideas as to how they might best use their time in the final week before the exam.

    Write the **article**.

3 You have been asked to prepare an information leaflet for school leavers who might be interested in joining your company. Make reference to any possibilities for training and career advancement and perks or benefits that might be available. Also include in the leaflet brief sections describing the main activities and achievements of the company.

    Write the **text** for the **leaflet**.

1 When you select the task to answer in Part 2, remember to:
   a) choose a text type which you feel confident about writing. (Ask yourself if you have written this kind of text before, if you can organise your material appropriately and if you can remember the appropriate style for this kind of task.)
   b) make sure you have definite ideas of what you will include as the content. (Do you know the key topic vocabulary you will need?)
   c) include all the points asked for in the task.
2 Discuss your choice of task with another student. Explain why you think this is the best choice for you.
3 Now write your answer in approximately one hour.

7 Now look at all the writing assessment bands on p.211 Writing reference. Give your work to another student so they can suggest which band they think your answer might come in. Discuss with your partner which areas of your answer could be improved.

8 Rewrite your answer. Try and improve it so that it would come in a higher band.

Certificate in Advanced English quiz

Attempt the quiz below to see how much you know about the CAE exam.

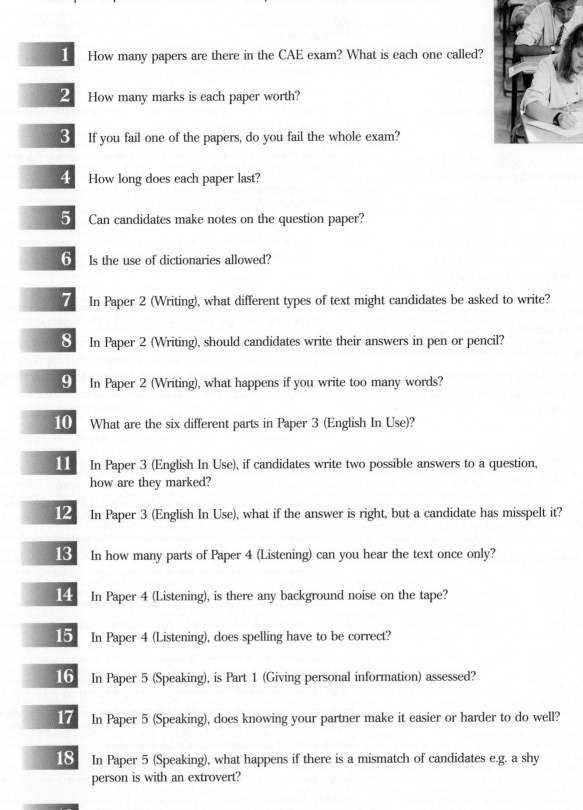

1 How many papers are there in the CAE exam? What is each one called?

2 How many marks is each paper worth?

3 If you fail one of the papers, do you fail the whole exam?

4 How long does each paper last?

5 Can candidates make notes on the question paper?

6 Is the use of dictionaries allowed?

7 In Paper 2 (Writing), what different types of text might candidates be asked to write?

8 In Paper 2 (Writing), should candidates write their answers in pen or pencil?

9 In Paper 2 (Writing), what happens if you write too many words?

10 What are the six different parts in Paper 3 (English In Use)?

11 In Paper 3 (English In Use), if candidates write two possible answers to a question, how are they marked?

12 In Paper 3 (English In Use), what if the answer is right, but a candidate has misspelt it?

13 In how many parts of Paper 4 (Listening) can you hear the text once only?

14 In Paper 4 (Listening), is there any background noise on the tape?

15 In Paper 4 (Listening), does spelling have to be correct?

16 In Paper 5 (Speaking), is Part 1 (Giving personal information) assessed?

17 In Paper 5 (Speaking), does knowing your partner make it easier or harder to do well?

18 In Paper 5 (Speaking), what happens if there is a mismatch of candidates e.g. a shy person is with an extrovert?

19 How and when do candidates get their results?

20 In what form will the results come?

1 There are punctuation mistakes in six of the following sentences. Find the mistakes and correct them.

1 What are the names of the three students, who have just arrived from Cyprus?
2 Saint Michel en Grève where my friend Gillian lives really took my breath away.
3 Most people are really taken with the islands which are all very different from one another.
4 My letter to which I have received no reply was sent on 1st December.
5 In 1975 she published her theory which met with immediate derision from other psychologists.
6 Is that your cousin, who's standing next to you in the photo.
7 Can you recommend a restaurant where we can get vegetarian food?
8 Kamakura, whose many attractions include Buddhist temples, gardens and a delightful beach, lies only a short train journey from Tokyo.

2 Use one of the adverbs in the box below to complete this extract from a speech. You can use some of the adverbs for more than one gap.

> frankly actually basically obviously
> personally generally clearly naturally
> surely presumably

(**1**) *Frankly* speaking, we found the people friendly and hospitable. (**2**) ... , they were a good deal more friendly and hospitable than we are here. (**3**) ... this is in part because their livelihood is even more dependent on tourism than ours is, though I met a number of people who were (**4**) ... very keen to help us even though there was nothing whatsoever in it for them. I was, quite (**5**) ... , very impressed by their attitude. (**6**) ... it's about time we realised that a friendly smile and the willingness to give up a few moments of one's time make a more positive impression on tourists than all the luxury resorts in the world. (**7**) ... , I would gladly forego the latter, especially if it means doing without the former, though I know not everyone will agree with me. (**8**) ... I see it as a question of balance. If we can maintain our identity and see growth in the tourist industry then, (**9**) ... , we all stand to benefit. (**10**) ... , this involves a little extra effort, but that's only to be expected.

Paper 3 English in Use: Part 2 (open cloze)

3 Complete the following article by writing each missing word in the space. **Use only one word for each space.** The exercise begins with an example (**0**).

The forty-three inhabitants of Pitcairn Island, situated (**0**) *between* Australia and South America, not only make up (**1**) ... of the most remote communities on earth, they are (**2**) ... all related. Cousins, nephews, uncles and aunts live together on a patch of ground (**3**) ... bigger than London's Hyde Park. Pitcairn was uninhabited (**4**) ... 1790 when the mutineers from the British ship, the Bounty, settled there. A year earlier, the crew, led by Fletcher Christian, had rebelled (**5**) ... Captain William Bligh, setting him adrift in a small boat. The mutineers then sailed for Pitcairn (**6**) ... they found a safe refuge (**7**) ... British justice. For two decades no one knew what (**8**) ... happened to the Bounty and its crew, but in 1808 an American whaler called at the island (**9**) ... chance. Only one mutineer, John Adams, was still alive. Living with him on the island were ten women and twenty-three children. The (**10**) ... of the original settlers, (**11**) ... Fletcher Christian, had died violently or (**12**) ... disease. Nevertheless, the community has survived. Today, the islanders, (**13**) ... most common surname is Christian, are extremely proud of having descended (**14**) ... those twenty-seven British seamen who mutinied on the Bounty (**15**) ... than two hundred years ago.

4 Rewrite these sentences beginning with the words in bold.

1 It was the first time I had set out on such a long journey alone.
   Never before ...
2 He's intelligent and kind-hearted and really good-looking too.
   Not only ...
3 There are very few occasions on which I have met a man as rude as Carl.
   Rarely ...
4 Don't ever let the cats out.
   At no time ...
5 I had only just got back from my holiday when I heard the news.
   Hardly ...

5 Complete the sentences below with one of the words in the box. You will need to use one of the words twice.

> away to upon as out
> for on in up

1 Even after three months it still really takes it .... of me.
2 You take me completely .... granted.
3 They're bound to be taking people .... there.
4 It completely took my breath ....
5 She's taken it .... herself to nurse her sick friend.
6 Take it .... with the committee.
7 I don't think I took .... more than half of what she said.
8 Amazing as it may seem though, they've really taken .... one another.
9 I think you must have taken me .... someone else.
10 We take people pretty much .... we find them.

6 Now match the remarks in Exercise 5 with those given below.

EXAMPLE: *1i)*

a) I don't believe we've met, actually.
b) It was such a dense lecture.
c) I didn't think Pete was Suzie's type.
d) I hear they're opening another supermarket in Morwell.
e) You won't have to go to any trouble for us.
f) I've had enough of you!
g) The Grand Canyon was definitely a highlight of our trip.
h) Margaret is a saint!
i) The doctor told me to swim three times a week.
j) You know what you should do if you feel so strongly about it?

Paper 3 English in Use: Part 3 (error correction – extra word)

7 In **most** lines in the following text, there is **one** unnecessary word. It is either grammatically incorrect or does not fit in with the sense of the text. For each numbered line 1–15 find this word and underline it. Some lines are correct. Indicate these lines with a (✓) at the end of the line. The exercise begins with two examples (**0**) and (**00**).

GETTING OLDER TELESCOPES YOUR PERCEPTION OF TIME

0	Does your birthday seem to come around faster <u>in</u> each year?
00 ✓	The common experience that time flies as you get older was
1	first noted more than a hundred years ago by the psychologist
2	William James. Now researchers have proved it that age really
3	does affect on your perception of time. They asked people in three
4	age groups to date the twenty major public events such as natural
5	disasters and political changes. The 18–21 age group who thought
6	the events had occurred more recently than they actually had to,
7	while the over-60s dated events too far back. The middle-aged
8	groups were the most accurate. These results are show that our
9	perception of time really it does depend on age, although no one
10	knows quite why this should be. One explanation for is that as
11	we get older we accumulate of generic memories of events such as
12	Christmas and holidays. Such a regular events may create the
13	impression of time is passing more quickly. Another explanation
14	is that we perceive time in relation to our own age – when you
15	are four, a year is a quarter of your life, but it's only a fortieth for a 40-year-old.

8 Complete these sentences with one word.

1 You'd better let that soup .... down before you drink it.
2 Could you .... up? We can't hear you.
3 .... down! Panicking won't get us anywhere.
4 Some new curtains would really .... up the living room.
5 The FBI eventually .... down the list of suspects to six computer scientists.
6 I plan to .... up with some old friends while I'm in Melbourne.
7 He spent two days trying to .... down a copy of the record.
8 We're doing our best to .... up your passport application.
9 You nearly gave me a heart attack! Don't .... up on me like that.
10 You should .... down on fatty foods and sweets.

9 Join the participle clauses below to one of the clauses in the box.

EXAMPLE: *1b)*

1 Nestling in the San Lorenzo valley,
2 Rising to their feet,
3 Not realising the phone was off the hook,
4 Rewarded for good behaviour rather than punished for bad,
5 Having saved every penny I earned while I was a student,
6 Having seen the weather forecast the night before,
7 Lightly tossed with an oil and vinegar dressing,

a) she thought he had forgotten to call.
b) is the sleepy village of El Bueno.
c) the audience burst into uproarious applause.
d) we knew to take our umbrellas.
e) baby spinach makes a delicious change from lettuce.
f) most puppies become obedient and lovable companions.
g) I had enough money to spend a year travelling.

10 Fill in the gaps using one of the verbs in the box below. You will need to use some of the verbs more than once.

take   get   be   go   work

1 to ... bankrupt
2 to ... on strike
3 to ... early retirement
4 to ... flexitime
5 to ... the sack
6 to ... laid off
7 to ... maternity leave

Paper 3 English in Use: Part 5 (register transfer)

11 Read the following advice for business travellers to Tahiti and New Zealand and use the information to complete the numbered gaps in the informal letter following. **Use no more than two words for each gap.** The words you need do not occur in the advice.

Dos and Don'ts for Travellers

Tahiti
General
Tahitian custom calls for removing one's shoes before entering a home.
Names/Greetings
If you are in a group of thirty or less, you are expected to shake hands with all those present.
Hospitality/Gift Giving
If you are invited to dine in a Tahitian home, you should express interest in your host's home and family. But be careful, your Tahitian host might make a gift of a prized possession if you express too great an interest in it. Food is sometimes consumed with the fingers. Observe your hosts and take your lead from them.

New Zealand
General
Tipping is extremely uncommon and will often be refused.
Names/Greetings
Shake hands on arrival and departure.
Hospitality/Gift Giving
Punctuality is highly valued. Visitors should arrive a little before the appointed time. A modest gift of chocolates or wine is acceptable, though not compulsory.

Dear Tony,

I've managed to get some good advice on Tahiti and New Zealand for you.

I hear you're (**0**) *having dinner* at Dr Lomo's the night you get to Papeete. You'll probably have to (**1**) ... your shoes when you get there so wear your best socks! And shake hands with (**2**) ... , not just your hosts. Do say nice things about their house, but try not (**3**) ... too interested or they might (**4**) ... whatever it is you've admired. You might have (**5**) ... with your fingers, but wait (**6**) ... what the Lomos do.

When you get to New Zealand, don't tip the taxi drivers. Hardly (**7**) ... and they probably won't (**8**) ... your money anyway! You should shake hands with the people at Government House when you (**9**) ... and when (**10**) ... . And make sure you get to the Johnsons' house a (**11**) ... 7.30p.m. For New Zealanders, being on time is apparently (**12**) ... ! The Johnsons will be happy with chocolates or wine if you want to get some, but don't feel you (**13**) ... .

All the best,
Jenny

Grammar reference

Index

1 Conditionals

1.1 Formal style

In more formal styles *if* can be omitted and the auxiliary verb placed before the subject.

If I had known → Had I known *you were planning to visit your grandmother, I would have given you something to take to her.*

If I had booked → Had I not booked *a return ticket, I would stay on for another couple of months.*

If Helen were → Were Helen *my sister, I would be only too happy to lend her the money.*

If you should decide → Should you decide *at some future time that you do require our services, please do not hesitate to contact us.*

1.2 if + should happen to

We use *if + should/happen to* to suggest that something is more unlikely or just a chance possibility. *Should* and *happen* can be used together.

If *you* **should happen to** *run into my old friend Peter Simpson in Berlin, do say hello from me.*

If *you* **should happen to** *pass a chemist shop, could you get me a packet of aspirin.*

If *you* **happen to** *see anything you think would be nice for Kathy's birthday, buy it and I'll pay you back.*

1.3 supposing/imagine

We use *supposing* and *imagine* in place of *if* with a similar meaning.

Supposing *you won the lottery, who would you give money to?*

Imagine *you had enough money to never work again. You'd give up your job, wouldn't you?*

1.4 if + was/were to

We use *if + was/were to* to make an event seem more hypothetical. This structure is not used with state verbs e.g. *believe*.

If *they* **were to** *find a way of extending the human life span to 200 years, would you want to live that long?*

If *I* **was to** *put it to you that you were in Smith Street on the night of June 4th, what would you say?*

1.5 if + will/would

We use *if + will/would* to make requests more polite. The auxiliary means 'be willing to' in this case.

If *you* **will** *just bear with us for a few moments, the Minister will answer your questions.*

If *you* **would** *be kind enough to let us have your account details we will send out a statement immediately.*

2 Emphasis

In order to emphasise particular words or phrases, we can put everything else in the sentence into a clause beginning with *what*. We can then start with the *what* clause and finish with the words we want to emphasise. The two parts of the sentence are joined by *is* or *was* since we think of the *what* clause as singular.

What *I like most about Sam* **is** *his willingness to talk about his feelings.*

What *Leo did* **was** *to arrange a surprise party for Alex.*

What *happened* **was** *that they told him it was a fancy dress party but it wasn't really.*

What *really gets on my nerves* **is** *people who keep dogs in small flats in the city.*

3 Emphasis with inversion

3.1 Negative adverbs/adverbial expressions

We can put a negative adverb or adverbial expression at the beginning of the clause for emphasis. When we do this there is inversion of the auxiliary and subject.

Under no circumstances should you let her into the house.
At no time did she consider any other possibility.
Not until they were convinced he was missing did they notify the police.

3.2 Restrictive words/expressions

We can also put certain restrictive words or expressions at the beginning of the clause for emphasis.

Hardly had I put down the phone *when* it rang again.
Scarcely could one have guessed what they were plotting.
No sooner had the children settled down to work *than* there was a bomb scare.
Seldom has she received such a positive response from an audience.
Little did I know that he planned to resign that very day.
Never has the city looked more magnificent.
Only when I saw him again did I fully come to terms with the separation.
Not only have you missed several classes, you have also failed to submit the written work.

4 Talking about the future

4.1 The future continuous tense is used:

- to say that something will be in progress at a particular time in the future
  *This time next month **I'll be sitting*** on the pier in Augusta fishing.
  *Sorry we can't make it to the wedding. **We'll** all **be thinking*** of you.
- to talk about events in the future that are fixed, decided or expected to happen
  *The Minister **will be visiting*** Community Health clinics and schools in the area next week.
- to make polite enquiries about people's plans
  Will you be coming into town at all over the next few days?
  Will** Doctor Newton **be attending tomorrow evening's seminar?

4.2 The future perfect tense is used:

- to say something will be completed at a particular time in the future
  *By next Christmas Mary **will have saved*** enough money to travel for a whole year.
  *By the end of this century many of the diseases that affect us today **will have been eradicated**.*
- to express an assumption
  *You **won't have been** told much about today's meeting so I'll just run through some of the main points.*
  *She **won't have** even **started** worrying yet.*

4.3 be + to + infinitive

We use *be + to + infinitive* in formal contexts to indicate that an event in the future has been officially scheduled.

*The examination session **is to begin** no later than 9.30 a.m.*
*Competing athletes **are to assemble** outside the Sports Hall at 10 a.m.*

4.4 about to + infinitive/on the point of + -ing

We use *about to + infinitive* and *on the point of + -ing* to talk about the next moment.

*We're **about to go** out actually, so I can't talk now.*
*I'm **on the point of telling** Jessica exactly what I think of her.*

4.5 due to + infinitive

We use *due to + infinitive* to indicate a time in the future that has been previously scheduled.

*The ceremony is **due to start** at midday.*
*When is your flight **due to leave**?*

5 It as preparatory subject/object

5.1 it as a preparatory subject

It is more natural to use *it* as a preparatory subject in the following situations:

- when the subject of a clause is an infinitive expression
  ***It** was really lovely **to see** Philip again.*
  ***It** is essential **to obtain** a visa before you enter Australia.*
  ***It** makes me sad **to see** her so frail and thin.*
- when the subject of a clause is another clause
  ***It**'s unlikely **that he'll arrive on time**.*
  ***It** is terrible **how many young people are unemployed**.*

*It's always a relief **when it rains after a period of hot weather**.*

- when we want to emphasise what comes first in the sentence
*It was **Sally** who introduced me to Kaye.*
*It is **on Wednesday** that the exhibition starts.*
*It was **in London** that they met.*

5.2 it as a preparatory object

We can also use *it* as a preparatory object in this pattern.

subject + verb + *it* + complement + infinitive/clause

*I find **it** a little hard to believe you met Bill Gates in Cambridge.*
*They made **it** perfectly clear they wanted a room with a sea view.*

We do **not** normally use *it* as preparatory object without an adjective or noun complement after the verb.

*I hate **it** to see people shouting at their children in the supermarket.* ✗
*She believed **it** that he really loved her.* ✗

6 Modal verbs

Modal verbs can be used to express the following:

- permission
Might I have the next dance?
May I ask you another question?
You can use my computer if you want to.
- theoretical possibility
I may be going away for the weekend of 26th.
The weather in Melbourne can be very changeable.
It might be a good idea to give Mary a call.
- strong obligation
All those wishing to attend tonight's lecture must leave their names at the front desk.
Need we say anything to Kathy about the present?
You will arrive on time in future or face dismissal.
We've got to get there on time.
- lack of obligation
You needn't drive Lucy to the theatre. Julia can give her a lift.
- prohibition
Cars may not be parked beyond this point.
You must not let her in under any circumstances.
You can't smoke inside the airport.
- deduction
You must be Mary's sister.

I can't have told him I'd be back this week or he would have been in touch by now.

- ability
All the members of Merrilyn's family can play a musical instrument.
Ann's little boy could talk when he was only nine months old.
- weak obligation
You really should have an early night.
We had better go and see Aunt Alice tomorrow afternoon.
Paul ought to start thinking about what he wants to do.

7 Noun phrases

Nouns combine in the following three ways so that one noun modifies another: in 7.1 and 7.2 the first noun acts like an adjective to describe or modify the second.

7.1 noun + noun

- when we describe a measurement e.g. *a 26-hour flight*
- when we name a particular thing and it is a well-known combination e.g. *a detective story*, *a tea cup*
- when we say what things are made of e.g. *a cotton blouse*
- when we talk about parts of inanimate objects e.g. *the door handle*

(In most cases the main stress is on the first noun.)

7.2 noun + 's + noun

- when we indicate possession e.g. *Michael's wedding*
- when the first noun is a user of the second e.g. *a young person's railcard*
- when the second noun is produced by the first noun e.g. *sheep's milk*

7.3 noun + preposition + noun

- when we describe a certain quantity of something e.g. *a litre of milk*
- when the nouns do not refer to a typical or well-known combination e.g. *a premonition of disaster*
- when we describe a container and its contents e.g. *a carton of fruit juice, a glass of wine*

(In 7.1 and 7.3 the main stress is usually on the first noun. In 7.2 it is usually on the second.)

8 Verb tenses

8.1 The perfect simple tense is used:

- to express completion or achievement
  *By this time next year Lucy **will have finished** school.*
  ***Have you finished** stacking the dishwasher?*
  *By the time he was thirteen he **had performed** in every European capital.*
- to emphasise duration with *for* and *since*
  I've known Diana since I was eleven.
  *I **hadn't** slept well **for more than a week**.*
  *By this time next month I **will have lived** here **for twenty years**.*

8.2 The perfect continuous tense is used:

- to talk about temporary situations
  ***I have been visiting** a friend in Spain.*
- to emphasise the activity rather than whether or not it is complete.
  ***He's been working** too hard.*

8.3 The past perfect tense

The past perfect is often used to show that one event happened before another.

*I **had only met** him once before I found myself sitting next to him at Sandra's wedding.*
*She was convinced that **he had been lying** to her.*

8.4 Continuous tenses

We often use continuous tenses to show that a speaker sees the event as ongoing or temporary.

***She's living** at home at the moment.*
*She **will be visiting** Britain next month.*

9 Participle clauses

We can combine other words and participles to form participle clauses. We often use participle clauses to give more information about the idea expressed in the sentence.

- They can be used after nouns.
  *There's a man **mowing his lawn** in the back garden.*
  *Most of the people **included in the list** were the ones who had not handed in all the necessary documents.*
  *All those **wishing to attend the reception** should ensure they reply by 29th February at the latest.*
- They can be used to replace words like *because, so that, after* etc.
  ***Having read the book,** I was disappointed in the film.*
  ***Thoroughly refreshed after a dip in the lake,** they went back to the hotel for lunch.*

10 Passives

- We use the passive when the active form would require the use of an indefinite or vague pronoun or noun.
  ***Someone** will process your application in the next few days.*
  *Your application **will be processed** in the next few days.*
  ***People** purchase the majority of new cars at the end of the financial year.*
  *The majority of new cars **are purchased** at the end of the financial year.*
- We often use the passive with verbs such as *think, believe, know* and *say* to show that it is a general opinion.
  *The escapees **are believed** to be somewhere in the area around the prison.*
  *She **is said** to be our greatest living writer.*
  *He **was known** to be particularly partial to smoked salmon.*
- We can use the passive to make a statement sound less personal and connected to a particular individual or group.
  *Education spending **was reduced** by a little over 2% last year.*
  *Offenders **will be prosecuted**.*
- By using the passive we can avoid an awkward change of subject in the middle of the sentence.
  *Hill published his first collection of poems in the early sixties and since that time **has been** constantly **praised** by critics and public alike.*
  *She placed the advertisement in the paper on a Tuesday and by Wednesday **had been** literally **inundated** with calls.*

11 Relative clauses

11.1 Defining relative clauses

Defining relative clauses say which person or thing (or kind of person or thing) we are talking about.

*The session **which/that started at 7.15** was more convenient for us.*
*The woman **who/that organised the event** lives with my friend Rosemary.*
*Hanging Rock is a place **(which/that) most people find magical**.*
*The photos **of which we made copies for everyone** are in the album.*
*The woman **to whom I was speaking** seemed somehow distracted.*

11.2 Non-defining relative clauses

Non-defining relative clauses say more about the person or thing we have already identified.

Next Friday, **which is the 3rd of March,** *we're having about twenty people round for drinks.*

Nanette, **who is one of my oldest friends,** *has just produced a film.*

Melbourne, **where I grew up,** *is now a really exciting city.*

The minister, **for whom a press conference had been organised,** *had to be rushed straight to hospital.*

The treaty, **under the terms of which a new border is to be established,** *was signed yesterday afternoon.*

12 Reported speech

- If the reporting verbs are in a past tense the modal verbs *would, should, could, might, ought* and *must* do not always change their form.
  I **would** *love to come to lunch on Friday if I* **could** *get some time off work.*
  She said she **would** *love to come to lunch on Friday if she* **could** *get some time off work.*
  You **should** *buy a weekly bus pass while you're here.*
  He recommended that we **should** *buy a weekly bus pass while we were there.*

- When the sequence of events is clear it is not necessary to report past tenses with a shift into the past perfect.
  Before the seventeenth century no one **knew** *what the function of the heart was.*
  The lecturer **explained** *that before the seventeenth century no one* **knew** *what the function of the heart was.*
  We thoroughly **enjoyed** *the wedding.*
  We heard you all thoroughly **enjoyed** *the wedding.*

- When the reporting verb is in the present, future or present perfect the tenses don't usually change.
  I **love** *children.*
  He **says** *he* **loves** *children.*
  I'm *a vegetarian.*
  She'll probably **tell** *you* **she's** *a vegetarian.*
  Racism terrifies me.
  She **has** *often* **said** *that racism* **terrifies** *her.*

- In informal speech we often drop *that* after common reporting verbs (e.g. *say, think, tell*). *That* is not usually dropped after nouns.
  He **said** *he'd be here by 9.30.*
  She **told** *me I shouldn't let the dog off the lead in the park.*
  They accepted **his claim that** *he had been nowhere near the scene of the crime.*

- Reporting verbs that express the importance of an action are often followed by *should*. In American English this is less common and the subjunctive is used.
  They **recommended that we (should) stay** *overnight in Madrid.*
  I **insisted she (should) accept** *payment for the work she had done.*
  We all **agreed that she (should) be** *asked to resign.*

- Certain reporting verbs can be used in the passive introduced by *it* e.g. *announce, believe, suggest, say, claim.* This structure is used when the speaker does not want to take personal responsibility for a statement or is reporting the views of a group of people.
  It is *commonly* **believed** *that there is life elsewhere in the universe.*
  It has been claimed *that jogging damages leg joints.*
  It was announced *earlier today that the Queen and Prince Philip would be visiting Australia next month.*

13 Substitution and ellipsis

We avoid repetition of words or expressions that have already been used by means of substitution and ellipsis.

13.1 Substitution

Substitution involves using other words such as *it, one, do, there, that, so, neither* and *not.*

We've been to **Thailand** *several times but as Alan had never been* **there** *he decided to join us on our last trip.*
Bill **doesn't** *really* **like** *formal occasions and* **neither do I.**
She looked at **the spilt milk** *on the floor, took a cloth and mopped* **it** *up.*
A: Would you like **a cup of tea?** *B: I'd love* **one.**
A: Are you **going skiing this winter?** *B: We might* **do.**
A: Would you like to come to **a picnic at Hanging Rock on Sunday?** *B:* **That** *sounds wonderful.*
A: **Is that all** *we have to do today? B: I hope* **so.**
A: She **won't be** *in the mood for festivities after what happened today. B: I expect* **not.**

13.2 Ellipsis

Ellipsis involves leaving out words to avoid repetition. We do this:

- after *and, but* and *or*
  She felt anxious **and** *confused about the situation.*
  He was excited **but** *a little apprehensive about starting the new job.*
  I'm thinking of taking some flowers **or** *perhaps some wine.*

- at the end of a verb phrase
  *She wanted to **visit her aunt in hospital** but she **couldn't**.*
  *She said she was going to **do her homework** and she **has**.*
- with infinitives
  *I didn't want to **give the puppies away** but my mother said I **had to**.*
  *He doesn't **play much tennis** now. He **used to**, though.*

14 Verb patterns

14.1 Transitive verbs followed by direct objects

Transitive verbs are usually followed by nouns and pronouns acting as direct objects.

*The thunder **frightened the dog** so much that he hid under the bed.*
Shut the door!
*Would you **advise us** to take the fast train?*

14.2 Transitive verbs can have passive forms

*She **was** so **frightened by** the prospect of flying that she decided to travel by ship.*
*When I got there the gate **had** already **been shut**.*
*We **were advised** not to bother booking in advance.*

14.3 Transitive verbs which can be followed by both a direct and an indirect object

- In most cases the indirect object is a person and comes first.
  *Could you **bring me some orchids** from Thailand?*
  ***Play me a tune** on your guitar.*
  *She **gave me** a **large slice of turkey**.*
- In some cases the direct object can be left out because it is obvious from the context.
  *You really should give up **smoking** (cigarettes).*
  *Lynne **rides** (her horse) at least once a week.*
  *I learnt to **cook** (food) by watching my mother.*

14.4 Intransitive verbs are not followed by a direct object

*Something very strange **happened**.*
*Please **wait** in the queue.*
*Did you **sleep** on the plane?*

14.5 Verbs which can be used transitively or intransitively

These verbs often describe change. When some of these verbs are used intransitively they can have a meaning similar to the passive.

*The sound of the rain on the roof **woke her**.*
*She **woke** early that first morning.*
*You haven't **burnt the toast** again, have you?*
*The cake **burnt** while I was talking on the phone.*

14.6 Verbs which require a preposition or participle before the object

*Can you **explain this grammar point <u>to</u> me** again?*
*I find it really distracting to **listen <u>to</u> music** while I'm working.*
*What are you **laughing <u>at</u>**?*

14.7 Different patterns when verbs are followed by other verbs

- The following verbs can be followed by -ing or the infinitive with *to* with different meanings:
  *I **forgot to tell** you. I'm going out tonight.*
  *He couldn't **forget seeing** the ship sinking before his very eyes.*
  *I **like living** here with you.*
  *I **like to get up** early in the morning and have a swim whenever I can manage it.*
  *I **regret to inform** you that your application has been rejected.*
  *He deeply **regretted having sold** the ring.*
  *I hope you'll **remember to write** to your aunt.*
  *He **remembered locking** the door with the key.*
  *We **stopped to buy** a newspaper on the way home from the park.*
  *I wish you'd **stop drumming** your fingers on the table like that.*
  *I've been **trying to get through to** her on the phone all morning.*
  ***Try sleeping** without a pillow. That might help.*
- When the verbs above are followed by -ing they often refer to an action or state before the main verb.
- *Begin, continue, intend, propose, start* can be followed by -ing or the infinitive with *to* with a slight difference in meaning.
  *I fully **intended going/to go** to the centenary lunch but I couldn't in the end.*
  *As I turned the corner he **started to run/running** away from the house.*
- *Attempt, deserve, expect, fail, manage, neglect, threaten* are normally followed by an infinitive with *to*. These verbs often refer forward to the future.
  *I **expect to receive** some kind of response in the next 24 hours.*
  *You **deserve to lose** your licence.*

- *Avoid, detest, keep on, mind, miss, put off, risk* are followed by *-ing*.
  *Isn't there some way we can **avoid having to wait** outside in the cold?*
  *I think we'll have to **put off going** to visit Melanie until tomorrow.*
- *Make, let, help* are followed by an object and an infinitive without *to*.
  *I **helped her pack** her suitcase.*
  *You **made me love** you.*
  *Do you think Dad will **let us go** to the party?*
- *Advise, beg, dare, encourage, invite, persuade, urge* are followed by an object and an infinitive with *to*.
  *He **encouraged me to take part** in my first tournament.*
  *I **urge you to give** the candidate your full support.*

Watch Out!

Watch Out! boxes

The following are items that appear in Watch Out! boxes:

responsible p.10
containers p.23
didn't need to/needn't have p.49
quite p.75
what p.134
No sooner . . . than / Hardly . . . when p.146

Language index

(*GR* refers to the *Grammar reference*)

Articles p.38

Conditionals p.58; (advanced forms) p.62; GR p.195 (1)

Countable/uncountable nouns p.176

Emphasis p.108; GR p.192 (2); (with inversion) p.145; GR p.193 (3)

Future forms p.64; (advanced features) p.69; GR p.193 (4)

Gerunds/infinitives p.42; (verbs +) p.94; GR pp.197–198 (14)

Have/get something done p.183

Hypothetical meaning p.96

It as preparatory subject/object p.118; GR pp.193–194 (5)

Linking words p.137

Making comparisons p.122

Modal verbs p.26; p.48; GR p.194 (6)

Noun phrases p.22; GR p.194 (7)

Participle clauses p.158; GR p.195 (9)

Passives p.154; (advanced features) p.180; GR p.195 (10)

Questions p.148

Relative clauses/pronouns p.40; relative clauses (advanced features) p.134

Reported speech p.96; (advanced features) p.170; GR p.196 (12)

Substitution/ellipsis p.84; GR p.196 (13)

Tenses p.111

Transitive/intransitive verbs p.6; GR p.197 (14)

Verb tenses p.34; GR p.195 (8)

Exam tasktype index

Exam Task	Training unit	Exam focus unit
P1, Pt2 (gapped text)	5, 9,12, 15	10
P1, Pt3 (multiple choice)	1, 7, 8, 13, 14	
P1, Pts1+4 (multiple matchng)	2, 3, 4	6, 11
P2, Pt1 (compulsory question)	1, 5, 6, 12, 13, 14	10
P2, Pt2	2, 3, 4, 9, 11, 12, 13, 14	15
P3, Pt1 (multiple-choice cloze)	7	8, 10
P3, Pt2 (open cloze)	10	13
P3, Pt3 (error correction – extra word)	1, 15	2
P3, Pt3 (error correction – spelling + punctuation)	4, 9	5
P3, Pt4 (word formation)	6, 12	14
P3, P5 (register transfer)	6	11
P3, Pt6 (gapped text)	2	3
P4, Pt1 (monologue: note taking/ sentence completion)	10, 15	
P4, Pt2 (monologue: note taking/ sentence completion)	6, 11, 14	7
P4, Pt3 (conversation: sentence completion/multiple choice)	1, 3, 5	4
P4, Pt4 (multiple matching/ multiple choice)	2, 8,	9, 15
P5 Pt1		1
P5, Pt2	2, 3, 4, 8	
P5, Pts 3+4	5, 6	
P5 (all)		12

Paper 2 Writing reference

Contents

Paper 2, Part 1

 Task

You are a member of the extra-curricular activities committee at your college. Recently you helped organise an 'end-of-course' trip. You and a group of classmates stayed at **Happy Valley Campsite**. Unfortunately, you were all very disappointed with your stay.

On the right is the brochure you received from **Happy Valley Campsite** before booking the trip and the notes you made while you were there.

When you got home you phoned a friend who works at the Consumer Protection League and told her about your experience. She has sent you the leaflet on p.201.

You have offered to write a letter (200 words) to the campsite director asking for compensation on behalf of your group. You are also going to send the campsite brochure and a copy of your letter to your friend at the Consumer Protection League. Write a covering note (50 words) to your friend to accompany the copy of the letter and the campsite brochure.

HAPPY VALLEY CAMPSITE

If you're planning to spend your holidays with a group of friends then camping is definitely an option to consider and at Happy Valley we make groups especially welcome. We offer the finest campsite facilities in Europe at very reasonable daily, weekly and group rates (generous student discounts available).

!!! Not to us!! Person on desk said this had changed since we made our booking six months earlier.

So small could barely get out of bed. VERY dirty!!!

✹ **COSY TRAILER ACCOMMODATION** ✹

✹ **HIRE A TENT OR BRING YOUR OWN** ✹

Sue and Anna not allowed to put up their own tents – had to hire them!!

✹ **MINI-MARKET** ✹

Open for ONE hour a day: AT LUNCHTIME!!! Everything twice the price of supermarket in the town.

✹ **METRES FROM CLEAN SAFE BEACH** ✹

2 KILOMETRES away!!

✹ **FANTASTIC NIGHTLIFE IN NEARBY GRIMSCIA** ✹

One cinema (same film throughout our stay) and a pub full of unfriendly locals.

WHEN WE WENT TO COMPLAIN MANAGER 'UNAVAILABLE'!

Make sure you book early so as to avoid disappointment!!!

We did!!!

Phone: 982019069
e-mail: hapvalcam@netexplor.com
or write to: Dan McNamara Campsite Manager
Happy Valley Little Bay
Gisborn GI79 F09

BUT THE ADVERT SAID ...

Have you ever paid for a product or service on the basis of an enticing advertisement or brochure only to be disappointed! Misleading advertising can be irritating but it can also cost the consumer money. If you find an instance of misleading advertising, let us know.

Here are some things to look out for:

- false claims about the qualities of the product
- false claims about special offers
- false claims about prices

Send us a copy of the advertisement or brochure concerned, noting any discrepancies you found and we will take up your case!

FAIR DEAL
CONSUMER PROTECTION LEAGUE
22 Albert Rd
Hambleside
Gisborough, GI3 S89

---

2 Model answer

a) letter

DO begin by identifying the situation you are writing about.

DO state the purpose of your letter.

DO make links between paragraphs.

DO say what you want the result of your letter to be in the final paragraph.

Dear Mr McNamara,

I am writing on behalf of the Gisborn College group that stayed at Happy Valley from 10th to 24th July. I am sorry to tell you that we were not at all satisfied with our stay and feel that we deserve some kind of compensation.

The most serious of our complaints is that we were charged the full fee despite the fact that we had originally been quoted a price with a student discount. Furthermore, group members who had brought their own tents were not allowed to use them.

If this were not enough, the trailers were extremely cramped and had obviously not been cleaned for some time. Another problem was the 'mini-market'. Aside from being extremely expensive, it was closed for most of the day which meant that we had to walk the two kilometres back from the beach at lunchtime so as to buy the things we needed. Finally, I would hardly call the pub and a cinema in Grimscia 'fantastic nightlife'.

If we do not receive a satisfactory answer to this letter, I will be forced to take the matter up with the Consumer Protection League.

I look forward to hearing from you in due course.

Yours sincerely,

Max Braun

Max Braun

DO use the person's name if you know it.

DO organise points from the input in a logical way.

DO make links between points within the paragraph.

DON'T use the same language as the input.

DO expand on the ideas in the input.

If you have used the person's name at the beginning of your letter, DO end your letter like this.

b) note

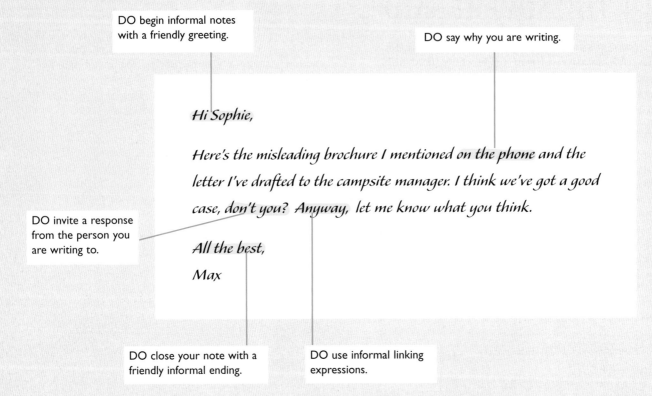

DO begin informal notes with a friendly greeting.

DO say why you are writing.

DO invite a response from the person you are writing to.

DO close your note with a friendly informal ending.

DO use informal linking expressions.

Hi Sophie,

Here's the misleading brochure I mentioned on the phone and the letter I've drafted to the campsite manager. I think we've got a good case, don't you? Anyway, let me know what you think.

All the best,
Max

INFORMATION SHEET

1 Task

Your local tourist office has asked you to write an information sheet (about 250 words) for visitors to your country. The purpose is to inform them about the main public holidays that occur throughout the year. Write your **information sheet**.

2 Model answer

DO think of a title for your sheet that will provoke the reader's curiosity. DON'T provide illustrations.

The Land of the Long Weekend

We're famous for our public holidays, many of which are on a Monday or Friday. Here are some of the main ones that fall in each of the four seasons. (Be warned: banks and most businesses are closed on the days marked with an *!)

Summer ———————————— *DO use section headings.*

Christmas falls in the summer in the Southern Hemisphere so there are lots of public holidays at this time. We celebrate our national day in this season too.

▶ Christmas Day (25/12)*
▶ Boxing Day (26/12)* ———— *DO use lists of bullet points.*
▶ New Year's Day (1/1)*
▶ Australia Day (26/1)*

Autumn

When the leaves begin to fall, Australians think of the Easter holidays and of another national holiday, ANZAC day. The latter is a day on which Australians and New Zealanders remember their compatriots who lost their lives in the First World War. Members of the armed forces as well as ex-servicemen and women take part in a parade.

▶ Good Friday*
▶ Easter Monday*
▶ ANZAC Day, April 25th (Australia and New Zealand)

DO think of an interesting way of introducing each section.

Winter

Winters are mild in Australia so if you don't like very hot weather this is a good time for visiting! The most important public holiday is 9th June* which is Queen Elizabeth II's official birthday.

Spring

In Victoria, one of the states, the most important public holiday of this season is Melbourne Cup Day. The Melbourne Cup is a horse race which takes place on the second Tuesday in November*. Many locals go to watch the race and people from all over Australia ... and beyond ... follow it closely on radio or television, especially if they have placed a bet!

So whenever you choose to come to Australia, you'll be able to join the Australians having fun on one of their many public holidays.

DON'T forget to add a conclusion.

INFORMAL LETTER

1 Task

Recently you went on holiday abroad and stayed with a friend. Unfortunately, you misread the departure time on your return tickets and missed your flight. You were able to get another flight the same day but had no money to pay for the ticket yourself. Your friend bought your ticket for you and you promised you would pay her/him back as soon as you got home. Write a **letter** to your friend explaining how you have arranged repayment and inviting her/him to stay with you when s/he visits your country.

2 Model answer

DO begin by telling your friend why you've decided to write.

Dear Clara,

Thought I'd better drop you a line straightaway to thank you for helping me out on Friday. I'm really sorry I had to bother you at such an unsociable hour and I'm sure you can imagine how embarrassed I was about having to ask you to pay for my ticket like that.

DO divide your letter into paragraphs, each of which should cover a different element from the task input.

I am now back home safely, as you can see. I went into the bank yesterday and arranged to transfer the price of the ticket from my bank account to yours, so you should find the money in your account any day now. I'm enclosing the receipt so you can see how much the ticket cost in dollars and check that the amount I've sent in pounds is correct. I hope it is, as I asked the people in the bank to double check.

DO expand upon the task input by using your own ideas.

Despite missing the plane like that, I had a really wonderful time in San Francisco. I particularly enjoyed meeting your niece and going out skating with her friends. I also loved the city, especially the bay and hope I'll get to go back some time.

DO close your letter by mentioning the next time you will see or speak to them.

I know you said you might be coming over to London in the summer. I really hope you do manage to get the time off work and that if you do, you will come and stay with my family. There's plenty of room here and you'd be very welcome, so just let us know when you're coming.

DON'T finish your letter with *Yours sincerely/faithfully*. DO use an appropriate INFORMAL phrase. There are various ways of closing letters to friends depending how well you know them. For very close friends or relatives you can use *With (all my) love*, *Love* or *Lots of Love*; with friends use *All the best*; with people you still don't know very well use *(With) best wishes*.

All the best ... and thanks again!

John

USEFUL LANGUAGE

BEGINNING THE LETTER

Thanks so much for your letter. It was really great to hear from you.
Sorry not to have written/been in touch for so long/such a long time.
I've been really busy lately.
Thought I'd better/drop you a line/write to let you know …

ENDING THE LETTER

I think that's all my news for the moment. Do write soon and let me know
what you've been doing.
Once again, thanks very much for being so nice to Susie …
Can't wait to see you *on the 24th/next week in* Cambridge …
Don't forget to say 'hi' to … *from me.*
Give my love to …

APOLOGISING

I'm really/terribly/awfully sorry about what happened the other night.
Sorry I couldn't/didn't manage to see you last time I was in …

INVITING

How about meeting up for a drink/coming over for a meal **some time**?
Why don't we try to get together some time soon?
I was wondering if you might like to get together with the rest of the old gang next
time you're in town.

RESPONDING TO AN INVITATION

Thanks very much for inviting us to your party. We're really looking forward to it.
I was really excited when I got your invitation. Unfortunately, I've now realised
it's the same weekend as my cousin's wedding so **I won't be able to make it / it
doesn't look as if I'm going to make it.**

MAKING A REQUEST

I was wondering if you happened to know anywhere in Dublin we could stay.
If you've got a spare moment, do you think you could find out when the music
festival is on this year?

REFERRING TO A PREVIOUS LETTER (TASK)

Do you remember that sports centre **you mentioned in your last letter**?
You said in your letter that you were thinking of applying for a scholarship.
Last time you wrote you asked how Tina was getting on.
You know that course **I told you** I had applied for. **Well,** …

REVIEW

1 Task

The editor of your college English language magazine has asked you to write a review of two films you have seen recently saying why one of the films is likely to be of particular relevance and interest to students at the college and why you believe the other is not worth watching. Write your **review**.

2 Model answer

DO indicate the structure of your review in the first paragraph.

DO start your review with a humorous or catchy comment to attract your audience's attention.

In reviews of more than one event, DO use the language of comparison and contrast.

DO use vocabulary specific to the event (film/TV/play/concert) you are reviewing.

DO give information about the cast, director or screenplay.

DON'T just describe the plot; offer your evaluation.

DON'T tell your readers about the ending if it will ruin the film or book for them.

DON'T forget to cover all the points mentioned in the task.

DO end your review with a recommendation.

Video of the Week

I rented 'Days of Wonder' and 'My Cure for the Summertime Blues' from my local video club last week. The first video I watched was well worth the money and time and has an important message for people like us; all I can say about the second is that you'd be better off spending your spare cash on a take-away pizza.

You'll be surprised I'm sure that 'Days of Wonder' was the second and not the first video I watched. Despite a star-studded cast including Caroline Nayra Smith, a director (Ann Champion) with a string of film successes behind her and a **screenplay** based on the novel of the same name, 'Days of Wonder' just doesn't work. Changing the setting from 17th century Paris to contemporary Sydney, while leaving the script in the baroque style of the original novel, is particularly ineffective. What's more, it's impossible to believe that a man would contemplate killing someone merely for speaking to his girlfriend.

Ten minutes into 'My Cure for the Summertime Blues', however, I was amazed to find myself laughing till I cried and nodding in agreement with almost every line of the script. I'd never seen any of the actors before but I found their portrayal of teenagers from a London comprehensive on holiday in Greece completely convincing. The film also has a clear message for young people: that caring about others and the planet mean a lot more than money or good looks.

So, if you're looking for a way to spend an evening with friends watching something that you'll all enjoy and which really does have something important to say then leave 'Days of Wonder' on the shelf and spend your money on 'My Cure for the Summertime Blues'.

USEFUL LANGUAGE

BOOK (FICTION)

Types: thriller, mystery, whodunit, romance, science fiction, fantasy, historical

Elements: character, plot, dialogue, setting, atmosphere, author, novelist, writer

BOOK (NON-FICTION)

Types: coffee table book, cookery book, travel book, encyclopedia, dictionary, textbook, manual

Elements: chapter, section, index, glossary, illustration, author, editor

FILM

Types: (as for fiction) + adaptation, comedy, animation

Elements: screenplay, script, set, role, costume, design, photography, special effects, animation, soundtrack

People: cast, actor, director, producer, scriptwriter

PLAY

Types: (as for film) + farce, musical

Elements: act, scene, set, role, costume, lyrics, music, design, stage

People: (as for film) + playwright, composer

CONCERT

Types of group or musician: rock group/band/musician, (lead, bass, rhythm) guitarist, (lead/backing) singer, drummer, **folk** singer/guitarist, **country and western** singer, **jazz** band/quartet/trio/singer, **orchestra,** quintet/quartet/ensemble/soloist/violinist/cellist

Elements: song, lyrics, tune, piece, symphony, concerto, cantata, score, stage, theatre, hall, auditorium

People: songwriter, composer, conductor

EXHIBITION

Types: painting, sculpture, photography, furniture, design, handicrafts

Elements: gallery, catalogue, displays

TV PROGRAMME

Types: series, documentary, soap opera, drama, situation comedy, chat show, debate, current affairs programme

People: compère, presenter, host, director, producer, scriptwriter, cast, actor

PROVIDING BACKGROUND INFORMATION

'A horse of a different colour' is Michael Gordon's **fourth novel / second film / first major role / second individual exhibition.**

'In the beginning was the word' **came on at** Odeon cinemas last week **and I went along** to see it.

INTRODUCING A BRIEF ACCOUNT OF THE PLOT

Set in 18th century London, the film **tells the story of/ recounts events** in the lives of three sisters.

In the breathtaking landscape of northern Canada, the book **examines the themes of** solitude and intimacy.

On the eve of the First World War, the series **introduces us to** the Wilson household.

COMMENTING CRITICALLY

I found the plot **rather conventional/predictable/contrived/ completely bizarre/absurd/incomprehensible.**

The novelist **has succeeded in** creating **an extremely intricate/complex plot/entirely believable/life-like characters.**

The characters are completely believable/unconvincing and the dialogue is witty/stilted and natural/artificial.

The ballerina was absolutely brilliant/was verging on the incompetent.

A particular strength/weakness of the production **was** the set design by Marcelo Camilleri.

The exhibition catalogue is economically priced/ ridiculously over-priced.

PROVIDING A RECOMMENDATION

I would strongly advise you not to **miss/waste your money on** 'Ain't got a clue'.

I would definitely recommend seeing/visiting/reading/having a look at 'Melbourne: a sentimental journey'.

For those who enjoy contemporary music, Tropical String Quartet are **not to be missed.**

Go and see 'Momix'. **You'll be amazed.**

COMPARING AND CONTRASTING (STRENGTHS OR TWO EVENTS)

While/Whereas/Although/Despite the fact that/In spite of the fact that characterisation was particularly strong, the plot gradually lost credibility.

The cast is brilliant; especially when you take into account **how truly dreadful** the script is.

'I remember what you did last winter' **is a masterpiece;** 'Looking for Sam' **is the opposite.**

Both films are likely to appeal to younger audiences, **but** 'Postmortem' **will be especially appealing.**

Neither the novel nor the film fully convinced me, **though** the character of Margo really **comes alive on the screen.**

REPORT

 Task

You were contacted by an international research company looking at sporting activities in your area. You agreed to interview fifty people using the questionnaire below and to write a report describing the existing level of participation in sporting activities in your community including any factors which discourage people from taking part in sport and recommending ways of encouraging more people to take up a sport.

QUESTIONNAIRE ON PARTICIPATION IN SPORTING ACTIVITIES

- Do you take part in sporting activities? If so, which ones?
- What prevents you from taking part or from taking part more?

Write your **report.**

2 Model answer

DO begin by stating the purpose of your report. **DO** use an impersonal formal style.	
DO use lists of points.	
DO develop the ideas in the input.	
DO use clear layout with headings. **DON'T** let your report look like a discursive composition.	
DO summarise information succinctly by using invented statistics.	
DO divide your report into sections according to the input.	
DO express opinions and recommendations in the last section of your report.	
DO use footnotes for extra information, definitions and clarification.	

Participation in Sport in Santa Maria

Introduction

The principal aims of this report are to:

1 provide an overview of participation in sporting activities by members of my local community (Santa Maria).
2 indicate factors preventing greater participation.
3 make recommendations as to how greater participation might be achieved.

I interviewed fifty people between the ages of 13 and 82 living in Santa Maria using the questionnaire provided.

Participation

Thirty-seven of the people interviewed took part in at least one sporting activity and seventeen took part in two or more. The most popular of these was football (20), followed by various keep fit activities e.g. jogging, aerobics, walking (17) and then by tennis (7), swimming (6), basketball (5) and martial arts (5).

Factors preventing fuller participation

There was a clear division between those who already took part in a sport and those who did not. The former group cited cost of equipment (17) and lack of facilities e.g. courts, football pitches (15) as the main factors preventing them from taking part more. Those who did not play a sport, on the other hand, cited poor health (6)*, lack of time (10) and lack of interest (5) as the main factors.

Recommendations

In my opinion, encouraging those who currently take no part in sports should be a priority. I recommend, therefore:

- an advertising campaign to promote keep-fit activities for the over-60s.
- more flexible timetables at council-run sports centres.
- introduction of new activities e.g. water aerobics.

Those who already take part in some sporting activity will be encouraged to do more by the creation of more sporting facilities.

* It should be noted that these individuals were all over sixty-five.

USEFUL LANGUAGE

STATING THE PURPOSE

The aim/purpose of this report is/was to describe/evaluate/present …
In this report, I will describe/evaluate/present …
This report provides a description/evaluation/presentation …

DESCRIBING HOW YOU GOT YOUR INFORMATION

I spoke to/interviewed several members of our sales staff …
Members of the local police force answered a questionnaire …
I visited three hotels: the Maritima; the Plage Royale and the Shackelton …
I conducted a survey among college graduates …
Car owners were invited to attend a focus group …

REPORTING YOUR RESULTS

Most people **said/expressed the opinion that** …
According to Dr Ann Wilkinson, the funding is inadequate …
A **high/small/significant proportion of those surveyed/respondents said that** …
25% of the older residents …
A small group (6) felt that the situation had deteriorated.

PRESENTING A LIST

The points in favour/against introducing genetically modified foods can be summarised as follows:
1 …
2 …

The following reasons were given for lack of participation in local festivals:
1 …
2 …

Arguments in favour of/against the introduction of a local television channel were:
1 …
2 …

There are a number of ways in which facilities for the parents of small children could be improved:
1 …
2 …

MAKING RECOMMENDATIONS

In the light of the results of the survey/questionnaire the introduction of a small fee would seem to be the best choice/option/solution.
I would recommend, therefore, the purchase of five more computers and laser printers.
My recommendations are the following:
- …
- …

ARTICLE

1 Task

You have been invited to write an article for an international magazine called 'Future Perfect'. The article should discuss expectations you and your friends had for the new millennium before it began and say to what extent these expectations have been fulfilled so far.

Write the **article**.

2 Model answer

DO think of an interesting title.

DO use language suited to your audience and topic.

DON'T forget to cover all aspects of the task.

DON'T forget to express your opinion. DO finish your article in an interesting way.

A New Millennium – A New World?

On the night of the 31st of December 1999 the world as a whole celebrated in style and we, here in Xania, were no exception. I don't know a single person who didn't greet the new millennium with at least some expectations that it would be better than the preceding thousand years.

Many of us hoped for an end to war, to hunger and to injustice. Another wish that we made that night was for a cleaner, less polluted planet. Almost all of us were fairly certain that the new millennium would bring with it more technological and scientific advances. Mobile phones with cameras and screens, faster, more powerful computers and further developments in genetics leading to the eradication of disease are just some of the things I can remember my friends mentioning as possibilities.

We woke, however, on the 1st of January 2000 to find that the world had hardly changed at all. Wars were still being fought, there was still hunger and injustice and the air didn't smell any fresher. On the positive side, the notorious Y2K (Year 2000) bug hadn't caused any significant damage either.

As time has gone on we've seen many of the technological and scientific advances we dreamed about come to be. Science continues to find cures for many of the diseases of the last century. As a result, there is a greater feeling of optimism than there was before. This, I believe, can help us find solutions to the world's problems and perhaps, as the century and millennium grow older, we can really change the world.

IMPROVING YOUR MARKS ON PAPER 2

1 Each of the two pieces of writing produced by a candidate for Paper 2
is given an impression mark as follows:

Band 5	Minimal errors: resourceful, controlled and natural use of language, showing good range of vocabulary and structure. Task fully completed, with good use of cohesive devices, consistently appropriate register. No relevant omissions. N.B. Not necessarily a flawless performance. Very positive effect on target reader.
Band 4	Sufficiently natural, errors only when more complex language attempted. Some evidence of range of vocabulary and structure. Good realisation of task, only minor omissions. Attention paid to organisation and cohesion; register usually appropriate. Positive effect on target reader achieved.
Band 3	Either (a) task reasonably achieved, accuracy of language satisfactory and adequate range of vocabulary and range of structures or (b) an ambitious attempt at the task, causing a number of non-impeding errors, but a good range of vocabulary and structure demonstrated. There may be minor omissions, but content clearly organised. Would achieve the required effect on the target reader.
Band 2	Some attempt at task but lack of expansion and/or notable omissions/irrelevancies. Noticeable lifting of language from the input, often inappropriately. Errors sometimes obscure communication and/or language is too elementary for this level. Content not clearly organised. Would have a negative effect on target reader.
Band 1	Serious lack of control and/or basic errors. Narrow range of language. Inadequate attempt at task. Very negative effect on target reader.
Band 0	(a) Fewer than 50 words per question. or (b) Totally illegible work. or (c) Total irrelevance (often a previously prepared answer to a different question).

This general impression mark scheme is used in conjunction with a task-specific mark scheme, which focuses on criteria specific to each particular task (e.g. report, article, formal letter), including relevance, range of structure, vocabulary and presentation and register.

2 Now look at the task below and the answer a student has written. The student's work has been annotated by their teacher. Look again at the CAE marking criteria on p.211. Into which band would you put this answer?

> The tourist authority want to encourage tourists and locals to spend more time walking around the capital city in your region or country. They have decided to prepare a leaflet on walks that people can take. Their intention is that the leaflet should include three walks taking in important buildings and monuments, parks and open spaces and a part of the city that is particularly interesting for cultural or historical reasons. You have been asked to prepare the leaflet.

Not a very interesting title and taken straight from the question. What about the tourists? It's not their capital city after all.

Try to make the idea of walking sound more inviting.

Another rather dull heading taken straight from the question.

Think about who you are writing for and why. People will presumably want to take these walks so it would be better to describe the buildings and monuments in the order in which they will see them during the walk. You could begin like this 'Start out from the magnificent Cathedral and walk straight on until ...'

Think of another more interesting way of saying this.

This sounds as if you don't like the park very much yourself. Try and make it sound more attractive. You could suggest that it is a good place to go for people who want to relax after shopping or taking the other walk.

This needs a heading that will make people want to take the walk. Do not just copy phrases from the question.

Make this more interesting. Describe the walk itself and introduce each of the buildings in order.

Is this relevant?

SPEND MORE TIME WALKING AROUND YOUR CAPITAL CITY!

There are lot of walks around your city you can take and get to know better. Here are three nice ones:

Important buildings and monuments

San Cristobal has many important buildings and monuments. There is the cathedral of the Immaculate Conception which were built in the seventeen century. There are also very nice houses that once belong to rich marchants in the area near to the market. You should also see the Bishop's Palace and the History Museum.

Parks and open spaces

This is a short walk because there are not so many parks and open spaces. You have to go out to the country or to the mountains for this. If your are stuck in San Cristobal the only green space is the Humboldt Park. This is not a large park and you can walk around it in about twenty minutes or half an hour. There is a pretty flower show in the park in April so it is better if you go then.

A part of the city that is interesting for cultural reasons

The area around the State theatre is very interesting, Apart from the theatre there is an important art gallery with a collection of peintings by famous artists. You can also find some small private galleries around here. Next door to the theatre is a very grand building. This is the State Library. You can't borrow any of the books though.

I hope you enjoy this walks.

Can you come up with a way of finishing that will have more of an impact on your audience?

3 Now check your assessment of this answer with the teacher's comments below.

Teacher's comments and advice on improvement

Obviously you know your city very well and you've got plenty to say. You've also thought carefully about the layout of your material. Nevertheless, this would be graded as Band 2 if it were an exam answer because you don't really expand on any of the ideas in the input task and you have taken a lot of language directly from it. Another problem is that a lot of the language you use is very simple (adjectives such as *nice*, *important* and *beautiful*; sentence structures with *There is/are ...*). I also don't think that someone reading this would feel like taking the walks, do you? I've made some suggestions on how your answer could be improved but you also need to edit your work thoroughly for grammar and spelling errors using the **Editing checklist**. Have another try and hand it in again.

4 Now look at the student's second attempt at the same task . This is now a Band 5 answer.

GETTING TO KNOW SAN CRISTOBAL ... ON FOOT!

The best way to get to know a city – even the one you grew up in – is by seeing it on foot. We've come up with three exciting walks that will show you just how varied our city is.

Walk 1: Architectural Marvels

Start out from the awe-inspiring cathedral of the Immaculate Conception, built in the seventeenth century. Walk down Santiago Street with its luxurious villas, once the homes of rich merchants trading in silks and spices. Perhaps the most magnificent of these are the Bishop's Palace and the Villa San Pedro which now houses the History Museum. At the end of the street you'll find the market with its wide variety of exotic fruits and flowers. Walk through, buying your picnic lunch on the way.

Walk 2: A breath of fresh air

Not so much a walk as a pleasant stroll, Humboldt park is our next destination. If you're lucky enough to be there in April, as you walk along the shaded paths, you'll also be able to enjoy the annual flower show. At whatever time of year the park is a wonderful spot for a picnic, so sit down on one of the benches facing the glorious central fountain and enjoy your lunch.

Walk 3: The art of the city

This walk takes you from the State Theatre and its imposing neighbour the State Library, through a series of quaint winding streets to the Municipal Gallery. The Gallery houses an impressive collection of works by local artists, but the many small galleries in the area also have plenty to offer.

Stop for a coffee in one of the many attractive cafes. You'll probably need to put your feet up, but we know you will have thoroughly enjoyed getting to know San Cristobal in this way!

EDITING CHECKLIST

When you have finished the first draft of a piece of work check that you have:

- done everything you were asked to do in the task input
- used language suited to your audience
- used appropriate layout for the task (sections, headings, bullet points etc.)
- used different language from the language of the input
- made links between paragraphs and between sentences in paragraphs
- written an accurate piece of work in terms of grammar, spelling and punctuation
  - Have a mental list of the kinds of errors you tend to make and pay particular attention to these errors.
  - Read your work at least three times and look for a different type of error each time e.g. the first time check for grammar, the second time for punctuation and the third time for spelling.

COMMON MISTAKES

GRAMMAR

Agreement: nouns and pronouns
*My brother works at home. ~~She~~ **He** has a computer and ~~her~~ **his** boss sends work through the Internet for ~~her~~ **him** to do.*

Agreement: subject and verb
People often find~~s~~ it difficult to adjust to change.
*Sarah and Jeff's three teenage children who had just got home from school ~~was~~ **were** surprised to find their grandfather in the kitchen.*

Verb tense
First I ~~had~~ washed the dishes and then I swept the floor.
*I ~~am~~ **have been** living in London for six months now.*

Word order
*Do you **often** go ~~often~~ to the cinema?*

Questions
*I wonder what ~~are~~ Bill and Alan **are** doing now?*
*Who ~~did come~~ **came** to the party?*

Irregular verbs
*Nanette has ~~teached~~ **taught** herself to play the guitar.*

Verb form
*I have ~~being~~ **been** meaning to write to you for weeks.*
*If I ~~would have~~ **had** realised the phone was out of order I wouldn't have been so worried.*
He suggested we ~~going~~ to a Mexican restaurant.
*~~To smoke~~ **Smoking** is not allowed in any part of the airport.*

Articles
I think that without ~~the~~ love we could not survive.
Design of the living room was blend of modern and classical styles. ✗
***The** design of the living room was **a** blend of modern and classical styles.* ✓

PUNCTUATION

Commas
My cousin who is coming to dinner tonight lives in New Zealand. ✗
My cousin, who is coming to dinner tonight, lives in New Zealand. ✓

Question marks
I've been meaning to ask you where you buy your coffee? ✗
I've been meaning to ask you where you buy your coffee. ✓

How often does the average student use the Internet. Our survey shows that it is more often than you might think. ✗
How often does the average student use the Internet? Our survey shows that it is more often than you might think. ✓

Apostrophes
The streets appearance had changed. ✗
The street's appearance had changed. ✓

The visitor's carpark was full so we had to park in the street. ✗
The visitors' carpark was full so we had to park in the street. ✓

Quotation marks
Soon 55% of households will be connected to the Internet,' said Mark Wilcox. ✗
'Soon 55% of households will be connected to the Internet,' said Mark Wilcox. ✓

Hyphens
My sixteen year old niece is studying fashion at school. ✗
My sixteen-year-old niece is studying fashion at school. ✓

SPELLING

Omission of silent letters
sychology ✗   **p**sychology ✓

Suffixes and prefixes
responsa**ble** ✗   responsi**ble** ✓
desadvantage ✗   **dis**advantage ✓

Homophones
here/hear there/their where/wear piece/peace

Letter doubling
nec**c**esary ✗   nec**ess**ary ✓
occurence ✗   occur**r**ence ✓

Letter order
recieve ✗   receive ✓
rethorical ✗   rhetorical ✓

Communication activities

Unit 1, Vocabulary Exercise 2, p.8

awe·struck /ˈɔːstrʌk‖ˈɒ:-/ *adj* feeling extremely impressed by the importance, difficulty, or seriousness of someone or something: *She gazed awestruck at the jewels.*

gasp /gɑːsp‖gæsp/ *v* [I,T] **1** to breathe in suddenly, quickly and in a way that can be heard, especially because you are surprised or afraid; *"My leg! My leg!" he gasped. "I think it's broken!"*

haunt·ing /ˈhɔːntɪŋ‖ˈhɔ:n-/ *adj* sad but also beautiful and staying in your thoughts for a long time: *a haunting melody* – **hauntingly** *adv*

pen·chant /ˈpɒnʃɒn, ˈpentʃənt‖ˈpentʃənt/ *n* [C] *French* a liking for something, especially something that is slightly disapproved of by other people [+ **for**] *a penchant for fast cars*

twirl /twɜːl‖twɜːrl-/ *v* [I,T] to turn around and around or make something do this: [+ **around/round**] *twirling around the dance floor* | **twirl sth around/round** *He twirled the gun around in his hand.*

(Longman Dictionary of Contemporary English – 3rd edition)

Unit 2, Reading Exercise 2, p.19

Answers to reading quiz

If you have answered only one of these questions with a *Yes*, then you are probably already a speed reading expert! And that one question was the first – **Speeds of 1,000 words per minute are possible.**

All the others should have been answered with a resounding *No*. These remaining 19 questions covered the full range of current misconceptions about reading.

If you believe these false assumptions, not only are you believing in something that is not true, you are believing in something that will actively make your reading habits worse and worse, your reading speed slower and slower, and your comprehension and understanding more and more difficult and unsatisfactory.

Unit 3, Reading Exercise 6, p.32

Student A: You have recently won £1m on the lottery. You have been thinking about what/who to spend it on. You are worried about how the money will affect the attitude of your relatives and friends towards you.

Unit 5, Listening Exercise 1, p.54

'Cryonics' is the 'art' of freezing the bodies of people who have recently died. The hope is that one day science will have discovered how to bring these bodies back to life again.

Unit 6, Grammar Plus Exercise 5, p.69

Student B

CAMBRIDGE SCHOOL Summer Party		
7p.m.	Welcome by director
7.50p.m.	Open buffet
8.20p.m.	Live band 'Delirious'
9.30p.m.	Disco
10p.m.	'Coolest couple' award
10.15p.m.	Surprise entertainment!
10.50p.m.	Live band 'RJE'
11.30p.m.	Fireworks
midnight swim!	

Unit 6, Vocabulary Exercise 1, p.74

USAGE NOTE: MAN
POLITENESS
Many people no longer use **man** to mean 'men and women in general' because it gives the impression that women are not included. They prefer to use **humans** or **human beings**: *abilities found in humans* (rather than *in man*). ...
It is also advisable not to use words that contain **man** in the names of jobs, because this seems to mean that only men do that job or that the person is a man. So say that someone is a **chairperson**, rather than a **chairman**, especially when it is a woman. Similarly it is better to say **spokesperson**, **businesspeople**, or **salesperson**.
Sometimes you do not need to use -**man**, -**woman**, or -**person** in the names of jobs at all. For example, people are more likely to say **firefighter** than **fireman**, **police officer** rather than **policeman**, and in British English, **headteacher** or **head** instead of **headmaster** or **headmistress**.

(Longman Dictionary of Contemporary English – 3rd edition)

Unit 3, Reading Exercise 6, p.32

Student B: You are a journalist who wants to interview a lottery winner and get an interesting story for their paper. You want to find out how Student A feels about having all this money and what they intend to do with it. You may need to persuade Student A to talk to you.

Unit 11, Speaking Exercise 5, p.130

Student B: You make lots of suggestions (some of them rather eccentric, impractical and expensive).

Unit 14, Speaking Exercise 3, p.174

Student A
- To what extent do people have a responsibility to look after the welfare of animals?
- Does it matter if certain animals become extinct?

Unit 10, Speaking Exercise 3, p.120

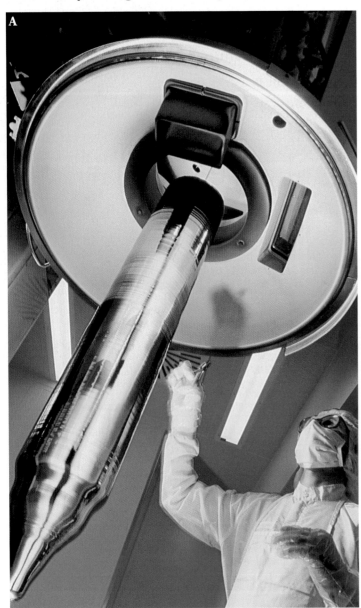

Unit 9, Speaking Exercise 3, p.109

Unit 11, Speaking Exercise 5, p.130

Student A: You are going to chair the meeting. It is your responsibility to make sure everyone has a chance to express their opinions and to arrive at a shortlist of the best three or four ideas by the end of the meeting.

Unit 2, Speaking Exercise 2, p.22

Unit 12, Exam Focus, Speaking, Paper 5, Part 2, p.146

Candidate B's photos

Unit 11, Speaking Exercise 5, p.130

Student C: You are concerned to make a good impression on the chairperson (who is your boss). You are very polite about other people's ideas but usually want to change them a little so they end up being YOUR idea.

Unit 12, Speaking Exercise 1, p.152

Unit 12, Speaking Exercise 3, p.152

Unit 14, Speaking Exercise 3, p.174

Student B

- In what ways can ordinary people help endangered animals?
- Do you think there are any fundamental differences between humans and animals? If so, what are they?

Unit 11, Speaking Exercise 5, p.130

Student D: You have worked in the tourist board for many years. You have heard most of these ideas before. You have a generally negative attitude and are quick to point out the downside of any new ideas.

Unit 13, Reading Exercise 6, p.158

⬤ **THIN PERSON**

1 words meaning thin
2 thin and strong-looking
3 thin in an attractive way
4 thin in a way that is not attractive
5 too thin, for example because of hunger or illness
6 words for describing a face that is thin
7 to become thinner

---

1 words meaning thin
thin
slight

---

thin /θɪn/ having very little fat on the body [*adj*]
Larry was tall but very thin with dark brown hair and bright blue eyes. | The war years had turned my mother into a thin, ailing old woman. | I wish my legs were a bit thinner!

slight /slaɪt/ thin, delicate, and often weak-looking [*adj*]
The girl's name was Juana, she was slight and delicate-looking. | Her father's figure was slight, which made him appear taller than he really was. | He pulled the little girl to her feet, marvelling that so slight a creature could have put up such a fight.

---

2 thin and strong-looking
lean
wiry

---

lean /liːn/ thin and physically fit, especially because you do a lot of exercise or physical work [*adj*]
He's a very handsome man: tall, lean and tanned with thick white hair. | At seventy-two my grandfather was lean and strong and I expected him to live forever. | She was looking lean and very fit today in training for tomorrow's race.

wiry /ˈwaɪəri/ a man or boy who is **wiry** is thin and strong, though often not very tall [*adj*]
Archie McNeile was a wiry, upright figure with an alert, intelligent face. | Jedd rolled up the sleeves on his wiry arms and was soon sawing the tree trunk with quick strong movements.

---

3 thin in an attractive way
slim   willowy
slender   keep your figure
trim

---

slim /slɪm/ [*adj*]
He was tall, slim and blond and really good-looking. | Mrs Ester was in her late thirties, about average height, with a slim figure. | "Does he look like Dan?" "He's slimmer than Dan, has chestnut hair and a neat beard."

slender /ˈslendər/ thin in an attractive and graceful way [*adj*]
Laurence was a tall slender young man with a light brown moustache. | Mandy had her mother's colouring, she was slender and very fair with long golden hair. | Although her face was quite plain, she had long, slender expressive hands, like a concert pianist.

trim /trɪm/ someone who is **trim**, especially a woman, has an attractively thin body and all her flesh looks very firm [*adj*]
Joan's trim figure suited the dark uniform she had to wear. | She strolled along the beach toward him, her body sleek and trim, without an excess gram of fat. | I play badminton regularly to help me keep trim.

willowy /ˈwɪləʊi/ a woman or girl who is **willowy** is attractively tall and thin in a graceful way [*adj*]
In contrast to Francesca, who was tall and willowy, Diana was small and curvy. | Anastasia was willowy and graceful, with grey eyes and long, straight red hair.

keep your figure /ˌkiːp jɔːr ˈfɪgər ‖ -ˈfɪgjər/ to manage to stay thin in an attractive way even though you are getting older [*v phrase*]
Lovely to see you again, Joan. You've kept your figure well all these years. | Superstars like Jagger and Nureyev must have worked incredibly hard to keep their figures into middle age.

(Longman Language Activator)

Unit 11, Reading Exercise 2, p.138

Group B

TRUTH BE TOLD SHE LIED

My curiosity about the sporting lie was piqued by an episode that took place in the US a number of years ago but came to light only recently, in Britain, when Ffyona Campbell, a distance walker, admitted that she had lied about a walk across the United States. During a 1,000-mile stretch, she said, she had cheated, accepting occasional rides from her companion and driver.

'Nobody knew, nobody was hurt, I rationalized,' Campbell wrote in her book *The Whole Story*, published amid controversy last November in Britain. Campbell's American crossing was the first of four tremendous walks, totalling 19,586 miles, that won her a place in the *Guinness Book of Records* with the longest distance ever walked by a female. But the lie preyed on Campbell for years.

Campbell is, to put it mildly, a difficult person. Restless, self-absorbed, and prone to moralistic pronouncements, she covers her body with the logos of corporate sponsors while castigating multinational corporations for destroying the earth. She walks farther than any woman before her but generally doesn't seem to notice a single pretty thing along the way.

Certainly, Campbell's childhood was hard. Her family moved 25 times in 12 years. Her mother seems not to have known how to handle Ffyona's ferocious spirit. Clearly Campbell's relations with her father, a tightly wound former Royal Marine helicopter pilot, were smouldering and remote.

As a young woman, Campbell frequently ran away from home and at age 16 somehow hatched the idea of walking the full length of Britain, a dream that slowly consumed first her imagination and then her energies. She was starved for attention in those days (she wore a sweatshirt that said 'Sponsor Me!').

In 1988 she walked Australia. In 1991–1993 she traversed Africa, a walk interrupted twice by political unrest. Along the way, she wrote two popular books that described her adventures. Then in 1994 she did Europe. Typically she would walk 30 miles a day on the shoulder of the highway. Every ten miles, a companion would be waiting for her in the supply vehicle. She'd take a break, eat, maybe drain some blisters with a syringe.

Her life between walks wasn't any easier, Campbell says. She flitted from job to job and seems to have alienated many supporters with her self-involvement and lecturing manner. But as she worked her way across Europe, a worm was turning inside her. She was being devoured by a lie that was now almost a decade old.

It all began back in Indiana, a little over a thousand miles into her east-to-west walk across America in the mid-eighties. Her pace had left her exhausted and weepy, and she started to fall farther and farther behind schedule. Her sponsor, Campbell's Soups, threatened to pull out. Then one afternoon she discovered why she was flagging: she was pregnant.

The moment Campbell gave in to Noel's offer to give her a lift, her misery faded. 'When things got too hard, I just got in the van till I was walking very little at all, just on the approach to a town to do the interviews,' Campbell writes in *The Whole Story*. 'A little farther past the town and I'd jump in again, all through Illinois and Missouri and Oklahoma and Texas.'

Campbell is still on the move. She lived with aboriginal women in northern Australia for a few weeks last year, and though gratified by the challenges of tracking in the bush, she felt called back to the developed world. 'I found out I had to go back, to find my home.'

'Ffyona, what are you going to do for a living?' I ask.

'I'm a retired pedestrian,' she says. 'But I really don't like people asking me what I'm going to do. It's limiting when you declare something.'

Unit 11, Speaking Exercise 5, p.130

Student E: You make some quite cautious suggestions. You are aware that the board has a limited budget and cannot afford to spend a lot of money on new ideas.

It was on a dreary night of November that I beheld the accomplishment of my toils. With an anxiety that almost amounted to agony, I collected the instruments of life around me, that I might infuse a spark of being into the lifeless thing that lay at my feet. It was already one in the morning; the rain pattered dismally against the panes, and my candle was nearly burnt out, when, by the glimmer of the half-extinguished light, I saw the dull yellow eye of the creature open; it breathed hard, and a convulsive motion agitated its limbs.

How can I describe my emotions at this catastrophe, or how delineate the wretch whom with such infinite pains and care I had endeavoured to form? His limbs were in proportion, and I had selected his features as beautiful. Beautiful! Great God! His yellow skin scarcely covered the work of muscles and arteries beneath; his hair was of a lustrous black, and flowing; his teeth of a pearly whiteness; but these luxuriances only formed a more horrid contrast with his watery eyes, that seemed almost of the same colour as the dun-white sockets in which they were set, his shrivelled complexion and straight black lips.

The different accidents of life are not so changeable as the feelings of human nature. I had worked hard for nearly two years, for the sole purpose of infusing life into an inanimate body. For this I had deprived myself of rest and health. I had desired it with an ardour that far exceeded moderation; but now that I had finished, the beauty of the dream vanished, and breathless horror and disgust filled my heart. Unable to endure the aspect of the being I had created, I rushed out of the room and continued a long time traversing my bedchamber, unable to compose my mind to sleep. At length lassitude succeeded to the tumult I had before endured, and I threw myself on the bed in my clothes, endeavouring to seek a few moments of forgetfulness. But it was in vain; I slept, indeed, but I was disturbed by the wildest dreams. I thought I saw Elizabeth, in the bloom of health, walking in the streets of Ingolstadt. Delighted and surprised, I embraced her, but as I imprinted the first kiss on her lips, they became livid with the hue of death; her features appeared to change, and I thought that I held the corpse of my dead mother in my arms; a shroud enveloped her form, and I saw the grave-worms crawling in the folds of the flannel. I started from my sleep with horror; a cold dew covered my forehead, my teeth chattered, and every limb became convulsed; when, by the dim and yellow light of the moon as it forced its way through the window shutters, I beheld the wretch – the miserable monster whom I had created. He held up the curtain of the bed; and his eyes, if eyes they may be called, were fixed on me. His jaws opened, and he muttered some inarticulate sounds, while a grin wrinkled his cheeks. He might have spoken, but I did not hear; one hand was stretched out, seemingly to detain me, but I escaped and rushed downstairs. I took refuge in the courtyard belonging to the house which I inhabited, where I remained during the rest of the night, walking up and down in the greatest agitation, listening attentively, catching and fearing each sound as if it were to announce the approach of the demoniacal corpse to which I had so miserably given life.

Unit 4, Speaking Exercise 4, p.46

UNIT 4, Vocabulary Exercise 5, p.43

MISSING

I step off the train, I'm walking down your street again, and past your door, but you don't live there any more. (**1**) ... Now you've disappeared somewhere like outer space, (**2**) ... and I miss you, like the deserts miss the rain.

Could you be dead? You always were two steps ahead of everyone. (**3**) ... I look up at your house, and I can almost hear you shout down to me (**4**) ... and I miss you, like the deserts miss the rain.

Back on the train, I ask why did I come again? (**5**) ... And the years have proved to offer nothing since you moved. (**6**) ... and I miss you, like the deserts miss the rain.

a) We'd walk behind while you would run.
b) You're long gone but I can't move on,
c) It's years since you've been there.
d) Can I confess I've been hanging around your old address?
e) where I always used to be,
f) you've found some better place,

Pearson Education Limited Edinburgh gate Harlow Esssex CM20 2JE England

www.longman.com

Set in 10/13pt Admark by Oxford Designers & Illustrators

First edition published 2001
Ninth impression 2006

Printed in Spain by Graficas Estella

ISBN-13: 978-0-582-33804-3
ISBN-10: 0-582-33804-2

Publisher Acknowledgements
The publisher wishes to express thanks and appreciation to the following reporters: Keith Greenwood, Brian Nield, Ana Gutiérrez de Francisco, Roy Norris, Susan Bolland, Joanne Johnson, Susan Cleveland, Brian Brennan, Nick Shaw, Lisa Girling, Spain; Carmel Engin, Emma Tuhill, Laura De Souza, Louise Leonard Cavalier, UK; Magdalena Wojdylo, Ewa Spirydowicz, Poland.

Author Acknowledgements
I would especially like to thank the following people: all the Longman team and, in particular, Ann Hislop (Project Manager) Therese Naber and Araminta Crace for their comments and advice at an early stage of the project.

We are grateful to the following for permission to reproduce copyright material: Atlantic Syndication Partners (Solo) for extracts from articles 'Blundering Bank..' by Roger Scott in *DAILY MAIL* 4/7/97, reading text based on article in *DAILY MAIL* 21.1.98, 'I'm Proud of my Dad..' by Lester Middlehurst 26.1.98, and an adapted extract from the article 'Alternative revision secrets' by Bonnie Estridge in *DAILY MAIL* 18/5/98; BBC Worldwide/the author's agents for an extract from *THE SPEED READING BOOK* 1997 by Tony Buzan pp14–15 . Copyright © Tony Buzan 1997; Cover Magazine for extracts from the articles 'Are you losing your memory?' in *COVER* Magazine Sept.1998, 'Computer commanded by brain power', extract from an article by Lisa Sykes (originally in 'Geographical') all in *COVER* Magazine Dec. 1998; Disneyland Paris for an extract from pp1–2 *Disneyland Paris OFFICIAL HOLIDAY GUIDE* Spring/Summer 2000; EMI Music Publishing/IMP for song 'Dr Heckyll and Mr Jive' from the album *Cargo* by Men at Work; European Magazines Ltd for extract from the article ' The Lost World..' by Simon Pradinas & Zhu Xiao Ling in *MARIE CLAIRE* February 1998; Gruner & Jahr Ltd/National Magazine Co for extracts from the articles 'The Laws of Freak Chance' by Robert Matthews in *FOCUS* July 1996, 'University of...' by Robert Matthews in *FOCUS* August, 1997, 'The art of survival' by Robin Hood in *FOCUS* Oct 1997, 'MOTIVATION: Are you up for it" in *FOCUS* March, 1998, 'First to conquer Mount Everest' by Nick Smith in *FOCUS* Sept.1999 (*FOCUS* 43) and 'Getting older telescopes our perception of time' in *FOCUS* March 2000; Guardian Newspapers Ltd for an abridged extract from the article 'The search for corporate identity' in *GUARDIAN EDUCATION* 20.4.93, extracts from the articles 'Basketball favourite...' by Richard Liston in *SUNDAY OBSERVER* 30.4.95, 'Stress takes toll on office staff' by Alison Daniels in *THE GUARDIAN* 21.10.97, 'Web of Intrigue' by Roger Dobson in *THE GUARDIAN* 3.2.98, 'Credit's due' by Muhammed Yunus in *GUARDIAN SATURDAY REVIEW* 31/10/98 and 'The living dead' by Michael Pitts in *THE GUARDIAN WEEKEND* 28.3.98; Independent Newspapers Ltd for extracts from articles 'Superwoman mellows out' by John Arlidge in *THE INDEPENDENT* 14.10.94, 'How the family pecking order affects you' by Elizabeth Udall in *THE INDEPENDENT* 16.9.96, Reading text based on an article in *THE INDEPENDENT* 21/1/98, adapted extracts from 'Does your pet have an inner life?' by Jerome Burne in *THE INDEPENDENT* 8/6/98, and 'Out for the Count' by Jane Feinmann in *INDEPENDENT ON SUNDAY* 19.4.98 and 'Smart move' by Meg Carter in *THE INDEPENDENT ON SUNDAY* 20.9.98; Levi Strauss & Co Archives for text extract about the history of Levi Strauss; IMP for the songwords 'When You Dream' Words and Music by Ed Robertson and Steven Page © 1998 Treat Baker Music/WB Music Corp, USA Warner/Chappell Music Ltd, London W6 8BS. Lyrics reproduced by permission of IMP Ltd; Minneapolis Star Tribune for an adapted extract from the article 'Borne to Bicker' by Maxine Abrams in *MINNEAPOLIS STAR TRIBUNE* 2/4/97; New Crane Publishing Ltd for an article on Trevor Bayliss by Lesley Dobson in *SAINSBURYS THE MAGAZINE* July 1998 pp49–51; News International Syndication for extracts from articles "Tycoons pull plug on rich kids" by Andrew Alderson in *THE SUNDAY TIMES* 29.3.98 © Times Newspapers Ltd 1998, "Used car dealer makes his first million aged 14" by Andrew Alderson in *THE SUNDAY TIMES* 8.3.98 © Times Newspapers Ltd 1998, 'New Review' and "The schoolboy spy" by Jonathan Ungoed-Thomas in *THE SUNDAY TIMES* 29.3.98 © Times Newspapers Ltd 1998, extract from story about Max Valentin by Christopher Hadley in *SUNDAY TIMES MAGAZINE* 8.11.97 © Times Newspapers Ltd 1997, 'Tiger teeth...' by Tony Barrell in *SUNDAY TIMES MAGAZINE* 15.2.98 © Times Newspapers Ltd 1998, 'cloning ' by Tania Unsworth in *SUNDAY TIMES MAGAZINE* 14.6.98 © Times Newspapers Ltd 1998, adapted extract from article by Robina Dam in *SUNDAY TIMES MAGAZINE* 15.12.98 © Times Newspapers Ltd 1998, 'The day I conquered my fear of flying' by Julia Gorst in *THE TIMES* 10.3.98 © Julia Gorst/Times Newspapers Ltd 1998, 'A generation born to conform' by Celia Brayfield in *THE TIMES* 24.6.98 © Times Newspapers Ltd 1998 and reading text based on article in the *THE SUN* 1/9/93; New York Times Synd. Sales Corp for extract from article by Marina Isola (The New York Times) in *COVER* Magazine 1998; Premier Media Partners for an extract from the article 'The bravest athletes in the World' by Pat Butcher in British Airways Magazine *HIGH LIFE* August, 1997; The Reader's Digest Association Ltd for extracts from the articles 'Did you Know?' in various editions of *THE READER'S DIGEST*, 1990; Realworld Music Ltd for song 'I Dont' Remember' from the album *Peter Gabriel* by Peter Gabriel; Sony Music Publishing for lyrics from 'Missing' by Ben Watts/Tracey Thorn; Telegraph Newspapers Ltd/Encyclopedia Britannica for extracts drawn from I article 'Outdoors....' by Sebastian O'Kelly 20/9/97 and *ENCYCLOPAEDIA BRITANNICA* 'Pitcairn Island' Copyright © 1996, extract from the articles 'Cupid's Target' in *SUNDAY TELEGRAPH* 14.2.97 and 'Study finds twins are also "Mirror Images"' by Katrina Creer in *SUNDAY TELEGRAPH* 2/1/00; Time Inc. for an extract from 'Winners: Sole Survivor' by Michael Neill/Lydia Denworth in *PEOPLE* © 1994 Time Inc; Time Inc/Newsday Inc. for extracts from article 'Cirque du Soleil Proves a Little Circus can make the Big Time' by M Small & D Lindeman in *PEOPLE* 25/88 / Aileen Jacobson in *NEWSDAY* 31/3/95; Director of Corporate Communications, University of Durham, for an extract from the *University of Durham's website;* Viking Penguin, a division of Penguin Putnam Inc for an extract from THE ROAD AHEAD by Bill Gates 'Copyright © 1995 by William H Gates III; The Week for an extract from the article 'Briefing' in *THE WEEK* 21.3.98; the author, Philip Weiss for an extract from his article 'Truth Be Told They Lied" in *OUTSIDE* Magazine May 1997.

We have been unable to trace the copyright holders of the article 'Sweet Nothings' by Belinda Wallis or the story from 'The Man who mistook his wife for a Hat' by Oliver Sacks and would appreciate any information which would enable us to do so.

We are grateful to the following for permission to reproduce copyright photographs: Ace Photo Agency for 19; Action Plus for 73; AKG London for 12 top middle; All Sport for 71 top (Clive Brunskill) and 74 bottom; Art Directors and TRIP for 20 (Helene Rogers) and 74 middle left ($ Grant); Aviation Images for 148 (Mark Wagner); BBC Photographic Library for 18, 101 and 157; The Body Shop International for 155; Bridgeman Art Library for 12 bottom (Musée Picasso, Paris), 13 (Mr & Mrs John Hay Witney, New York) and 143 (Peggy Guggenheim Foundation); British Telecom for 155; Britstock-IFA for 131 middle; Bubbles Photo Library for 109 bottom right (Shona Wood) and 185 (Jennie Woodcock); C.M. Dixon for 178; Colorific/Philippe Bourseiller for 172 left and 172 right; Corbis (UK) Ltd for 156; Mary Evans Picture Library for 104 right; Sam Faulkner for 31; Firepix International for 96; Focus Magazine for 149; Getty One Images for 14, 27 top, 46 top left, 46 top right, 46 bottom, 66, 74 top, 80 middle right, 80 top, 80 bottom, 80 middle left, 83, 120 bottom, 130 top, 130 middle top right, 147 top right, 172 bottom (background), 218 bottom right, 219 top middle, 219 bottom right, 223 top left and 223 top right; Ronald Grant Archive for 47 top, 47 bottom, 56 and 81 top; Sally & Richard Greenhill for 120 middle, 147 middle right and 174 top; Robert Harding Picture Library for 6 bottom left, 28 bottom, 130 middle bottom left, 130 bottom, 136 and 137 middle; Hulton Getty for 40; The Hutchison Library for 24; Image Bank for 109 bottom left, 131 bottom, 217 bottom left, 218 top left and 218 bottom left; Images Colour Library for 219 top right and 219 bottom left; Katz Pictures for 216 right; Moviestore Collection for 81 bottom; NASA for 55 left; National Geographic/Michael Nichols for 168 and 169 Network Photographers for 9 and 216 left; NHPA for 91 (Nigel J Dennis); Nokia for 54 left; The Oldie for 32, 36, 45, 50, 61, 118, 162 and 163; PA Photos for 32 top (David Giles), 32 bottom (Brian Little) and 53 (David Jones); Pearson Education/Gareth Boden for 99 top, 99 bottom and 151; Peugeot Motor Company for 155; The Photo Library, Wales for 130 middle bottom right (Steve Benbow) and 131 top (Richard Davies); The Photographers Library for 26, 28 top left, 74 middle right, 76, 82, 89, 109 top left, 181 bottom left, 219 top left, 219 bottom middle; Pictor International for 27 bottom, 125, 147 left, 181 bottom middle and 218 top right; Popperfoto for 59, 70, 71 bottom, 105, 119 and 181 top; Powerstock Zefa for 217 right and 223 bottom; reproduced by permission of Punch for 90 and 106; Rex Features for 6 right, 12 middle, 12 top right, 28 top right, 54 right, 60, 98 top, 98 bottom, 104 left, 123, 137 top, 137 bottom, 138 left, 138 right, 139 and 181 bottom right; Science Photo Library for 30 left (Jorge Sclar), 55 right (Peter Menzel), 58 (Geoff Tompkinson), 120 top (NASA) and 179 (British Museum/Munoz); The Shakespeare Birthplace Trust for 130 middle top left; Frank Spooner Pictures for 30 right (Gamma) 68 left, 68 right and 68 middle (Jimmy Bolcina); Superstock for 142; Swift Imagery for 88 top and 88 bottom; Tate Picture Library for 12 top left; Telegraph Colour Library for 49 and 217 top left; Times Newspapers for 33 (David Jones)and 117; University of Sussex/Stuart Robinson for 10/11; John Walmsley for 188 and Woburn Safari Park for 174 bottom.

We regret that we have been unable to trace the copyright holder of the photograph on page 42 and would welcome any information enabling us to do so.

Illustrated by Nigel Axtell, Aldo Balding, Rowan Barnes-Murphy, Warrick J Cadwell (East Wing), Linda Clarke (Ian Fleming & Associates), Doug Gray, Louise Morgan (Arena), Mark Oldroyd (Arena), Oxford Designers & Illustrators, Brian Sweet (Arena), Shaun Williams.